1983

How Mongolia Is Really Ruled

How Mongolia Is Really Ruled

A Political History of the
Mongolian People's Republic, 1900–1978

Robert Rupen

HOOVER INSTITUTION PRESS
Stanford University • Stanford, California

Hoover Institution Publication 212

©1979 by the Board of Trustees of the
  Leland Stanford Junior University
All rights reserved
International Standard Book Number: 0-8179-7122-X
Library of Congress Catalog Card Number: 78-59865
Printed in the United States of America

to Yongsiyebu Rinchen
1905–1977

Contents

Tables

Editor's Foreword

Studies of the sixteen ruling communist parties, from their origins to the present, have been undertaken in order to fill a gap in modern English-language historiography. When completed, they will include histories of these movements in Albania, Bulgaria, Cambodia, China, Cuba, Czechoslovakia, (East) Germany, Hungary, (North) Korea, Laos, Mongolia, Poland, Romania, the Soviet Union, Vietnam, and Yugoslavia.

Professor Robert Rupen's monograph on the Mongolian People's Revolutionary Party, fifth in this series, covers the following:

- Historical background, early leadership, and impact on domestic political life.
- Interwar years and the Comintern (purges, stalinization, training of cadres in the Soviet Union).
- World War II and its aftermath (integration with the USSR's Far East defense system and beginnings of the personality cult).
- Developments since the death of Stalin (rise and decline in Chinese influence).
- Party problems in the late 1970s, impact on transformation of the country, and relations with the CPSU.

As editor of the series, it is a pleasure to present this study on Mongolia by such a distinguished scholar as Dr. Robert Rupen.

RICHARD F. STAAR
Director of International Studies

Hoover Institution
Stanford University

Preface

Professors Nicholas Poppe and William Ballis were very influential in setting me on a Mongolian road, and it is my pleasure to record publicly the considerable debt I owe to them. But it was my family that bore the brunt of my removal from normal activity required by the extended time spent in preparation of this book: for this I extend to them both apologies and appreciation.

To friends, colleagues, and critics in Mongolia and the Soviet Union, I can only express a hope for better and more complete communication. What often appears to you to be negativism and complaint is only a bourgeois nationalist's troubled and inadequate search for truth. It is impossible for me to substitute your judgment for my own.

PART ONE

BEGINNINGS

1. Introduction

Five layers comprise Mongolia's historical stratigraphy. The base layer represents the era in which the indigenous nomadic society prevailed. Above this lie the Buddhist-Tibetan, Manchu-Chinese, and tsarist Russian strata. The surface layer, representing the present time, is that in which Communist Russian domination is the key element. Tsarist Russian influences had been interacting with Buddhist-Tibetan and Manchu-Chinese ones long before the outbreak of the Bolshevik Revolution. The Manchus had been eliminated in 1911, and a Russian-Chinese accommodation that recognized tsarist Russia's political predominance had been reached in 1915. A longtime historical shift of Outer Mongolia away from China toward Russia seemed to be the dominant trend before the Communists came to power.

The Mongolian People's Revolutionary Party (MPRP) was thus by no means the first extension of Russian influence and control in Outer Mongolia. Many other tools of expansion had already been in use for a long time, and they continued to be used. The Party was always only one of several instruments of Soviet control, but the way in which it was used provided a clear example of the difference between tsarist and Soviet policy in Mongolia: it illustrated the more systematic and activist commitment of the Soviets. The function and role of the Party can be made much clearer through an examination of Mongolian history before 1921.

Mongolian developments occurred in, and were significantly affected by, a variety of situations. One was a long-term constricting pressure on Mongols by Chinese threatening invasion from the south and Russians from the north. Even before 1911 Buryat Mongols had feared assimilation by Russians, and Inner Mongols by Chinese. Those fears had not yet penetrated Outer Mongolia, but Buryat anti-Russian nationalism and Inner Mongolian anti-Chinese nationalism would significantly affect developments in Outer Mongolia. It was not long before Khalkhas (eastern Mongols), too, began to fear for their long-term survival. While the Mongols saw this only as a Mongolian phenomenon, it must be considered in a larger context of the whole of the "Inland C" of minority ethnic groups squeezed between and threatened by expansionist Chinese, Russians, and Indians. A giant letter "C" in Asia starts with Mongols; goes westward to Uighurs and Kazakhs in Turkestan, southward to Tibet, and then eastward to Nepal, Sikkim, and Bhutan; then on to Meo and other tribal-minority groups in Burma, Thailand, Laos, and so on. The traditional societies inhabiting this whole vast territory are all under pressure not only from their neighbors but also from the related forces of Westernization and modernization that are affecting traditional societies everywhere. Compromises, surrenders, and defeats are commonplace among these societies.

The main immediate political context for Mongolia is the Sino-Soviet dispute. Twentieth-century history would have to show Mongolia as an integral part of Russo-Japanese and Russo-Chinese relations. There could be no Mongolian policy for Russia independent of its concern with Japan and China. Since Japan before 1945, and China always, have been so much more important to Russia than Mongolia, the country has inevitably been used as a pawn and bargaining chip repeatedly, with very little control over its own fate.

Since the defeat of Japan in 1945, the story of Mongolia has been part of the story of Sino-Soviet relations, and events in the Mongolian People's Republic (MPR) have proved to be sensitive indicators of the state of those relations. The likelihood of Chinese recovery of the MPR has not been very great, however, although such a development seemed possible during the period 1952–1962. Since 1962 the Soviet Union has substantially tightened its control in Mongolia, and developments in the 1970s suggest an irreversible and comprehensive process of integration of at least the northern MPR with Eastern Siberia. Certainly the pace and kind of Siberian development is a directly relevant factor in any view of Mongolia.

Since its original formation in June 1920, the Mongolian Party has been an active participant in Soviet domination in the MPR, but never the sole instrument. To find out how Mongolia is really ruled, many factors and institutions besides the Party must be examined.

The questions of the reality of Mongolian independence and the integrity of Mongolian nationalism, as well as of the extent to which the Party has been simply an instrument of Soviet control, are vexing ones on which considerable difference of opinion exists.[1] When the Party was not simply a medium for Soviet domination, the Russians used other instruments; this was the case much of the time during the 1920s. After the Party was extensively purged and reshaped, it became a more important tool for the Russians. The Comintern issued and enforced directives that the Mongols were unable to resist effectively, but it eventually lost influence and power in Mongolia as elsewhere.

The Mongolian and Russian secret police and military often exercised significant control, with the Mongolian functionaries usually carrying out Soviet instructions. Little of importance has occurred in the MPR since 1921 that did not originate with, or was not approved by, the Russians. The shared interest in opposing the Japanese and the Chinese, however, provided a commonality that meant no simple description of Mongolia versus Russia would be adequate. Moreover, many Mongols were not last-ditch opponents of destruction of the Buddhist Church as it operated in all its superstition and corruption. Neither can it be forgotten, however, that Mongolia was wracked by massive rebellion and what amounted to civil war in the early 1930s; the regime's contention that the rebels were all Japanese agents and vestigial feudal remnants is not credible. So much of what the Mongolian regime says of itself,[2] and what the Russians say of it, is clearly false that it is easy and tempting to discredit the regime entirely, but the great progress it has achieved in education and health alone shows that care is required in assessing its record. The very lack of economic development for so long and the limited manpower available to the Russians in the Baikal area have protected the Mongols and permitted them to have Mongolian Communists at least as their visible overlords. By now the Mongols have received enough economic largesse from the Soviet Union that any allegation that the Russians exploit the Mongols economically cannot be justified.

The nagging "bourgeois" conviction persists that a great deal of blood was spilled wantonly, that a great deal of unnecessary physical violence occurred, and that spiritual and/or intellectual violence is still being done to the truth and to integrity. There has also been a marked shortage of "bourgeois" compassion, pity, decency, and humanity. Nevertheless, the restoration of the old regime would be unthinkable. No romantic view of the past can overlook the fact that in traditional Mongolia life was nasty, poor, dirty, brutish, and short.

Another sad conclusion is that realistic alternatives to Soviet control were virtually nonexistent. The choices that were actually available were few: the Manchu warlord Chang Tso-lin might have disposed of the anti-Bolshevik Russian military leader Baron Roman von Ungern-Sternberg who controlled Urga, and that might have forestalled the Soviet-Mongolian invasion in 1921; or even less likely, on some later occasion Chang Tso-lin might have taken over Mongolia militarily. Feng Yu-hsiang, the warlord opposing Chang Tso-lin in north China, might have changed history if he had defeated his rival in 1925 instead of being defeated by him. The Japanese might have won at Nomonkhan in 1939; and the Chinese Communists might have succeeded in reversing Mongolia's orientation in the 1950s or in 1960–1962. Whether the Mongols would have benefitted from any of these alternatives is debatable, but on balance they probably emerged in a more favorable position the way things actually turned out.

Any future reorientation to China seems extremely unlikely, since the infrastructural connections between Russia and Mongolia have become so numerous and so strong and intimate. There has been a distinct increase in the intensity and volume of Soviet-Mongolian ties in the 1970s. Even in the unlikely event of Sino-Soviet detente and the restoration of cooperative-collaborative relations, the situation in 1978 differs substantially from that twenty years ago, making a reversion far less likely. The MPR is probably lost to China forever. The process began before the Communist period; the Mongolian Party played a significant role in continuing it, but the most important role was played by the Red Army.

2. Roots: 1900–1920

The roots of the MPRP and of Soviet dominance in the MPR were formed long before 1920-1921.[1] Russian activity and influence in Outer Mongolia go back at least to 1861, and, it could be argued, even farther back—to the first stirrings of Russian relations with China in the seventeenth century.[2] The Russo-Japanese War of 1904-1905, however, will be taken as the starting point here.

MILITARY-STRATEGIC CONSIDERATIONS

The difficulty experienced in maintaining a supply line across or around Lake Baikal in the Russo-Japanese War deeply etched in the minds of the humiliated Russians a perception of the vulnerability of the Baikal Corridor and of all the scant population and vast territory beyond the lake. When the Chinese began to plan permanent settlement in northern Mongolia, and started construction of barracks to house an augmented military garrison in Urga, the Russians began to fear the growing threat of bisection at the lake. Count Serge Witte, negotiator of the Russo-Japanese peace treaty at Portsmouth, New Hampshire, in 1905, was accompanied at that meeting by a secretary, Ivan Korostovets, who went to Peking as minister in 1907-1911, and then to Urga as special diplomatic representative in 1912-1913. Gerard Friters justly referred to Korostovets as "the most important supporter of an active Russian policy in Outer Mongolia."[3] Korostovets's experience in the treaty negotiations and his subsequent involvement in Chinese and Mongolian affairs provided a direct and personal link between the logistical and strategic lesson of the Russo-Japanese War—the vulnerability of the Baikal Corridor—and Russia's Mongolia policy.

The Chinese, suffering their own brand of humiliation, wanted to apply what they perceived as the strategic lesson of the Russo-Japanese War: that Russia was a paper tiger unable to sustain military operations in Asia. They moved to consolidate their control in Outer Mongolia. That led to the humiliation of the Mongols, who resisted the Chinese pressure and feared the ultimate result of a large Chinese population. The humiliated Mongols turned to the humiliated Russians for relief from the humiliated Chinese. The "lessons" of other battles in other places permeated the perceptions of all parties. The Mongols wanted to avoid a repetition of the fate of the Inner Mongols at the hands of the Chinese; the Russians wanted to avoid a repetition of their defeat at the hands of the Japanese; and the Chinese wanted to avoid a repetition of their loss of territory at the hands of the Europeans. The Russians perceived protection of the Transbaikal area and people as their vital interest; the Chinese believed that effective control over all they considered Chinese territory was their greatest concern; and the Mongols were most interested in avoiding their own absorption and disappearance.

The 1911 revolution in China that overthrew Manchu rule began on October 10, 1911 (the Double Tenth), when Chinese military commanders refused to obey the orders of the Manchu rulers. The Mongols were able to "declare independence" and the Russians were able to help them with at least temporary impunity since China was then a pitiful, helpless giant. Whether Russia would have acted vigorously to restrain Chinese settlement and militarization of Outer Mongolia if there had been no Double Tenth and Chinese Revolution will never be known.[4]

From the beginning of their relationship with the Manchus in the seventeenth century, the Mongols had appealed to Russia for assistance against both Manchus and Chinese. In 1895, the Jebtsun Damba Khutukhtu, who was the most influential Mongolian Buddhist spiritual leader and who also exerted considerable temporal power, sent an envoy to Russia to raise the question of support. Specific Mongolian requests for Russian assistance were also sent in 1905, 1907, and 1910. In 1907 there was a request from the Barguts in Manchuria to the Russian consul-general at Harbin. An activist secular aristocrat, the Sain Noyan Khan, inspired the Jebtsun Damba Khutukhtu to call a congress of princes and lamas in July 1911. This congress resolved to turn to Russia for help, and sent a small delegation (Khangda Dorji Wang, Da Lama Tseren Chimet, and Khaisan) to St. Petersburg with a letter to the tsar, dated July 17, 1911, and signed by the four Khalkha khans, lay princes in Mongolia. The letter specifically requested "rapid assistance and protection." It included a complaint that the Chinese officials interfered in Mongolian affairs, sent in permanent population, mistreated the Buddhist Church, and limited the jurisdiction of Mongolian officials. The arrival of the Mongolian delegation in St. Petersburg in August 1911 was an embarrassment to the Russians, and only vigorous efforts by Prince Esper Ukhtomsky (a confidant of the tsar, an influential publicist, and an enthusiast of the Far East) and Kokovtsev (Witte's successor as minister of finance) persuaded Stolypin to receive them.

On the Russian side, Count Murav'ev-Amursky, the energetic governor-general of Eastern Siberia, wrote in 1853: "In case the Manchu Dynasty fell and decided to retreat into its homeland Manchuria, we should act at once to take steps to prevent a new Chinese Government in Peking from extending its authority over Mongolia, which in such an event could be proclaimed our protectorate." Petr A. Badmaev, a Buryat Mongol, enjoyed the favor of Tsar Alexander III and later became a friend of Rasputin's and an adviser to Nicholas II. Badmaev formulated elaborate schemes, and in 1893 he proposed "annexing Mongolia and Tibet to Russia." Prince Ukhtomsky had written, "It is high time that the Russians should recognize the heritage bequeathed to them by Chinggis Khan and Tamerlane."[5]

Thus, Mongols were accustomed to turn to Russia for relief from Manchu and Chinese pressure, and many Russians were eager to oblige. In 1911, however, official Russia still remembered the disaster of 1905, so a commitment was made only very cautiously. Perhaps the Russians would have moved overtly against China even if the Chinese Revolution had not erupted, but the evidence suggests a marked unwillingness ever officially to order Russians to shoot at Chinese. Thanks to the Chinese Revolution of 1911, the Russians were able to substitute their occupation troops for Chinese-Manchu occupation troops in Outer Mongolia without firing a shot.

Russian troops in the Far East included the Transbaikal Cossacks, and they included many Buryat Mongols. Organized Transbaikal Cossacks had existed since the middle of the eighteenth century, and in 1851 the Transbaikal Cossack Army was formed. By 1897, 15 percent of the total native population in the area—twenty-seven thousand Transbaikal Buryats—served on the Mongolian border. Cossack units had crossed the border into Mongolia in 1873, when six hundred had been sent to Urga to defend Russians and Russian interests against the Dungan threat. (The Dungans were ethnic Chinese who were Muslims. Their massive revolt in north China in the 1860s and 1870s caused tremendous damage to life and property. They had taken and destroyed Ulyasutai in 1870 and Kobdo in 1871, and no one knew how far they would come.) In 1900, during the Boxer Rebellion, two hundred Cossacks had been sent to Urga.

Concern with preventing Manchu reprisals against the Mongolian envoys returning from St. Petersburg in August 1911 led the Russians to send a Cossack detachment with them for protection. This detachment was soon to save the Manchu Amban, Sando, from rioting Mongols when they proclaimed their independence in December 1911. (The Manchu Amban was one of the top officials sent by Peking to rule its Mongolian "colony"—a kind of governor-general. Sando was an especially activist Amban who was particularly unpopular among the Mongols.) Among the Cossacks was the twenty-year-old Semenov, who was later to become a notorious figure. It is very likely that von Ungern-Sternberg was with these Cossacks, too.[6]

The Chinese garrison in Urga was supposed to have attained a strength of 2,000 by the end of 1911, and an ultimate strength of 10,000, but in actuality, at the time of the Mongolian declaration of independence the garrison numbered 250 and was without hope of reinforcement; thus 200 Cossacks were enough to assure Russian control of the situation.

In the most important military operations of 1911–1912, Ja Lama, a Kalmyk Mongol who became a legendary figure in western Outer Mongolia as a defender against foreign oppression, rendered Russia an inestimable service when he defeated the Chinese at Kobdo in August 1912 and then pursued them and broke up their reinforcements and encampments early in 1913. His fighting permitted the Russians to move in Cossacks and take over western Mongolia while avoiding the necessity of confronting the Chinese in battle. The Cossacks did not kill any Chinese; they actually saved nearly a thousand of them from almost certain massacre at the hands of the Mongols. They then shipped them back to China and established a presence that was sufficient to deter the Chinese from returning. It was only after Ja Lama's victory at Kobdo that Korostovets went to Urga, and thus extended Russian "recognition" to Mongolia as an independent entity. The victory at Kobdo was more important than the declaration of independence of December 1911 in Urga in establishing *de facto* Mongolian "independence."

The areas north, west, and south of Kobdo each had their own special ethnic, cultural, and political features. Compared with Urga and the Baikal Corridor, Kobdo contained fewer people and was of far less strategic importance; usually it had little effect on Russian-Chinese relations. The ethnic and cultural variety and the vigorous energy of its local native population, however, were greater. The western Mongols, or Oirats, had always been considered far more activist, less passive and stoic, than the Khalkhas. In 1911–1912, moreover, the military operations at Kobdo were far more important than the very minor ones at Urga.

From Kobdo connections went to Biisk and Barnaul in the Russian Altai and Western Siberia, to Belotsarsk (which was actually founded only in 1914) in Uryanghai (now Kyzyl in Tuva); and to Shara Sume in Sinkiang-Altai, and on to Urumchi. In the first decade of this century, the Russians were moving politically and economically eastward from Western Siberia into Eastern Siberia and Mongolia and the Chinese were moving northward from Urumchi. Substantial Russian permanent settlements in the Siberian Altai had already inundated the native "Altai Oirats" and in 1903–1904 the Russians improved the rugged and tortuous Chuisk Road to Kobdo for wheeled traffic. At Urumchi in 1905 le Coq wrote: "There were many Chinese troops in Urumchi just then, when the Japanese were continually routing the Russians; a very little more and the Chinese would have invaded Russia. They would undoubtedly have been able to occupy all Siberia without more ado."[7] Urumchi was quite independent of Peking at that time, and the

Chinese there were not paralyzed by rebellion in the fall of 1911. Kobdo was reinforced.

It is very unlikely that the Russians would ever have frontally assaulted the thousands of Chinese troops at Kobdo, but thanks to Ja Lama, that was never necessary. The forty-five-day siege of Kobdo he led ended in August 1912 and solved Russia's problem. The Russians moved against Ja Lama, but not against the Chinese, and occupied Kobdo, warning the Chinese not to try to return. The Chinese were no more eager for a frontal assault on the Russians than the Russians were for one on the Chinese. Ja Lama provided a convenient instrument for the Russians.

While Ja Lama was a remarkable personality, idiosyncratic and charismatic, he also represented larger forces at work. He was a Kalmyk born at Astrakhan in 1860. The Kalmyks in European Russia were beginning to develop connections with other Mongols by the turn of the century, and Buryat leaders were consciously appealing to Kalmyks in a nascent pan-Mongolism.[8] Ja Lama, however, resisted the ambitions of Urga, the Jebtsun Damba Khutukhtu, and Khalkha Mongols to control western Mongolia. He demanded autonomy for the Kobdo District, and thereby lessened the prospects for a united Mongolia under centralized political control.

Ja Lama also represented the close connection of western Mongolia with Uryanghai. The pressure of Russian settlement caused Tuvan and Mongolian resistance, and "nationalistic" Tuvans joined Ja Lama's forces.[9] The Manchus administered Uryanghai from Kobdo, and the defeat of the Chinese at Kobdo briefly gave independence to the area. Ja Lama also dislodged Kazakhs from western Mongolia, driving them into Russia and China. That action dramatized the conflicts between Mongols and Kazakhs, Buddhists and Muslims, that had prevailed in Central Asia especially since the Islamic Dungan rebellion of the 1870s when Chinese Muslims had ravaged Mongolian lands and desecrated many Buddhist holy places.[10]

Ja Lama also established a camp and sometimes took refuge near Shara Sume, across the Chinese (Sinkiang) border but in a district populated by non-Chinese: the ethnic melange in this area, which formed a junction for Russia, China, and Mongolia, included Oirats, Uryanghaits, Kazakhs, Dungans, and Uighurs.

Ja Lama was a traditionalist revolutionary—a fascinating combination of Mongolian and Russian influences embodying cultural transition. He employed primitive superstition and indulged in savage violence with an ultimate aim of cultural transformation. During his brief period of rule, from his victory at Kobdo in August 1912 until his arrest by the Russians in February 1914, he tried to remake western Mongolian society. He had announced that he would follow the example of Peter the Great, erecting a new capital city and forging a disciplined and orderly regime under his unquestioned autocratic domination. He had no hesitation about indulging in personal cruelty and harsh punishment. His strictures on lamas and the Buddhist Church especially caused apprehension. He enforced unaccustomed standards of sanitation and cleanliness; he ordered princes around him to wear Russian boots and clothing, and sometimes colorful Russian-style uniforms; he excommunicated lamas who drank alcohol or smoked; he publicly humiliated, excoriated, and occasionally beat to death those who violated the order he proclaimed and enforced. He seemed to be a mad genius, credited by the Mongols as a "rebirth of Amursana." The Mongols believed that bullets could not kill him and that he had supernatural powers, and they feared him.

The Mongolian Revolution of 1911 actually comprehended both the demonstrations and proclamation of independence in Urga in December 1911 and the siege of Kobdo in August 1912. It came to an end only with the arrest of Ja Lama by the Russians in February 1914 and the Tripartite (Russia, Mongolia, China) Treaty of Kyakhta in June 1915.

The suspension of authority between the Wuchang revolt of October 1911 and the formal announcement of the end of the Manchu dynasty in February 1912 constituted an interregnum in China, making it easier for the Mongols to declare independence and for the Russians to support them. A Khalkhan decree announced the formation of an autonomous government in December 1911, but the official Russian reaction to this action was delayed. The Chinese surrender of Kobdo to Ja Lama on August 19, 1912, was quickly followed by a letter of August 23 from Sazonov, the Russian foreign minister, instructing Korostovets to proceed to Urga, and a note to the Chinese government in October warning them not to try to return to Kobdo. Russian-Chinese discussions about the status of Mongolia began in December 1912, but the Russians opened a consulate at Kobdo (it had previously been refused by the Chinese authorities) on July 1, 1913, and the Sain Noyan Khan's delegation was received in St. Petersburg in October.

In December 1913, the Russian consul at Shara Sume, Kuzminsky, concluded a truce agreement with the Chinese who controlled Altai-Sinkiang, Prince Palta, establishing a demarcation line. Thus an official of the Russian government negotiated an agreement that had in fact been won by the armed force of the "rebel" Ja Lama.

The Mongolian delegation led by the Sain Noyan Khan left St. Petersburg for Urga on January 22, 1914, and a Russian captain, V. G. Gabrik,[11] departed St. Petersburg for Kobdo. Ja Lama was arrested by the Russians on February 8, 1914, and Gabrik was named secretary of the Kobdo consulate on February 9. On April 5, 1914, the tsar announced the establishment of a Russian protectorate over Uryanghai (Tuva). By the time the Tripartite Treaty of Kyakhta was concluded in June 1915, World War I was already draining Russian power in Mongolia.

The common connections and separated jurisdictions of Central Asia were basically the same before and after 1921, and the borders of 1978 differ surprisingly little from those established by 1915. In November 1913 Russia and China had divided Mongolia into Outer and Inner, with Outer Mongolia autonomous but under the sovereignty of China. Inner Mongolia remained an integral part of China without any restriction on the authority of the Chinese government. In December 1913, "Sir Henry McMahon . . . conceived the idea of applying a Sino-Russian solution reached in respect of Mongolia a month earlier, to the Tibetan problem. . . . McMahon devised his plan for the partition of Tibet into inner and outer zones in December 1913."[12] In April 1913 Sazonov had affirmed the Anglo-Russian agreement of 1907, which recognized a special British interest in Tibet, and indicated that "our interests in Tibet are limited and based exclusively on the fact that the Russian Kalmyks and Buryats profess the Lamaist religion, the head of which is the Dala Lama."[13]

After the military victory at Kobdo, Maksorjav, a Mongolian, turned to Inner Mongolia and attempted to extend the Urga government's authority there. He occupied Dolon-Nor, but had to retreat because of a lack of weapons and an excess of Chinese soldiers. Maksorjav was about to occupy Küke Khoto when the Kyakhta Conference (September 1914–June 1915)[14] concluded the treaty that required Outer Mongolia to forego any extension into Inner Mongolia. Once again Maksorjav had to return to Urga.

Meanwhile, Japanese plans to overthrow Yuan Shih-k'ai, the ruler of China, included two versions, one of which was to support a Mongolian prince, Babojab, in an attempt to restore the Manchu empire, which would rule Manchuria, Mongolia, and North China. The alternate plan relied on Chang Tso-lin. At the end of 1915, Babojab's army retreated to Hailar in the face of attacks by Maksorjav near Dolon-Nor and Küke Khoto. Although Yuan Shih-k'ai died on June 6, 1916, Babojab and his troops (about three thousand cavalry) raided and ransacked the Tamtsag Bulak monastery in Outer Mongolia.[15] In July–August 1916 Babojab moved south from Hailar, but was in danger of losing in fighting with the Chinese. Japanese protection was withdrawn, and Babojab was killed in early October. Maksorjav reoccupied Tamtsag Bulak in November.

Thus Tibet had a special relationship with Mongolia, and events in the one country had some impact on the other. Russia retained limited interests in Tibet. The autonomous government in Urga desired to extend its authority over Inner Mongolia, but the Russians blocked that plan and forced the Mongols to accept separation. The Japanese in Manchuria supported the Mongols against China and encouraged Inner Mongolian attempts to move into Outer Mongolia, but they also supported Chang Tso-lin and a Chinese regime in Manchuria. Interactions among Britain, Russia, Japan, and China, including British-Tibetan, Russo-Mongolian, and Japanese-Manchurian negotiations and machinations taking place at the same time combined in an intricate and complex way to erode Chinese sovereignty.[16]

IDEOLOGICAL CONSIDERATIONS

The most important issues concerning Mongolia that later emerged more clearly as Marxist-Communist ideological concerns lay in the areas of (1) religion, (2) nationalism, (3) the class struggle, (4) economic development, and (5) racism and prejudice. Buddhism so permeated Mongolian society, and religious leaders exercised so much political and economic power, that the most critical questions concerned the retention or elimination of the church, or some degree of compromise with it. Mongolian nationalism was almost inseparable from Buddhism, since it was difficult to imagine a secular society that would be compatible with Mongolian culture and tradition. Class struggle was for the most part a concept used in subsequent Communist analysis to explain Mongolian history, but certainly there were exploiters and exploited. "Feudal" is a term commonly applied to traditional Mongolian society.[17]

Economic development, Western education, the idea of progress, modernization generally, were inherent in the Russian influence in Mongolia. Many Russians also had racist or Yellow-Peril attitudes; they commonly assumed that they were superior to the Mongols and harbored an inchoate and "atavistic" fear of the masses of China.

In 1892 the famous Russian explorer A. M. Pozdneev described the popular appeal of the Jebtsun Damba Khutukhtu: "Crowds of worshippers stretch toward the Khutukhtu from all sides, and not only Khalkhas, but also southern Mongols as well, Solons, Oolots [Oirats], Durbets, Tanguts, and finally Buryats and Kalmyks."[18] He was perhaps the only Mongolian personality known to all the generally illiterate and often apathetic Mongols throughout the land—practically the only recognized rallying point for all the Mongols.

Pozdneev also pointed out the significance of Erdeni Dzu: "Here almost every column and hill, every temple and every burkhan, calls to mind some individual or holds the tale of some event close to the heart of every Khalkha. The very mention of Erdeni Dzu arouses love for his native land in the heart of every Mongol, and ultimately, moves him to fall on bended knee in trembling delight before this holy place."[19] Erdeni Dzu was the first Buddhist monastery in Outer Mongolia, constructed in 1586. It lies within a few miles of the ruins of the old capital of the Mongolian empire, Kara Korum. Thus the locality bore concentrated nationalistic-religious symbolism for the Mongols.

The living influence of the Buddhist religion was further demonstrated in Urga in November 1904 when the Dalai Lama arrived from Lhasa: "Having 700 persons in his suite, his baggage was carried by a small army of camels. Over 10,000 citizens went several miles out of the town to meet him and prostrate themselves before him. Pilgrims flocked in from all parts of Mongolia, from Siberia, and from the steppes of Astrakhan, to do him homage."[20] Thousands of Buddhists converged on Urga from all over Central Asia.

The tsar sent a telegram to the Dalai Lama concerning the many Buryat Buddhists who had made the pilgrimage to Urga:

> A large number of my subjects who profess the Buddhist faith had the happiness of being able to pay homage to their great High Priest, during his visit to northern Mongolia, which borders on the Russian Empire. As I rejoice that my subjects have had the opportunity of deriving benefit from your salutary spiritual influence, I beg you to accept the expression of my sincere thanks and regards.[21]

At that time a number of Buryats volunteered to form an honorary guard to escort the Dalai Lama back to Lhasa. The British were increasingly apprehensive and skittish. Their old nemesis in Tibet, the Buryat Agvan Dorjeev, was with the Dalai Lama in Urga. (Dorjeev's presence in Lhasa had been in part the cause of the British occupation of the Tibetan capital in 1904.) The Dalai Lama invited the leading Russian and Buryat academic experts on Buddhism (Shcherbatskoi and Badzar Baradin) to return with him to Lhasa and pursue Buddhist studies there,[22] but the tsarist government exerted pressure to insure that no funds were available for the scholars to make the trip.

In August 1907 the Anglo-Russian agreement publicly confirmed that Russia was no longer pursuing an active policy in Tibet. The British believed that the outcome of the Russo-Japanese War had caused the reversal of the formerly aggressive policy; in any case much of the political importance of Agvan Dorjeev evaporated. Ideas about Shambhala[23] and pan-Buddhism lost much of their impact.

Although the importance of the Tibetan dimension in Agvan Dorjeev's career fell precipitately in 1906-1907, he continued to represent Buddhism to Russians and to Buryats and Kalmyks. He won the tsar's support in March 1909 for construction of a Tibetan-style monastery in St. Petersburg, and Prince Ukhtomsky, the eminent scholar V. V. Radlov, and many others helped to raise funds for it. Despite strong and vocal opposition from conservative Orthodox Church circles, the temple was completed, and portraits of the tsar and of the Jebtsun Damba Khutukhtu of Urga hung there.[24]

In 1913 Korostovets had ordered the Buryat intellectual Jamtsarano to cease printing "radical" criticism of the church in his Mongolian-language newspaper, and a few years later the government in St. Petersburg refused to sanction the anti-Buddhist coup proposed by Aleksandr Miller, Korostovets's successor as diplomatic representative. The tsarist government kept ideological or political interference with Buddhism and the Jebtsun Damba Khutukhtu to a minimum. Some individual Russians and some Buryat Mongols did criticize the church and the Khalkha officials of the Mongolian government, but the policy of the Russian government was to avoid any confrontation.

A solid stratum of superstition underlay the Buddhism of most Mongols. All sorts of primitive beliefs and customs inherited from shamanism persisted even among the lamas who had fought and in theory destroyed the older religious cult. Buddhism made war on and tried to eliminate shamanism from the time Buddhism began to spread in Mongolia in the sixteenth and seventeenth centuries. They were bitter enemies fighting for possession of the Mongolian soul, and the struggle was often presented in the form of virtue combatting the forces of evil. In the seventeenth century lamas were burning ongons[25] and destroying shaman paraphernalia among the Khalkhas, and much the same struggle raged bitterly in Buryat Mongolia early in the nineteenth century. Buddhism won, but shamanism was extremely persistent.

Shamanism continued to exist alongside Buddhism to some extent, with some practicing shamans also accepted by the Buddhist Church as lamas. Many shamans and shamanists saw no incompatibility in "converting" to Buddhism without abandoning any aspect of their former beliefs and practices. Shamanism also survived within Buddhism, becoming an integral part of it. In fact, Buddhism was almost neoshamanism, since it continued many customs and practices derived from the earlier faith. In some parts of the Mongolian culture shamanism continued almost untouched by Buddhist influences: the Irkutsk Buryats, especially those on Ol'khon Island in Lake Baikal, and the indigenous inhabitants of Uryanghai vigorously maintained their shamanism long after most Mongols and related natives had accepted Buddhism and foresworn the earlier belief.[26]

Shamanism was generally regarded by Russians and educated Mongols as superstitious, irrational, backward, primitive, even barbaric and savage. It was antimodern and antiprogressive; it was the lowest rung on the ladder of modernization. Buddhism was commonly seen as a higher step on an evolutionary scale leading to civilization and progress. Shamanism also reflected and expressed populism, however, in that it represented simple nomads against august princes and high priests. It also reflected and expressed Mongolian nationalism in a form that was still relatively pure and uncorrupted by Tibetan influences and by the sellouts and compromises of princes and priests who often made self-serving deals with the Chinese at the expense of their poor and oppressed subjects.

The limitation of Chinese settlement and militarization corresponded to Mongolian desires, and the anti-Chinese thrust of Russian policy was generally endorsed and approved by the Mongols. Russian scholarship and academic interest in Mongolia, particularly the discovery and description of Mongolian historical monuments, greatly strengthened Mongolian nationalism. Small but nonetheless significant beginnings in modernizing Mongolian education, in publishing a Mongolian-language newspaper, and in providing Russian education to some Mongols were important. Russians working in Mongolia took on Mongolian protégés and offered entirely new and previously undreamt-of opportunities to some of them. The Buryats helped to interpret and to bridge the gap between the two disparate cultures, and provided a model for adaptation to new ways and new things. The Kobdo District became more closely united with Khalkha than it had previously been.[27]

From the Mongols' point of view, however, there were negative and disappointing aspects, too. Full independence and sovereignty were denied them: the Russians insisted on retaining certain areas of control for themselves (for example, foreign affairs), and other areas for the Chinese, so that "Mongolia" was circumscribed in its jurisdiction. It was also limited in territorial extent, since Russia's prior arrangements with Japan, compromises with China, and protection of some of its own particular interests (such as Tuva) restricted the extent of the new Mongolian entity. There was a limited and weak Mongolian nationalism, and the Russians nurtured it and even indulged it to a significant degree; yet they also limited and circumscribed it, and disappointed Mongolian hopes. The principal aim was to serve *Russian* interests.

World War I soon weakened Russian influence in Mongolia, and the Chinese exclusion acts were before long rendered inoperative. The period of Russian domination had not been long enough to draw definitive conclusions about its effects on the Mongols and on relations with China. There were some signs that Mongolia was breathing on its own, but there were also some discouraging ones. A few more Mongols had been drawn into activity, commitment, and involvement, but massive apathy remained. No great change had occurred in the way things were done, or in the people who did them.

Those who espouse the misleading class-struggle interpretation of the Mongolian Revolution stress the cooperation of the Mongolian secular and religious leaders with Chinese authorities in exploiting the poor Mongolian nomads before 1921. Princes spent huge sums of money in Peking, running up gambling debts and carousing wildly, but the burden of the debts had to be borne by the subjects of these princes. Although high-church figures sometimes wasted large sums in dissipation, they often spent them for sincere religious purposes too—for the glory of Buddha. Nevertheless, the expenditures for gold and for great temples far exceeded the ability of the poor subjects of the church to pay. Then the Chinese took over the secular or religious land and property, and the masses sank even deeper into misery and despond. Significant resistance came only from the poor exploited arats who finally exploded in righteous anger against the princes and churchmen who had betrayed them. Uprisings of the exploited against the exploiters increased in frequency and intensity, and coalesced into a popular revolutionary movement. The exploited included Chinese peasants as well as Mongolian nomads, and the two groups joined together in resisting their exploiters, who were Chinese officials and merchants as well as Mongolian princes and khutukhtus. This picture, however, is very misleading; it omits many important historical facts and thus gives only a partial and distorted view.

Supporters of the "bourgeois-nationalism" interpretation of the revolution insist that Mongols made common cause against Chinese irrespective of their class background or status in property, wealth, and power, and that land-hungry Chinese peasants were the most direct enemies of the ordinary Mongolian nomad. The Chinese threatened to absorb and eliminate Mongolia's land and its people, and the Mongols resisted as a "national" group. Nationalism provides a better explanation for what occurred than class struggle, because cultural and ethnic loyalty supplies a stronger motivation for human behavior than identification with a social or economic group.

Certainly the Buddhist Church allied itself with the secular aristocracy in Mongolia from the beginning.[28] Indeed its leaders sometimes joined with Chinese officials and merchants to extort everything they could from their subjects. There was also considerable popular support for the church, however—even approval of its extravagant expenditures. Likewise, many princes fought the Chinese and defended their arat subjects; and they tried to hold on to the lands where herds were pastured.

In reality, the Mongolian gamblers and dissipaters and fornicators did not always turn out to be the enemies of the people, and the heroes of Mongolian nationalism were not always poor and clean-living. Two of the most important leaders of Mongolian nationalism and resistance to Chinese pressure were the Sain Noyan Khan and the Jebtsun Damba Khutukhtu. The Sain Noyan Khan ran up huge debts for dissolute living and gambling in

Peking, and the Jebtsun Damba Khutukhtu was a notorious drunkard and lecher; yet they quite effectively defended Mongolian rights and goals against Chinese threats and incursions.

The theory of bourgeois nationalism also explains more satisfactorily the great importance of the comparatively sudden shift around 1900 in Chinese policy toward Mongolia—from gradual expansion and slow acculturation to broad-front assault and the threat of total absorption. In the new accelerated policy, Mongolian lands were expropriated and confiscated whether or not Mongolian princes sold out their nomad subjects.

The source of the trouble was not the feudal class structure of the Mongols, but the rapid increase in the number of Chinese coming into Mongolia, which did not depend on treasonable or reprehensible acts of betrayal by Mongolian princes. The limited aim of the tsarist government in Outer Mongolia was to control and strictly limit permanent settlement by the Chinese and the Chinese military presence—a policy that corresponded to Mongolian wishes. The Mongols wanted more, however—to be completely free of China and to incorporate Inner Mongolia, Barga, and Tuva, as well as Khalkha and the Kobdo District in an independent Mongolia. Russia would support neither of these desires.

Russia did not want direct responsibility for the Mongolian government, and treaties with Japan limited the area of Russian influence to Outer Mongolia. The Mongols were further disappointed by the inability of Russian merchants to replace the Chinese, and by the weakening of the Russian position because of diversion of attention to Europe and the requirements of World War I.

Inner Mongols and Barguts had been especially active leaders in the Mongolian Revolution, and they occupied many secondary official positions in the Urga government. Some of them had fought with Ja Lama against the Chinese. They felt that the Russians had used them for Russian purposes and then discarded them. The tsarist government also refused to assume any commitment to social revolution. It supported a few small-scale efforts at modernization and change, but it did not formulate or promulgate any coordinated program or make any extensive effort in that direction.

The most important division in the autonomous government was between pro-Russian and pro-Chinese Mongols. The split thus occurred along "national" rather than class lines. It was not a matter of the people against the princes or the church, but a choice between reliance on China or reliance on Russia. The primitive characteristics of the autonomous government tended to favor China's claim to Mongolia and led Russia to interfere overtly more than it would have if the Mongolian government had shown greater competence. The Jebtsun Damba Khutukhtu's "cabinet meetings" were often drunken brawls: a Russian long resident in Mongolia, A. V. Burdukov, indicated that one of the government ministers, Khangda Dorji Wang, who met daily with the Jebtsun Damba Khutukhtu, often found the head of the government drunk by early afternoon.[29] Death by poisoning was the fate of several Mongolian officials.

ECONOMIC CONSIDERATIONS

Financial irresponsibility seemed to mark all Mongolian relations. Large debts to the Chinese binding Mongolian princes to Peking, forcing them to give up hereditary lands, and encouraging some of them to ally themselves with Russia against China just to forestall enforced collection were notorious. Church leaders committed huge sums of money for the construction of religious buildings and the importation of cult objects—statues and icons of all sorts.[30] Alienation of land because of accumulated debts was a particularly serious and widespread phenomenon in Inner Mongolia.

In 1913 W. W. Rockhill, the American explorer and diplomat in the Far East, emphasized the Chinese trading advantage over Russia and the radical measures it would probably take to change that situation: "exclusion of all possible foreign competition . . . and the forcing of all Chinese imports to come by the Vladivostok-Verkhneudinsk-Kyakhta route. . . ." Little development of Mongolian resources occurred. A new gold-mining venture soon faltered and collapsed financially, and coal mining near Urga (at Nalaikha) was on a small scale and yielded little. The Mongolian Expedition (ME) purchased livestock for the Russian army from 1915–1917: 63,000 head in 1915, 175,000 head in 1916, and 100,000 head in 1917. A protégé of the noted geographer and explorer N. M. Prjevalsky, P. K. Kozlov, headed the M.E. and was later to conduct extensive exploration in and around Mongolia.[31]

ORGANIZATIONAL CONSIDERATIONS

About two hundred princes represented the top aristocratic hierarchy in Mongolia; just over half of them were rulers of *hoshuns,* the administrative-territorial units into which the country was divided. The *hoshun*-prince enjoyed practically unlimited control over the population and property in his jurisdiction. Khans, princes, and *taiji* (the lay aristocracy) comprised about 4 percent of the total male population.[32]

The huge Buddhist sector consisted of 115,000 lamas and 750 resident-monasteries (another 1,850 temples were not ordinarily lived in); it included large amounts of livestock as well as many other forms of property. In Urga alone, thirteen thousand lamas lived at Da Khure, and another seven thousand at the Gandang.[33] The population of Urga itself had grown from thirty thousand in 1876 to nearly a hundred thousand in 1918 (the hundred thousand included sixty-five thousand Chinese, three thousand Russians, and the twenty thousand lamas).

Russia's official representatives in Urga played a very large and even governing role in Mongolian affairs, as this description of Shishmarev, the principal Russian diplomatic representative in Urga from about 1872 to 1907, indicates: "He was practically the leading man of Urga, for he was not only much esteemed and looked up to by the Mongols, but was actually consulted by them in most State affairs."[34]

A remarkable Russian Orthodox priest was assigned to the Russian consulate in Urga from 1914 through 1921. F. A. Parnyakov had served in and around Irkutsk from 1891 through 1914, organizing a school for girls and helping to carry out the 1897 census in Siberia. In Urga he organized the construction of nonsectarian schools and a library, and arranged lectures and concerts. In 1919–1920 he founded and edited a newspaper for the Association of Urga Cooperatives. He had ten children, one of whom was Pantaleimon, a leading East Siberian Bolshevik.[35]

Out of thirteen of the most important tsarist Russian official representatives in Mongolia, nine had been trained in Oriental languages, most of them in Mongolian. Six served at posts in both Sinkiang (Kulja, Kashgar, Urumchi, Chuguchak, Shara Sume) and Mongolia. Of the thirteen, one served for thirty-five years in Mongolia; another, for twenty years; four for between five and ten years; and only one for less than a year. One of the officials with the longest record of service, V. F. Lyuba, participated actively in the work of the Troitskosavsk-Kyakhta section of the Russian Geographical Society, as had Shishmarev. Lyuba doubted that Mongolia could survive independently; he did not believe that a viable Mongolian national consciousness existed. Similarly, Aleksandr Miller had complained in 1914: "The Mongolian ministers completely fail to think of their future, or on reforms; they have only their personal material interests in view."[36]

In 1907, four hundred Russians were engaged in some sort of economic relations in Urga. M. I. Bogolepov, an economist and professor at Tomsk University, helped to organize the 1910 Tomsk Expedition, which produced a detailed report that was basically in agreement with the conclusion of the 1911 Moscow Trade Expedition (MTE)—that "this market is slipping from our hands." The ministry of trade and industry, supporting the merchants and trading firms, appointed its own representative as special trade agent in Urga in 1913, A. P. Boloban. He and his constituency attempted to influence the Russian government to show greater political interest in Mongolia.[37]

Russians important in formulating and implementing Mongolian policy ranged from the conservative Kuropatkin to the Communist Kucherenko, along with Korostovets, Kokovtsev, Kotvich, and Kozin. General Kuropatkin was the commander in the Russo-Japanese War, and minister of war; his most notable reference to Mongols occurred in a notorious blustering and threatening speech to the Buryats in 1903 in which he warned them not to dare to organize against any official policies: "If you want liberation, if you think that your people might show any will to oppose the commands of the State, then know that you will be rubbed off the face of the earth, and there will remain no trace. You see here many Russian soldiers, they could become hundreds of thousands, and in the twinkling of an eye you would be crushed and annihilated. You must *demand* nothing. You may only ask mercy."[38] This "Kuropatkin threat" was often recalled by nationalistic Mongols in later years as the ultimate example of Russian prejudice and arrogance.

Kucherenko was a little-known worker in the Urga printing plant who came to Mongolia in 1912. He was one of Choibalsan's mentors and one of von Ungern-Sternberg's victims. Korostovets was, of course, the brilliant tsarist diplomat. Kokovtsev, minister of finance, inherited from Witte a special role in Far Eastern policy; he firmly supported Korostovets in matters concerning Mongolia. S. A. Kozin was appointed economic adviser to the Urga government, which seemed to the Russians to be irresponsibly wasteful of Russian money, by the ministry of finance.

V. L. Kotvich was a scholar who had taught at the University of St. Petersburg and also worked in the ministry of finance. He recommended Kozin for the job as financial adviser to the Urga government; he trained and then singled out Jamtsarano to run the school and to publish the Mongolian-language newspaper in Urga; he encouraged the unschooled but eager Burdukov to pursue serious study of the Mongols from his vantage point as a merchant in Kobdo; and he counselled Korostovets. In a quiet and inconspicuous way he affected Russian policy in Mongolia as much as did Korostovets himself.

Kotvich's protégés, Jamtsarano and Kozin, were both with the Sain Noyan Khan's delegation in St. Petersburg from November 1913 through January 1914, and immediately following that visit, Kozin assumed the duties of administering the thirty-million-ruble loan the Russians extended to the Mongols at that time. Jamtsarano returned to his Urga newspaper and school, then served as an adviser to the Mongolian delegation in the tripartite Chinese-Russian-Mongolian negotiations at Kyakhta from September 1914 through June 1915.

Burdukov, the unusually curious and sensitive Russian merchant in Kobdo, wrote to Kotvich in December 1909, and the sympathetic and encouraging reply led to a longtime close relationship. Kotvich, who represented the ministry of finance on the board of the scholarly Russian Committee (Korostovets represented the ministry of foreign affairs on it for a time), arranged stipends and minor assistance for Burdukov to pursue his ethnographic and other investigations, and undoubtedly helped to arrange the appointment of Burdukov as official interpreter for the Kobdo consulate in 1914. Burdukov knew Ja Lama personally; indeed he knew every personage in western Mongolia. He supplied Kotvich with a steady stream of information. Kotvich was not at all patronizing to him, and he encouraged the self-made scholar who was so isolated in a remote place to keep working and studying.

Thus Kotvich's own academic and official government jobs commingled; he placed people he knew in key spots and kept in close contact with them. Scholarship, the ministry of finance, and Russian-Chinese-Mongolian politics were all intimately involved with one another.

1911–1919

During the period of Mongolian autonomy, Mongols and Russians agreed in their desire to stop Chinese incursions and to control the extent of the Chinese presence and influence. The overthrow of the Manchus and the Chinese Revolution of 1911 had provided a favorable opportunity for the Russians to assist the Mongols to act, with little risk of effective reprisals. Ja Lama had employed military muscle in western Mongolia and defeated the Chinese, opening the way for Russia to exploit his military victory and move into Kobdo without having to fight the Chinese. The period of Russian influence, and the duration of Mongolian autonomy, were limited because Russia's involvement in World War I drew its attention away and led to a drawdown of the Russian presence; as the Russians left, the Chinese returned. The Bolshevik Revolution further weakened the Russians in Mongolia, while the confused situation and the temporary victory of the anti-Bolshevik forces in Eastern Siberia permitted the Chinese arbitrarily to eliminate Mongolian autonomy.

Mongolian anti-Chinese nationalism was strengthened by refugee Inner Mongols and Barguts who had been the victims of Chinese exploitation and who hoped to enlist support of Urga for the liberation of their homelands. The Khalkha Mongols were willing and even eager, but the Russians adamantly opposed ideas of pan-Mongolism (partly because of their treaties with Japan).[39]

Strong Buddhism and weak nationalism characterized most of the Khalkha Mongols at that time, but dreams of centralization and unification, and a growing recognition of the Jebtsun Damba Khutukhtu and the city of Urga as the political center of a Mongolian-Buddhist world did take on a modicum of reality. Very little social change took place, since the government was theocratic and unlikely to attack the church; hence Westernization and modernization moved very slowly.

The substantial debts owed to Chinese by some of the Mongolian leaders undoubtedly fortified their anti-Chinese nationalism, since return of the Chinese to effective power in Urga would probably mean vigorous debt collection. Few Khalkhas were educated or experienced enough to function effectively as government officials, and they relied heavily on the Inner Mongols, Barguts, and Buryats. Their active participation strengthened the desire for a Greater Mongolian State, but the Russians firmly blocked that plan. A handful of Khalkhas began to learn Russian: a few attended Jamtsarano's Mongolian school in Urga and a small number went to Russian schools in Irkutsk.

Russian involvement in World War I and then the 1917 Revolution obviously weakened the impact and slowed the pace of the changes that were just beginning to occur.

PART TWO

THE AGE OF CHOIBALSAN

3. Revolution. Buryats, Comintern, and Revsomols: 1920–1928

THE 1921 REVOLUTION

The addition of significant ideological and organizational dimensions differentiated the Mongolian Revolution of 1921 from that of 1911. Military-strategic considerations continued to be important, but they were now accompanied by these new concerns. Integral to the revolution in 1921 were Marxism-Leninism and Communism, including not only philosophical, historical, political, and sociological orthodoxy, but also organizational aspects such as a Mongolian Communist Party, a Communist-oriented government, and a Communist-directed army, as well as the active participation of the Comintern. The army was subject to a Communist-oriented political administration.

The Bolshevik Revolution and the Russian Civil War spilled over into Mongolia, and events there became part of Siberian developments. Japanese support of anti-Bolshevik Russians involved both ideological and military-strategic factors. The Japanese not only supported these Russians, but influenced regional and central authorities in China as well—and the Japanese intervention at Vladivostok added yet another thrust.

Although Russians and Buryats continued to be the most closely involved in Mongolia, the interference of the Comintern, the international Communist body, sometimes caused the inclusion of other groups among the participants. An Altai Oirat was an important Comintern agent in Mongolia in 1920-1921,[1] and Kalmyks were used more in Outer Mongolia in 1921 than in 1911. A true "international Communist" was the famous Czech who was then at Irkutsk, the author of *The Good Soldier Schweik,* Hashek.[2] He met some of the Khalkha Mongolian "revolutionaries" in Eastern Siberia in 1920. A small group of Mongols who met Lenin in the fall of 1920 found themselves in a group including the Turkish military leader Enver Pasha and many other illustrious revolutionary figures.

The Russians had sent troops into Mongolia in 1911-1912, but the Red Army dispatched there in 1921 was much larger, and the presence of the Red Army, with its important political administration, had ideological as well as military impact. The added ideological and organizational factors and the greater Japanese involvement of course made the 1921 revolution quite different from its 1911 predecessor. There was also a striking list of similarities in developments and policies, however, and a few of the actors were the same.

By defeating the Chinese at Urga in January-February 1921, and establishing himself as the ruler of Mongolia, von Ungern-Sternberg greatly aided the Bolsheviks.[3] He thereby permitted the Russians to move in and take over without having to confront the Chinese in battle. Not only did the Russians fail to kill any Chinese, they actually saved many of them from being massacred by von Ungern-Sternberg's forces and shipped them back to China. They then eliminated von Ungern-Sternberg, but their presence posed a serious dilemma for the Chinese, who were no more willing to confront the Red Army already ensconced in Urga than the Red Army had been prepared to confront the Chinese when they still occupied Urga.

By defeating and expelling the Chinese in 1921, von Ungern-Sternberg aided the Russians just as Ja Lama had at Kobdo in 1912. The similarity was not entirely coincidental: Burdukov recorded that von Ungern-Sternberg came to western Mongolia eager to know all about Ja Lama and how he did things. He was obviously fascinated with the earlier leader, and deliberately copied his flamboyant and cruel ways; both von Ungern-Sternberg and Ja Lama became tyrants.[4]

The underlying similarity between the situations in 1911 and in 1921 that enabled Ja Lama and von Ungern-Sternberg to win and the Russians to exploit their victories was the state of weakness and near-anarchy that existed in China in each case. The Chinese Revolution in 1911 had made possible the takeover by Ja Lama and the Russians, and the lack of unity among the Chinese in 1921 set the stage for their defeat by von Ungern-Sternberg and the Russians. Briefly it had worked the other way: the Bolshevik Revolution in Russia in 1917 had made possible China's return to Urga.

The cruelty and arrogance of the Chinese, and their total lack of empathy with the Mongols, were symbolized by Sando, the Manchu representative in Urga in 1910, and by Hsü Shu-ch'eng, the representative of the Peking government there in 1920. The period of extreme Chinese pressure on the

Mongols—from October 1919 to July 1920—was the time when the first "revolutionary circles" were established by two Khalkhas, Sukhe Bator and Khorlain Choibalsan; the conference officially forming the Mongolian Party met clandestinely in Urga in June 1920. The Chinese squeeze on the Mongols reached a climax just as the Bolsheviks returned to Baikal and Eastern Siberia, whence they had been ejected by Admiral Aleksandr V. Kolchak, the leader of the anti-Soviet army, in the summer and fall of 1918. The Bolsheviks returned in the spring of 1920, when the Mongols were groaning under the worst Chinese oppression and desperately looking for relief.[5]

Mongols had sent a delegation requesting Russian help against the Chinese in August 1911, and in a comparable move the Sain Noyan Khan went to see Bolshevik authorities at Irkutsk (Sergei Lazo) in June 1918. The Ataman Semenov, a lieutenant of Kolchak's who continued to lead an autonomous anti-Bolshevik army even after his commander's death in 1920, was already in Chita in June 1918, however, and the Czechs occupied Irkutsk in July, so nothing came of the visit, except that the Sain Noyan Khan was mysteriously poisoned in Urga in the spring of 1919. Bolsheviks were not in charge in Irkutsk again until February 1920.

During the period when Kolchak was winning and the Bolsheviks were fleeing westward, February 1919, the Japanese, Semenov, and Neisse Gegen, an Inner Mongolian Buddhist Khutukhtu collaborating with the Japanese and the anti-Bolshevik Russians, held a so-called "Dauria Conference"; its most important meeting opened at Chita on February 25. A few Buryats, Barguts, and Inner Mongols were present, but no Khalkhas. The Jebtsun Damba Khutukhtu ignored the meeting. A rather vague Japanese sponsorship of anti-Bolshevik pan-Mongolian movements became a pattern in and around Mongolia.[6]

An undated letter that must belong to this period was sent by Rinchino, the Buryat leader, to Dashi Sampilon, the Buryat representing native interests in Petrograd at that time. It argued that "the most basic necessity to fulfill our program for Buryat autonomy is to establish contact with the Japanese and the Semenov groups. . . . Behind Semenov stands Japan. . . . Japan and Semenov support our autonomistic tendencies."[7] Contradictions in contemporary accounts of Rinchino's role probably stemmed from his mistake in expecting permanency where there was only transience. His commitment to Bolshevism was to be more successful for him than his endorsement of Japan and Semenov.

MILITARY-STRATEGIC CONSIDERATIONS

At the Politburo meeting in Moscow on October 14, 1920, Lenin drew attention to Mongolia as a potential platform for aggression against Russia, underlining the importance of Mongolia to Russia's national security. At about this same time, Semenov's anti-Bolshevik units were being forced out of Chita, and von Ungern-Sternberg's troops were raiding across the Mongolian border into Eastern Siberia. Japan was supporting both Semenov and von Ungern-Sternberg. The Japanese threat appeared not only indirectly—in Japan's support of anti-Bolshevik forces, and of factions and warlords in China such as the Anfu Clique and Chang Tso-lin—but also directly—in its intervention at Vladivostok.[8]

The ease with which von Ungern-Sternberg occupied Urga and eliminated the Chinese presence in Mongolia emphasized the weakness of the Chinese government and its vulnerability to even very slight pressures. The Chinese had only recently bungled their chances to operate effectively and efficiently in Urga. Whenever they had been in control there, they had antagonized the Mongols and seemed unable to organize a military defense or a civil order.[9] From the Soviet point of view, the realistic alternatives to a Russian-controlled Mongolia were very unattractive; perhaps the most likely of these was the army of Chang Tso-lin.

The precipitating factor in the Soviet Red Army's advance into Urga in July 1921 was the threat of a similar move by Chang Tso-lin. Chang was ordered to destroy von Ungern-Sternberg and to liberate Urga on May 30; Uborevich, commander of the Fifth Red Army, was ordered to accomplish these same objectives on June 15. At the beginning of July both Chang Tso-lin's thirty thousand troops and the ten thousand troops of the joint Soviet-Mongolian force began to move toward Urga. There was nearly a collision of the Russian and Chinese revolutions in Mongolia in July 1921: the armies were almost eyeball to eyeball, but the Chinese blinked. The Soviet Red Army occupied Urga, while Chang Tso-lin did not even cross the Mongolian border.

Three factors inhibited Chang Tso-lin (Bertrand Russell, who was then in China, judged of the apparent preparations for the move on Urga: "No one for a moment supposed that he would undertake such an expedition"). The first was that the Japanese supported von Ungern-Sternberg as well as Chang Tso-lin. A move on Urga against von Ungern-Sternberg might easily have caused a crisis in Chang's relations with the Japanese.[10] The second inhibiting factor was the situation in Peking, where rivals were struggling for power; the diversion of Chang Tso-lin into Mongolia might cost him a chance to win control of China. The third, and immediately decisive, factor was the preemptive occupation of Urga by the Soviet-Mongolian forces.

Twice before July 1921 it appeared that Soviet troops might enter Mongolia. In November 1920 von Ungern-Sternberg besieged Urga, and Commissar of Foreign Affairs Georgyi Chicherin offered to dispatch Soviet military assistance to Peking. The offer was rejected, and the Chinese garrison succeeded in driving away von Ungern-Sternberg at that time. In February 1921 von Ungern-Sternberg succeeded in taking Urga, and the Chinese representative, Ch'en Yi, fled to Maimaichen on the Soviet border and requested help from Makstenek, the Soviet consul at the border, there. The Peking government disavowed that request, but in July 1921 the Soviets took action without asking for Peking's concurrence.[11]

The official Soviet explanation for the move into Urga in July 1921 was expressed by the noted Soviet diplomat Ivan Maisky in a letter to the American scholar George Murphy in July 1963: "The main consideration for taking such a decision consisted in the necessity to destroy Baron Ungern-Sternberg . . . who tried by force of arms to defeat the Soviet Government or at least to make for it as much harm as he could."[12] In November 1976 the Mongolian newspaper *Novosti Mongolii* indicated that von Ungern-Sternberg had advanced to the southern shore of Lake Baikal in an attempt to cut the Trans-Siberian Railroad and split the Far Eastern Republic away from the Russian Soviet Federated Socialist Republic (RSFSR). Henry K. Norton, a foreigner on the scene who was sympathetic to the Bolshevik cause, expressed the official view of the Far Eastern Republic:

> The effect of the presence of the Semenov and Ungern bands has been to keep the republic [Far Eastern Republic] in a state of war since its inception. It has necessitated keeping an army constantly mobilized, equipped, trained, and ready for action. The size of this army has necessarily been out of all proportion to the reactionary forces. Operating from Chinese and Japanese controlled territory, the latter were beyond the reach of the Russian[s]. . . . They might attack at any point from Kyakhta to Iman, a line over 2,000 miles in length, and the republic must be ready to defend itself against attack anywhere along the line. 5000 men at Urga means at least five times that many Republicans under arms along the Mongolian border. . . . By the middle of 1921 it was apparent that if the menace of the reactionary forces could not be removed, their very existence, even without an attack, would drain the lifeblood from the country, and make it an easy prey. China was powerless even to restore her own authority, let alone to protect her neighbor against aggression from her territory. Small wonder then that when Ungern did attack in June, the Republican troops followed up their victory by entering Chinese territory to dispose once and for all of this menace, and left the questions of violation of Chinese sovereignty to the diplomats to straighten out later as best they could.[13]

The Soviet military momentum probably made the move into Mongolia and the final elimination of the White opposition easier. The Red Army was winning all across Siberia, but complete victory was denied it as long as sanctuary was readily available to the enemy. The Fifth Red Army was on the scene: most of its hard fighting had already been done, but it had not had time to disband and demobilize, so the operation in Mongolia would be easy. It was a simple thing for the politicians to tell the army to move, since no forces had to be created or moved great distances, and no special equipment or even commanders had to be dispatched.

IDEOLOGICAL CONSIDERATIONS

At the Politburo meeting on October 14, 1920, Lenin and Stalin warned the Mongols of the deceptive attraction of anti-Chinese nationalism. They stressed the need for class solidarity and for the union of the world's oppressed, including the oppressed of Mongolia and of China, on the same side of the barricades. Mongolian speeches at international Communist meetings suggested that this advice made little impact: Mongolian-Chinese revolutionary cooperation for the common cause would not be easy to obtain.[14]

The list of the attendees at the Politburo meeting, as well as the attendance list and the substance of the Second Comintern Congress, which took place July–August 1920, and of the famous Baku Congress of the Peoples of the East (which had met just a month before the Politburo meeting), illustrated the intended global nature of Communist "liberation." The Mongols heard from Lenin and Stalin at the Politburo meeting about a global vision, and Mongolia's place in it, but they also saw how much farther toward understanding this goal were the Buryats and the Kalmyks, and of course the Russians.

On the other hand, the pan-Mongol movement supported by Japan promulgated another slogan: "Mongols of the World, Unite," and while the Mongols knew they were Mongols, they were not so sure they were proletarians. There was, however, an unlikely attendee at the Politburo meeting, Agvan Dorjeev, and backing him in the same room with Lenin and Stalin that day was the Kalmyk Amur-Sanan. Agvan Dorjeev and Amur-Sanan offered yet another slogan: "Buddhists of the World, Unite." Apparently Lenin and Stalin were interested. Tsarist Russia had essentially abandoned Tibet as a Russian target in 1907, but in 1920 the Communists showed interest in it. Perhaps the attention was anti-British in origin.[15]

Such discussions crystallized in the deliberations and decisions of the First Mongolian Party Congress at Kyakhta in March 1921. At that meeting, where the specific details were far less global, Jamtsarano won his argument that the Jebtsun Damba Khutukhtu should be retained in the new revolutionary government—that the elimination of the Jebtsun Damba would cause immense unrest and opposition and risk the success of all the other plans for revolution and change. Compromise was far more prudent than confrontation.[16]

For the Russians involved, the strong ideological opposition of Reds and Whites had been fanned by the Civil War and the cruel violence committed by both sides. There was still an ideological component in the drive to eliminate von Ungern-Sternberg and the last vestige of the enemy; likewise, von Ungern-Sternberg and the Whites still harbored a fanatical last-ditch opposition to Communism. These sentiments were still operative factors in decision making in Eastern Siberia in 1920–1921.[17]

ORGANIZATIONAL CONSIDERATIONS

The Mongolian Party was officially born on June 15, 1920, at a clandestine conference in Urga. Its first congress was held on Russian soil, at Kyakhta on March 1–3, 1921. Even before the Red Army's entry into Urga in July 1921, moves toward the formation of the Revolutionary Union of Youth (Revsomols) had begun.[18] Participation and direction by the Comintern and by Russians and Buryats accompanied every step. Many compromises were reached, and the early party documents and program were moderate and "bourgeois nationalist."[19] Nevertheless, a radicalization was occurring, and the potential for conflict between moderates and revolutionaries was growing.

A provisional Mongolian government was also formed at Kyakhta in March, and a Mongolian army was formally established. Preliminary steps had been taken toward all these developments, but the takeover of Urga by von Ungern-Sternberg obviously hastened their completion. A new sense of purpose and immediacy prevailed. The Mongolian army, though very small, was symbolically important. The plan was to achieve Mongolian "liberation" with Russian assistance. When ten thousand Red Army troops entered Mongolia alongside seven hundred Mongolian ones, however, it was hard to avoid the interpretation that Russia was directing events.

The three who made a satellite, those involved in the most critical events and meetings, were Comintern officials and citizens of the RSFSR: the Russian Boris Shumyatsky; the Altai Oirat S. S. Borisov; and the Buryat Mongol El'bekdorj Rinchino.[20] No Khalkha Mongols were as intimately involved in the significant decisions affecting the fate of their country as were these three "outsiders." Their function was to stimulate the "requests" of the Mongols and then accede to them; thus they acted as a medium for Russian control. Of the three, Shumyatsky was undoubtedly the most important. Thus, if the process by which Mongolia was transformed into a Soviet satellite can be traced to a single individual, that individual was Boris Shumyatsky.

The most important Khalkha, of course, was Choibalsan, and it is directly relevant that he was the Khalkha with the most Russian education and the one most fluent in the Russian language. Choibalsan maintained close contact with Russian Bolsheviks in Urga,[21] and the East Siberian section of the Comintern maintained close contact both with those Bolsheviks and with Moscow.[22]

Rinchino met Amur-Sanan at the October 1920 Politburo meeting attended by Lenin and Stalin; at that time he arranged for Kalmyks to act as military instructors to the Khalkha Mongolian army that was then being formed (Kalmyks seem to have participated in the Mongolian affair only in this capacity).[23]

The East Siberian towns of Irkutsk, Kyakhta, and Verkhneudinsk (Ulan Ude) dealt more directly and significantly with Urga in 1921 than had been the case in 1911. St. Petersburg officials dealt with Mongolia more directly in 1911 than Moscow officials did in 1921, perhaps because of the military situation at the later date and because the attention of the central authorities in Moscow was being diverted in so many other directions then. Shumyatsky was very much in control in 1921, and he appears to have exercised wide latitude on the scene; certainly he did not wait for instructions before acting. He checked with his superiors and made certain that Lenin and Stalin knew what was going on, but he was not being prodded from above.

1921–1928. MILITARY-STRATEGIC CONSIDERATIONS

In August 1922, thirteen months after the new regime was established in July 1921, fifteen major political figures—including the prime minister and two members of the Khalkha Seven (Sukhe Bator, Choibalsan, Bodo, Chakdor-jav, Danzan, Doksom, and Losol—the Mongols who formed the first group to enter the USSR and request assistance in July–August 1920)—were shot, and twenty-six others were arrested. Two years later the head of the Party (who had also been one of the Khalkha Seven) and a leader of the youth organization were executed. Four years after that, in 1928, the top three leaders were removed and replaced but not killed. Several other important political figures and other members of the elite lost their positions.

The army, the secret police, the Revsomols, the apparatus of "justice," and key Russian and Buryat officials representing the Comintern and/or the Narkomindel (the Commissariat of Foreign Affairs) successively eliminated "enemies" and controlled the political situation. Accusations against victims were always largely couched in national-security terms. The political figures arrested and executed in August 1922, including the top Mongolian leader Bodo, were charged with having dealt with Ja Lama, the White Russians, the Chinese generally and Chang Tso-lin in particular, the Japanese, and even the Americans.

Danzan, Bodo's successor, was himself shot in August 1924 for having negotiated with the Chinese warlord Feng Yu-hsiang and for plotting against Russia; he had attempted to recapture the Mongolian army from foreign control. Damba Dorji, another of the top Mongolian leaders, was removed in October 1928 for alleged contacts with the Japanese.

A special military delegation headed by Choibalsan and including Jadam-ba, a chairman of the Revsomol, the Mongolian Party's youth group, and a member of the Revolutionary military council, was in Moscow early in June

1922. On July 2 the GVO (the Mongolian version of the Cheka-KGB secret-police organization) was established under Soviet direction. Choibalsan and Jadamba returned to Urga at about the same time a new Russian representative, I. M. Lyubarsky, was named (on July 7). The First Revsomol Congress took place July 18–22, 1922, and Choibalsan and Jadamba were on its Central Committee, along with Gursed, a leading Khalkha official in the 1920s, Bavasan, a supporter of Danzan, and Bat-Ochir. The execution of the fifteen occurred on August 7.

When Sukhe Bator died on February 20, 1923, Choibalsan was in Moscow studying at the Red Army Academy; he did not return for the funeral. A few months before, in December, Sukhe Bator had been named commander in chief and Maksorjav minister of the army. In March 1923, Danzan assumed both these positions. In July 1923, Maksorjav went to Moscow and conferred with Red Army authorities, including Sorkin and the other eleven Red Army instructors who were preparing to go to Urga;[24] they arrived on September 23, 1923—the same day a new Russian diplomatic representative, A. N. Vasil'ev, was named. He arrived in Urga in January 1924, after serving as minister of justice in Turkestan.

The Third Party Congress (August 1924) was marked by discord, especially between Rinchino and Danzan: Danzan had tried to deprive the Revsomols of their special relationship with the army and subject them to the Party. Danzan also showed a reluctance to endorse the USSR uncritically. He seems to have tried to use the Urga military garrison to support his position, but Choibalsan and the Soviet instructors were able to frustrate that effort, and he was doomed.[25] Maksorjav appeared in Moscow again in December 1924, when he signed a treaty providing a Soviet loan to the Mongolian government.

In November 1924, after the elimination of Danzan, Rinchino was chairman of the Military Council; Choibalsan was commander in chief of the army; Maksorjav was minister of war; and Jadamba was the head of the political administration of the army and the chairman of the Revsomols. Gursed became the chairman of the Mongolian Supreme Court in 1926, after having served a year in the legation in Moscow. Bavasan was charged with having supported Danzan in trying to limit the role of the Revsomols, and was executed along with his mentor on August 30, 1924.

Joseph Stilwell, who was then U.S. military attaché in Peking, went to Urga in June 1923; his judgment has been summarized by Barbara Tuchman: "In Urga the hand of Russia was everywhere visible. Five hundred Red troops, both infantry and cavalry, equipped with some machine guns, dominated the situation. Their ammunition was meager. Owing to lack of railroads and deficiency of other transportation, campaigning in the area would present great difficulty."[26] Ten thousand Red troops had gone into

Urga in the first week of July 1921; six weeks later the Far Eastern Republic's contingent had withdrawn, leaving about three thousand soldiers. In August 1922 all but a battalion had left. The newborn Mongolian army, however, was extremely weak.[27] The American consul at Kalgan, Stanton, visited Urga at the time of the Third Party Congress, which culminated in Danzan's execution, and he noted the growing power of the secret police: "something of an air of terrorism hangs over the whole situation."[28]

The major military-strategic considerations for the Bolsheviks—the groups they repeatedly categorized as enemies and threats (in approximate chronological order)—were: the White Russians; Ja Lama; Chang Tso-lin and Feng Yu-hsiang; China; and Japan. In 1921 the greatest problems had been the anti-Bolshevik forces in Mongolia and the uncontrollable Ja Lama in western Mongolia. It was beginning to be evident that in 1928 the key problem was Japan.

The justification, or perhaps excuse, for the entry of Red Army troops into Mongolia in 1921 was that China had failed to control the remnants of the White forces that had taken refuge in Mongolia.[29] These forces continued to harass Eastern Siberia, and the Red forces desired to silence them totally and forever. That job was essentially completed by the end of 1921. Von Ungern-Sternberg was captured and shot; none of the Whites survived in Mongolia and only an exception like Semenov had the remotest prospect of ever leading a force again. The Civil War was really over, but the Red Army did not leave Mongolia.[30]

After Ja Lama had been arrested by the Russians at Kobdo in February 1914 he had been sent to prison at Tomsk, then at Alexandrovsky, near Irkutsk, and finally to Yakutsk. In 1916 he had been returned to Astrakhan, where the eminent Russian specialist in Mongolian affairs Vladimirtsov met him in September 1917. Vladimirtsov was astonished at his appearance, and wrote to Burdukov: "Of the Ja Lama we knew, nothing remains"; he now looked every inch the Russian dandy, complete with modish Russian clothes and gleaming boots. He told Vladimirtsov that he wanted to forget about Buryats, Kalmyks, and Mongols, and just be totally Russian. By that time he spoke Russian fluently and said that he was ready for complete assimilation. His appearance suggested that the process had already taken place; the wild primitive had apparently become a drawing-room ornament of Western civilization.

The Bolshevik Revolution, however, permitted him to flee his restricted exile and house arrest, and he returned to Mongolia in the summer of 1918. He tried to raise an anti-Chinese rebellion in the Selenga Valley north of Urga, but there was little response from the Khalkha population or from the Jebtsun Damba's government in Urga, so he returned to western Mongolia and his old haunts. There the response was far more satisfying. The Oirats had nursed their resentment for years (Burdukov reported that "the Khalkha Government [autonomous Mongolia] looked on Oirats not as equal partners but as slaves"[31]), and they still clung to rumors of the coming return of Ja Lama. The Urga government had confiscated all of Ja Lama's considerable property and removed it to Urga after the Russians had arrested and deported him, even though most of that property had originated in Kobdo monasteries. Because of this animosity, the Khalkhas failed completely to assimilate the Oirats and western Mongolia, and these groups remained independent and defiant even after the new regime assumed power in Urga. This time, however, the Mongols themselves dealt the blow to Ja Lama.[32]

In mid-1921, messengers of the new government in Urga who had been sent to Ja Lama's headquarters near Shara Sume on Chinese territory (Sinkiang) disappeared without a trace. In February 1922 a special decree called for the elimination of Ja Lama and his forces. Almost a year later the director of the Mongolian police personally led a special group that tracked him down and killed him. To prove the deed to Mongols who believed Ja Lama to be magically protected, the posse brought back with them and publicly displayed the severed head.[33] Sukhe Bator reportedly danced for joy.

The meeting between Feng Yu-hsiang and Borodin, the most important Soviet agent in China in relations with Sun Yat-sen and the KMT, at Kalgan in February 1925 (at which they talked for forty-four hours) initiated Russian military support of the "Christian general" and transformed Outer Mongolia into a bridge connecting the Russian and Chinese revolutionary move-ments.[34] The Russians wanted a direct geographical as well as ideological connection with the Chinese revolutionary movement. They wanted the cooperation of the Kuomintang-Chinese Communist Party (KMT-CCP), a successful Northern Expedition to take Peking, a victory by Feng Yu-hsiang over Chang Tso-lin, and Feng's adherence to the KMT-CCP alliance. If these conditions had been met, Outer Mongolia might have become negotiable, and the subsequent history of both Mongolia and China might have been substantially different.

The last Soviet Red Army troops left Mongolia in March 1925, and Khalkha representatives—Damba Dorji and Buyannemekh, a writer and active political figure—attended the Inner Mongolian Congress sponsored by Feng Yu-hsiang at Kalgan in October. At that time the Soviet Union was encouraging this particular expression of "pan-Mongolism," and Damba Dorji was not surreptitiously contacting Inner Mongols in an anti-Soviet move.[35] About the same time, the Tsetsen Khan (the minister of the interior in the MPR government) and Amor (who was then deputy prime minister) called on the Panchen Lama in Peking. (The Panchen Lama was second in the Tibetan hierarchy; he was usually closer to the Han Chinese and dominated by them more than the Dalai Lama was.)[36]

Many Chinese still hoped to wrest Outer Mongolia from the Russians, and Feng himself refused to recognize Outer Mongolian independence.[37] Feng's ally, Tuan Ch'i-jui, told Damba Dorji at Kalgan in October 1925: "Now it is important [for you] to get away from Russia and return closer to us." And pan-Mongolism was always double-edged: the Russians might employ it to separate Inner Mongolia from China and add that territory to the jurisdiction of the MPR. The Mongols themselves hoped for a united Mongolia that would limit the influence of both Russia and China. Tsedenbal claimed a few years ago that Jamtsarano wanted Mongolia to be "neutral like Switzerland."[38] The amount of traffic crossing the border between Inner and Outer Mongolia depended on the relations between Russia and China; when relations broke down, control over the border tightened.

Feng Yu-hsiang was no eager champion of Mongol rights. He simply hoped to use the native population against Chang Tso-lin in some way. His schemes for mass settlement by Chinese peasants on Mongolian lands[39] posed once again the persistent threat of the Han Chinese to the continued existence of Mongolia. Despite the obvious manipulation of the Mongols by both the Russians and Feng in 1925, the Party congress in Kalgan was a landmark—one of the outstanding events in modern Mongolian history. It was fraught with potential significance that never materialized—one of those turning points of history at which history failed to turn.

It failed to turn because Chang Tso-lin won and Feng Yu-hsiang lost. Support for Chang from Japan was of critical importance. In late 1923 and early 1924 Chang Tso-lin, Lu Chan-kuei, one of several leaders in Manchuria whose fortunes were intertwined with those of Chang Tso-lin, a Mongolian prince named Darkhan, and a Japanese missionary-adventurer who planned to work with Mongolian Buddhists reportedly planned an armed liberation of Urga. This simply never took place. But in 1925, at the time of the maneuverings between Feng Yu-hsiang and Chang Tso-lin, the Japanese army minister Ugaki Kazushige indicated the strong commitment of the Japanese to their ally: "The complete destruction and collapse of Chang would be disadvantageous to our country in its Manchuria-Mongolia policy. . . . The existence of Chang Tso-lin, holding power in North Manchuria . . . is necessary to our Manchuria policy, and especially to our North Manchuria policy. . . ."[40] When Kuo Sung-lin defected from Chang and joined Feng in November 1925, the Japanese quickly extended massive aid to assure Chang's victory. Soviet troops apparently massed near Manchuli in December 1925 to divert Chang's pressure away from Feng, and the manager of the Chinese Eastern Railway (CER), A. N. Ivanov, pressured Wu P'ei-fu on December 24 to refuse any assistance to Chang Tso-lin. Ivanov also raised bureaucratic and monetary obstacles to the movement of Chang Tso-lin's forces on the CER. On January 22, 1926, Chinese troops arrested Ivanov briefly.[41] Despite these efforts, however, Feng was defeated by the end of 1925.

Chang Tso-lin's victory over Feng increased pressure on the Soviet Union to solidify its control in Outer Mongolia and to eliminate all doubtful elements. Russian hopes that Mongolia would serve as a bridge to China faded, and Russian policy began to concentrate on building Mongolia into a protective barrier against Chang Tso-lin and his Japanese supporters. A distinct shift in the USSR in 1926 toward radicalism reflected a new policy toward Outer Mongolia: the odds of a geographic connection between Outer Mongolia and the USSR on the one hand and the KMT-CCP and Feng Yu-hsiang's Kuominchun on the other began to seem less favorable.

The political shift in 1926 was underlined and intensified when a split developed between the KMT and the CCP in April 1927, and it became increasingly clear that the Northern Expedition and the KMT's takeover of Peking would not be under Russian influence at all. Radicalization and a policy of tightened control in Outer Mongolia continued in the USSR, reaching a climax in the Seventh Mongolian Party Congress, held October–December 1928. The foundation for the triumph of radicalism and the cutting of ties to China, however, had been laid in 1926. The outcome of the Feng Yu-hsiang-Chang Tso-lin struggle in late 1925 had been more decisive than the KMT-CCP split in 1927 in changing Soviet policy and influencing Outer Mongolian developments. The important Comintern directive to the Mongols insisting on compliance with a new set of orders had come in January 1927, before the KMT-CCP split in April; thus the split strengthened the justification for an Outer Mongolian policy that was already being implemented.

Feng had lost to Chang Tso-lin about the time Amagaev, a prominent Buryat political leader, and Natsov, a Buryat who was an important Comintern agent in the MPR and in Tuva in the 1920s, were assigned as Comintern representatives to the Fourth Mongolian Party Congress, which was held September–October 1925. Thus Amagaev and Natsov serve as convenient symbols of a new and more radical course and the beginning of a concerted assault on moderates. They attacked Rinchino and Jamtsarano, and Choibalsan's power increased at the expense of Damba Dorji.

Ma Ho-tien, a Kuomintang representative, was in Urga from December 22, 1926 through February 12, 1927. Referring to Damba Dorji, he advised that "the Kuomintang should find a way to work with him so as to strengthen his hand." He quoted the Mongolian leader as having stated at a party celebrating Damba Dorji's return from Europe and Ma's forthcoming departure in February 1927: "There is no need to institute Communism. . . . Outer Mongolia is very anxious to join with China."[42] Nevertheless, the events of 1926 had already gone a long way to foreclose that possibility.

Stalin, Borodin, and Blyukher (a military colleague of Borodin's in China and Soviet military adviser to the KMT) had retained interest in Feng and continued to support him even after his defeat. They still hoped to be able to employ him against Chang Tso-lin. This led to the unusual choice of Urga as the locus for Comintern policy toward China for a short time. Feng left Kalgan on March 16, 1926, and spent the period March 22–April 27 in Urga. Borodin joined Feng in Urga April 3–7, and spent many hours briefing and teaching Feng and feeding him propaganda about Russia, Communism, cooperation with the KMT, and many other matters.[43]

The chairman of the Inner Mongolian Party and head of its army, Buyantai (Pai Yun-t'i) took refuge in Ulan Bator when Chang Tso-lin threatened Kalgan at the end of 1925, and a member of the Central Committee of the Inner Mongolian Party, Merse (Kuo Ta-fu), fled to the MPR a month or so later (early in 1926). At the time of the KMT-CCP split in 1927, Buyantai supported the KMT, but one of those who had been a delegate to the 1925 Kalgan congress, Ulanfu (Yun Tse), chose the CCP. Ulanfu attended Sun Yat-sen University in Moscow, from 1927 through 1930.

In the interregnum in Manchuria between the murder of Chang Tso-lin on June 3, 1928, and his son Chang Hsueh-liang's endorsement of Chiang Kai-shek in December, "a small body of Outer Mongolian troops officered by Russians" crossed into Barga, and in mid-August Merse led a "Young Barga" revolt; speculation at the time suggested that Barga would be incorporated into the MPR. Chang Hsueh-liang drove back the Mongols, however, and suppressed the uprising, which remained an isolated incident.[44] In 1929, Natsov labeled Buyantai and Merse renegades and traitors.

An iron curtain was descending over Mongolia. The famous American explorer Roy Chapman Andrews judged that 1925 was the last year that any work could be carried on in Mongolia by a non-Russian foreigner.[45] A Chinese-exclusion policy began to be applied. Patterns of trade and other relations shifted markedly beginning in 1926. Most of the measures were economic, but the causes and effects were clearly political.

IDEOLOGY, INDOCTRINATION, AND EDUCATION

Sukhe Bator met Lenin once, on November 5, 1921. At that meeting Lenin made a few points that became significant parts of Mongolian ideological development. One point, a military-strategic observation, was that Mongolia was a platform for aggression, and therefore important to Russia. He also pointed out that Mongolia should bypass capitalism by forming modest "islands of socialism" in the economy. The country had to develop a proletariat, since it was not possible to have a true Communist Party without one. Until such a class existed, however, a name other than "Mongolian Communist Party" should be employed.[46]

The small proletariat that did exist was largely Chinese, and Party members in the 1920s included representatives from such unlikely categories as lamas and princes, as well as many illiterates. In a pamphlet distributed at the Third Party Congress (1924), Rinchino stressed the need for the development of socialism and Communism, and alleged that Danzan was trying to build capitalism. The officially adopted policy of opposition to capitalism served in practice to exclude Chinese and other non-Russian competition from the market.

The legitimacy and the spiritual as well as temporal power of Buddhism were the key ideological problems, and the fate of the Jebtsun Damba Khutukhtu was one of the earliest dilemmas for the new regime. The Oath-Taking Treaty of November 1, 1921, imposed strict limits on exercise of any secular power, but it could not destroy the Jebtsun Damba's legitimacy and authority, which did not rest on the authorization of the Russian-influenced government. The revolt of the Saji Lama, the Jebtsun Damba's Tibetan bodyguard, in December 1921 ended with the arrests of forty-eight people, but apparently the Jebtsun Damba retained enough authority to get Saji Lama released for a time; nevertheless, he was executed with Bodo in the fall of 1922.

The Jebtsun Damba Khutukhtu died on May 20, 1924, and two important problems resulting from his death were handled with some care by the regime. His extensive property was not simply confiscated, but distributed by a special commission, and a third of it was retained to be used for religious purposes. The question of a successor khutukhtu was treated gingerly in 1925 and 1926, with reliance on a prophecy that the eighth Jebtsun Damba would be the last one. Only in February 1929 were any and all reincarnations of khutukhtus (not just the Jebtsun Damba) flatly forbidden.[47]

Anonymous pamphlets explaining and extolling neo-Buddhism circulated in 1926, and Natsov ascribed their authorship to Jamtsarano, who had argued for this sort of modification and modernization of religious practice instead of its suppression.[48] Sorkin, the Soviet military instructor in Ulan Bator at that time, indicated that the lamas opposed the army. One of their more effective appeals to the soldiers was through Tibetan medicine: until Russian doctors were available, the lamas effectively used their monopoly of medicine to sabotage attempts at forming an army.[49]

Mongols sponsored by Russia appeared in Lhasa in 1927 and 1928, and a 1926–1927 Buddhist congress in Moscow issued an "Appeal to the Buddhists of Mongolia, Tibet, and India."[50] Nothing came of that move, however; it was apparently a vaguely anti-Chinese, anti-British propaganda gesture that was neither serious nor enduring.

The radical turn to the left at the Seventh Party Congress (October 23–December 10, 1928) was forecast by increasingly threatening Comintern letters and directives from Moscow that began in late 1926. The resolution of January 24, 1927, laid out in detail the requirements: replace old officials by "younger and more suitable members"; abandon all compromise regarding the church or anything else; employ only convinced and experienced Communists. Especially to be eliminated were those bourgeois elements who "might appear superficially to reflect national interests." Stalin's definition stated on August 1, 1927, would apply:

> An internationalist is one who unreservedly, unhesitatingly, and uncondi-
> tionally is prepared to defend the USSR because the USSR is the base of the
> world revolutionary movement, and it is impossible to defend or advance the
> world revolutionary movement without defending the USSR. Whoever thinks
> of defending the world revolutionary movement without the USSR and against
> it, opposes the revolution, and must be considered an enemy of the revolution.[51]

The triumph of the left in Mongolia by December 1928 was engineered by the Comintern in Moscow, carrying out Stalin's orders, and it was part of a general phenomenon that was occurring inside the Soviet Union as well as affecting all Communist Party members everywhere. The period 1926–1928 marked a significant tightening of control by Moscow, an intensification of Stalinism and totalitarianism—what the Soviets called purification. It might also be termed rigidification. The Stalinist control that was steadily increasing in the USSR was extended to the Comintern, which in turn transmitted it to Mongolia. The driving force was Joseph Stalin in Moscow, not events in Mongolia or in Asia. Thus the pathology could not be cured in Ulan Bator; there was really no way for Mongols to respond sensibly. In *Soviet Russia and the East, 1920–1927,* Eudin and North, referring to 1927–1928, interpreted Stalin's goal as extending his control until it covered all Communist parties and all Communists: "the non-Soviet Communist Parties were primarily instruments for helping the Soviet Union attain its foreign policy objectives." Separation of Communists from social democrats and bourgeois elements was the Stalinist line then, and it was applied in the MPR as it was all over the world.

Just as Stalinization was transforming the way Communism worked in the USSR in these years, so it was transforming Communism in Mongolia, and the mirroring and mimicry became increasingly marked. Policy changes in the Soviet Union were reflected in Mongolia more mechanically in 1928 and thereafter than ever before. What had been a general and often imperfect correlation of Mongolian policies and procedures with Soviet ones became a meticulous and exact correspondence. Flexibility and adjustment to local conditions were increasingly interpreted as deviations and defiance, and were increasingly suppressed. In Mongolia that process was related to the failure to achieve collaboration and an alliance with the KMT-CCP, but the policy was transmitted to Mongolia from Moscow and not from China.

Ma Ho-tien had himself taught in the Mongolian-Tibetan Institute in Peking, and was commissioner of education for Kansu Province. He was especially interested in propaganda, indoctrination, and education. He found in Mongolia in 1926-1927 that " 'partyized' education receives more emphasis and is more widespread than in China." Radical training of young people and their indoctrination to a revolutionary outlook were already systematic and evident in remote local areas as well as in Ulan Bator. He observed that "the Red influence permeated everything." "It is Russians who direct everything"; "Mongolia was now modeling itself entirely after the government of Soviet Russia." He also noted the ubiquitous presence of the secret police. Ma reported a severe shortage of Khalkha teachers and a heavy reliance on Inner Mongols and Buryats, and observed that "the Mongols are prey to a host of superstitions . . . even the teachers, officials and students."[52]

The minister of education, Erdeni Batukhan, had been the interpreter and guide for Ivan Maisky in 1920 and the interpreter for Sukhe Bator and the Mongolian delegation that met Lenin in November 1921. He was actively involved in the program that had sent thirty-five Mongolian students to Western Europe, and he himself went to Berlin with them.[53]

ECONOMIC CONSIDERATIONS

Ma Ho-tien described graphically the harassment and discriminatory treatment suffered by Chinese in Mongolia in 1926. They were subjected to high taxes, long delays, insulting behavior, lack of any official protection, unfounded accusations, and currency restrictions: "It seems that the Chinese merchants are about to be entirely eliminated."[54] It actually took until 1931 for the Soviets to complete the job of eliminating China from Mongolian trade. To do this the Russians sent special trade representatives, employed the Comintern, used a network of consular officials around the country, and established and controlled a Mongolian trade bureaucracy.

At about the same time—the end of 1925 and the beginning of 1926, corresponding to Chang Tso-lin's victory over Feng Yu-hsiang—came a series of economic developments that suggest a marked shift in Mongolian trade and financial relations from China to Russia. A new Comintern representative, Amagaev, occupied the Mongolian governmental positions of minister of finance and chairman of the Economic Council; along with three Russians Amagaev was also on the editorial board of a new journal, *Khozyaistvo Mongolii*.[55] A Mongolian state bank was established, with equal numbers of Russian and Mongolian board members, but no Chinese; and a new Mongolian monetary unit, the *tughrik*, was introduced, for the purpose of "squeezing foreign capital out of the country's economy."[56] A new decree prohibited shipping livestock southward. Of total exports of Mongolian wool in 1925, 86 percent went to China and 13 percent to Russia. In 1926 these figures were turned around: 78 percent went to Russia and 22 percent to China. A major shift in the country's trade pattern had occurred, due to political pressure on the Mongols by the Russians. W. W. Rockhill had concluded from a trip he made to Urga in 1913 that Russia would have to adopt radical anti-Chinese measures if it expected to wrest control of the Mongolian trade; in conditions of free competition, the Chinese would be certain to win. His advice was followed and free competition ceased to exist.[57]

ORGANIZATIONAL CONSIDERATIONS

The radicalization of Mongolia in 1928 was one of the most important developments in the country's "Soviet" history, and some aspects of the decision-making process are known. It may be said to have begun in September 1926, with Comintern suggestions which the Mongols ignored.[58] It culminated at the Seventh Party Congress, which closed on December 10, 1928, with the complete rout of moderates and conservatives and a total victory of the left. That congress also registered the near-total subjection of Mongolia to the USSR.

A detailed Comintern directive of January 24, 1927, told the Mongols specifically what they were supposed to do.[59] The Mongols appealed for cancellation or substantial modification of the directive on May 26, 1927. The two representatives who were sent to Moscow to present the Mongolian case for gradual evolution instead of immediate revolution were Ganjuuryn Geliksenge and Magsarjavyn Dugarjav. In 1926 they ranked, respectively, third and sixth among the full members of the Central Committee of the Party. In 1925 Geliksenge had been a member of the Special Commission for Religious Affairs, which favored the neo-Buddhism that was discredited as rightist; he was purged from the Party by the Seventh Congress in 1928. Dugarjav, who had been a member of Sukhe Bator's original revolutionary circle in Urga in 1919, served for a time as deputy minister of foreign affairs. He was a well-known singer and composer, and one of his songs was "The First Party Congress."

On June 8, 1927, the Executive Committee of the Comintern (ECCI) rejected the Mongolian appeal. At the Sixth Mongolian Party Congress in Ulan Bator, which took place September 22–October 4, 1927, an honored guest was the famous Borodin, who was then returning from China after the failure of the policy he had recommended and represented. He spoke at the congress and published an article in the Ulan Bator newspaper,[60] but no substantial policy change ensued at that time. The letter the Comintern sent to the Central Committee of the Mongolian Party in January 1928 was undoubtedly impatient in tone. In April a plenum of the Central Committee of the Mongolian Party called for the removal of moderates, but this directive was not actually carried out. In June the ECCI appointed a special commission of seven members to get results in Mongolia. The chairman was Bogumir Shmeral, and the other known members were Borodin, Amagaev, Vartanian, and William F. Dunne (two members were not identified).

At least three of the members of this special commission were losers: Shmeral had lost to Klement Gottwald, who served many years as president of Czechoslovakia, in September 1925; Borodin had lost in China in about April 1927; Amagaev ("Amuga"), the former Comintern representative in Ulan Bator, had in 1927 been demoted to "Vostokkino" (an organization for the distribution of Soviet films in Far Eastern countries) in Moscow. Vartanian represented the Communist Youth International; nothing further is known about him. William F. Dunne (using the name MacDonald at the time) was a delegate to the Comintern from the Communist Party of the United States (CPUSA). The composition of the commission suggests that it did not originate Mongolian policy but enforced a Comintern directive.

"One of the most important in the history of the Comintern" is the way Eudin and North described that organization's Sixth Congress, which was held July 19–September 1, 1928. The affair was thoroughly dominated by Stalin and the leftists. In October a plenum of the Central Committee of the Revsomols of Mongolia met, and the resolutions it adopted were endorsed at the subsequent party congress. The Fourth Mongolian Party Congress had opened on September 23, 1925; the Fifth on September 26, 1926; and the Sixth on September 22, 1927; but the Seventh did not open until October 23, 1928. The Fourth Congress had lasted nine days; the Fifth, eight days; and the Sixth, twelve days; but the Seventh Congress, requiring preparation for significant policy changes, lasted seven *weeks.* The official *History of the MPR* indicated that "the Comintern Commission actively participated in assisting the preparatory work for the MPRP Congress and in exposing fundamentally and defeating the Rightists."[61]

The meetings with Lenin, which were frequently cited as evidence of Mongolian-Russian friendship, strengthened Mongolia's orientation toward the USSR. The symbolic significance of Sukhe Bator's meeting with Lenin on November 5, 1921, was underlined by numerous later paintings and recreations in the cinema and on the stage. That meeting embodied Russo-Mongolian friendship in just the way the Communist regimes of the USSR and the MPR want it presented and remembered.

The Mongolian delegation received by Lenin had met with Narkomindel officials in Moscow on October 26, 28, 30, and 31, and had worked out the Russo-Mongolian Treaty signifying recognition—and thereby infuriating China.[62] In addition to Sukhe Bator, the delegation included Danzan, Tseren Dorj, and Shirnin (representing the Jebtsun Damba Khutukhtu), plus Dava as secretary and Batukhan as interpreter. Tseren Dorj was one of the most durable Khalkhas; he had served in the autonomous government, then under Hsü Shu-ch'eng and von Ungern-Sternberg, and was to become minister of foreign affairs and prime minister of the MPR before his death in 1929. Dava became the first Mongolian diplomatic representative in Moscow, and his official reception by Kalinin in 1922 added to Mongolia's independent status and weakened its connection with China. Erdeni Batukhan had been Maisky's guide and interpreter, and became minister of education of the MPR. Boris Shumyatsky, who had proposed the meeting, also participated in it, along with Russian Narkomindel authorities.[63]

Mongols met with Lenin on two other occasions—in October 1920 and January 1922. Danzan, the only Khalkha who was present at all three meetings, was executed as an enemy of the people in August 1924. Chakdorjav, the other Khalkha who had been present in October 1920, was shot in August 1922 with Bodo. Buyannemekh, yet another Khalkha, who had met Lenin in January 1922 when Lenin was receiving delegates to the First Congress of the Toilers of the East then meeting in Moscow, accompanied Damba Dorji to the Inner Mongolian Party Congress at Kalgan in 1925; he was purged with Damba Dorji in 1928 and killed in 1937. Davajav, an official of the Mongolian government in the 1920s, also met Lenin in January 1922.[64]

An especially important organizational factor in Mongolia in the 1920s was the importance and independence of the youth group, the Revsomol, vis-à-vis the Party. The Revsomols were more radical, more rural, more "Communist," more pro-Russian, more progressive, better educated, and often better organized than the Party. Russians in Mongolia, plus the Russian-influenced army and the secret police, added effective power to the Revsomols and tilted MPR politics leftward, with this trend culminating in the Seventh Party Congress in 1928. The Revsomols emerged as opponents of Damba Dorji, pan-Mongolism, and China. When Feng Yu-hsiang was defeated by Chang Tso-lin at the end of 1925, the Russia-oriented radical Revsomols benefitted and the regular MPRP organization lost.[65]

Conrad Brandt's analysis of the relationship between the Youth Corps and the Communist Party in China showed that it closely parallels the Revsomol-Party relationship in Mongolia. He describes the Youth Corps as having been "a fortress of Jacobin intransigence." The Revsomols radically opposed Buddhism, condemned neo-Buddhism or any variety of compromise with the church, called for immediate collectivization, abandoned the del (the robe commonly worn by Mongols) and other traditional accoutrements, and derided tradition.

Both the Mongolian Revsomols and the Chinese Youth Corps were far to the left of the dominant parties, both of which were far from "Communist." Democratic socialists, bourgeois nationalists, all kinds of moderates and compromisers, and in Mongolia, church leaders and secular princes, were still Party members in the late 1920s. The Revsomols and the Youth Corps, however, never permitted as much latitude in beliefs as the larger organizations; in 1923 they specifically insisted on complete independence from their respective parties. Both "junior" organizations were in fact independent and autonomous entities. The Revsomols retained their independence until they were dissolved in 1932; the Youth Corps "managed to retain some autonomy (a very unusual state of affairs) until the late 1920s."[66]

Damba Dorji tried to capture the Revsomol organization and keep it under Party control, and Ma Ho-tien, representing the Chinese KMT, recommended dealing with Damba Dorji to avoid having to deal with the more radical Revsomols. Because the Chinese Youth Corps wanted to maintain its revolutionary purity, it offered the strongest resistance to compromise and alliance with the KMT. Feng Yu-hsiang's loss to Chang Tso-lin and the failure of Borodin's CCP-KMT alliance hurt the moderates and compromisers both in China and in Mongolia.

Conrad Brandt referred to the Youth Corps in 1926 as the cadres of rural revolution, indicating that students aroused and organized the peasants. At that same time in Mongolia, the Revsomols were better organized than the Party; they included many students and formed what came to be called the *khudon* opposition against the more moderate and urban regular Party organization. The "packing" of the party by the Revsomols resembled the capture of rural Party organization in China by the Youth Corps described by Brandt.[67]

The Communist Youth International sent an emissary from Moscow to Mongolia in the fall of 1921, and one to China in 1922, but while the Komsomols enjoyed a brief period of semi-independence from the Russian Communist Party, the Soviet Party established control over its youth organization several years before the Mongolian and Chinese Parties did so.[68] It was not very long before the Comintern itself, not the Youth International, was determining the relations between the Party and the Revsomols in Mongolia.[69] The Comintern deliberately encouraged the Revsomols to revolt against, and to infiltrate and subvert, the Mongolian Party.

In the 1920s several Buryats, one Kalmyk, one Altai Oirat, and a number of Russians directly occupied governmental and official posts in the MPR while they simultaneously functioned as Comintern agents in Mongolia and of course maintained their Soviet citizenship. Specific cases included: the minister of finance and chairman of the Economic Council; the head of Mongol'stroi (Mongolian construction); most of the top officials of Montsenkoop, the domestic trading organization; the head of the secret police and one of its inspectors; the chairman of the Military Council; the minister of war; the chief of staff of the army; and the military commandant of the city of Urga. Ma Ho-tien reported that there were four Russian advisers in the ministry of finance and eight in the ministry of war and a Russian heading the secret police, along with six Russian advisers.

Several of these Soviet citizens active in the MPR at that time were also key figures in Tuva who occupied official positions there at some time during the 1920s.[70] The Soviet and Comintern officials and representatives who dealt with Mongolia often also had relations with Tuva, and some of them with Tibet, but they seldom had anything to do with China. Mongolia was bureaucratically united with Tuva and Tibet, and bureaucratically separated from China. Borodin's trip to Ulan Bator to negotiate Chinese matters was very unusual. The Narkomindel and the Comintern at that time contained sections for Mongolia, Tuva, and Tibet, but the Comintern usually kept its dealings with China entirely separate.[71]

SUMMARY

Von Ungern-Sternberg's control of Urga and the Russian Civil War provided justification for the Red Army to enter Mongolia without challenging or confronting the Chinese. Once established in Urga, the Red Army stayed, acting as a barrier to a Chinese return to Urga. Numerous executions and considerable violence seemed aimed at assuring sole Soviet control in Mongolia and at eliminating any connection with China. Developments in north and northeast China, in Inner Mongolia and Manchuria, however, opened a new possibility of a Soviet-influenced Chinese movement. Significant developments in Sino-Soviet relations might have occurred in 1925, but Chang Tso-lin's defeat of Feng Yu-hsiang cut off this possibility, and from then on Stalinist restrictions, controls, and political radicalization unfolded in Mongolia with seeming inevitability, just as they were developing in the Soviet Union itself. Mongolian radicalization was directed by, and followed the pattern in, the USSR. What would have happened if Feng Yu-hsiang had been victorious in 1925 must remain unknown.

The KMT-CCP split, the Stalin-Trotsky feud, and the imposition of repression and Moscow-inspired "left deviations" (as they were soon to be labelled) subjected the MPR Communists, along with Communists everywhere, to a pattern of political development that was inspired from the outside rather than chosen by the domestic leadership.

4. Stalin and Japan: 1929–1939

MILITARY-STRATEGIC CONSIDERATIONS

The prospect of a Japanese attack across Mongolia cutting the Trans-Siberian Railway was a Russian nightmare. As Stalin put it in 1945, "It was necessary that Outer Mongolia be independent because of its strategic position, highly important for the Soviet Union; if a military power were to attack through Mongolia and cut the Trans-Siberian Railway, the USSR would be finished."[1] There was a related concern that Japan might separate Russia from China by forming a strategic cordon across Manchuria, Inner Mongolia, and Sinkiang. The Russians wanted to keep Japan out of the MPR to maintain it at a substantial distance from the Trans-Siberian Railway at Lake Baikal, and they wanted to maintain direct contact with China wherever possible. They hoped that Japanese-Chinese fighting in the south would divert troops and arms away from North China and Mongolia, thereby reducing pressure on the Russians. Strategically, Manchuria, Mongolia (the MPR and Inner Mongolia), and Sinkiang were interrelated, as were the Japanese-Chinese War and the threatened Japanese-Russian one. The Mongols were in the middle of a struggle of escalating proportions involving Russia, China, and Japan.

The Japanese succeeded in forcing the Russians out of Manchuria and creating a line across Inner Mongolia and North China separating Russia from China and breaking the connection at Kalgan that had been a major route of communication between China and Russia. They proved unable to penetrate the MPR, however, and they failed in their attempt to dominate Sinkiang.

Although the Russians surrendered the Chinese Eastern Railway (CER) and their position in Manchuria to the Japanese, they acted to deny Sinkiang to Japan and fortified their position in the MPR by sending in regular Red Army units, especially during 1937–1939, and enforcing the rapid build-up of the Mongolian army.[2] Increasingly they incorporated the MPR into the Soviet Transbaikal and Far East defense system; it served not simply as a buffer, but also as a forward defense line.

The culminating event in this period was the Battle of Nomonkhan in the fall of 1939, a battle in which combined Soviet-Mongolian forces thoroughly defeated the Japanese. Edmund Clubb attributed great importance to this battle and its outcome:

> The battle of Nomonkhan proved to be one of those critical turning points in history. . . . It led directly to the defeat of the Japanese faction that gave priority to a war with the Soviet Union, and the consequent rise to predominance in the Japanese Government of those who favored a grand strategy built around a plan for collision with the sea powers.[3]

The USSR had implemented a single integrated operational plan that contained significant MPR, Buryat Mongolian, and Eastern Siberian components.

On August 6, 1929, Blyukher was named commander of the newly formed Special Far Eastern Army (ODVA) at Khabarovsk. A test of general mobilization in the MPR that was attempted at about that time was a fiasco, with two thousand instead of thirty thousand men responding to the call-up. Early in 1930, A. I. Gekker was sent as an adviser to correct the deficiencies. Reportedly he barely escaped an assassination attempt in Ulan Bator.[4] Stricter enforcement of tougher military-service laws followed, and Mongolia began to be incorporated directly into the Soviet Far East defense system, in a process that was sometimes painful.

In 1934–1935 there were clear signs of the failure of the Japanese to penetrate the MPR and their loss of any realistic chance to exert influence in Sinkiang, but the Japanese alliance with the Inner Mongolian leader Teh Wang and Japan's effective control of Kalgan cut that potential Russian-Chinese connection. Russia's sale of the CER to Japan in 1935 marked recognition of the end of Soviet influence in Manchuria. The lines were drawn.[5] On March 1, 1936, Stalin stated to Roy Howard of the Associated Press in a widely publicized interview: "If Japan should venture to attack the MPR and encroach upon its independence, we will have to help [it]. . . . We will help the MPR just as we helped it in 1921. . . ." On March 12, the "gentlemen's agreement" made in 1934 was raised to the level of a Soviet-Mongolian treaty of friendship, including a mutual-defense protocol. Soviet tanks and armor moved into the MPR in 1937.

The Mongolian army slavishly copied the Red Army in many ways. The Red Army reintroduced ranks in September 1935; the Mongolian army did so in February 1936. The Russians appointed five marshals in November 1935; the Mongols appointed two (Choibalsan and Demid) in February 1936. The Soviets reimposed control by commissar on May 8, 1937, and the Mongols followed suit in November. Unitary command began to be introduced again throughout the Red Army in 1942, and in the Mongolian army after July 1943.[6] The Russians purged and executed three of their five marshals; the Mongols eliminated one of theirs (Demid).

Russians filled significant military positions in Mongolia. F. N. Voronin directed the Mongolian army's political administration and its political commissars. Pliev instructed the army staff from 1936 through 1939. Rokossovsky apparently served for a time as an instructor with the First Mongolian Cavalry Division. Sudets established the Mongolian Air Force during the years 1933–1937. Soviet regular units entered Mongolia: the 57th Rifle Corps, under N. V. Feklenko, established its headquarters in Ulan Bator in September 1937. Jamyangiin Lkhagvasuren attended the Lenin Military-Political Academy, 1935–1939, and later became the Mongolian minister of defense and the commander of the army. Demid attended the Tver Cavalry School, 1926–1929. Sorkin, who had been a Soviet military instructor in Ulan Bator through the 1920s, met with Demid in Moscow in the fall of 1936, and referred to Sambu as a close friend of Demid's. Sambu, the former chief of the political administration of the army, became diplomatic representative in Moscow, 1937–1946. Zhukov (who was at Tamtsag Bulak and Nomonkhan from June 5, 1939, through May 1940), Konev, and Fedyuninsky led the forces at Nomonkhan to victory over the Japanese. The Russian-Mongolian military connection was very close.

The NKVD played a role in Siberia and the Far East: it was at least partly supportive of the army and the USSR's national security. Its projects and preparations possessed some logic, though of course its methods and procedures were totally reprehensible. NKVD projects included double-tracking the Trans-Siberian Railway from 1933 through 1935 and constructing the new rail lines between Ulan Ude and Kyakhta, and between Borzya and Bayan Tumen (with a narrow-gauge extension to Tamtsag Bulak after 1939). The NKVD also did most of the construction at Komsomol'sk.

A large project that was close to the Mongolian border and partially shielded the vulnerable Trans-Siberian Railroad at Lake Baikal was the mining of molybdenum at Jida-Zakamensk. The Jida camps were notoriously inhumane, and Solzhenitsyn described their particularly awful conditions,[7] but the project bore some relation to real requirements. Siberia and the Far East belonged in great part to the military and the secret police.

The Soviets desired an unbroken corridor from Baikal to the Pacific so that there would be virtually no empty spaces nor possible political sympathizers for the Japanese to exploit. Walter Kolarz, a BBC analyst, indicated that the reason for establishing Birobijan in 1934 was:

> to increase the defense potential of the Soviet state by recruiting settlers for an exposed Far East border sector and to provide more manpower for the Soviet Far East in general . . . [at] an important strategical point where the decisive struggle for the domination of the Far East might flare up one day. The security aspect of the Birobijan experiment can hardly be overstressed. The Soviet

Government felt uneasy at the existence of a practically empty frontier zone bordering on a populous Manchuria.[8]

The administrative separation of two exclaves of the Buryat Mongolian Republic in September 1937 was also strategically motivated. The Aga and Ust-Ordya districts were separated so that native Buryat strength would be weakened and the Irkutsk and Chita areas would be solidified into unbroken units.

The NKVD did not always support the army, however, and it did not always act logically—and the Mongols slavishly copied its irrational maneuvers. From 1936 through 1939, the MPR was just as "unbelievable" as the USSR was in those years, and for basically the same reason—Joseph Stalin. The Great Terror overflowed Soviet borders. The famous Soviet military leader Marshal Tukhachevsky was shot in Moscow on June 12, 1937, and Rokossovsky, who was then commander of the Fifteenth Cavalry Division at Dauria, was arrested about that time. Rokossovsky was beaten and imprisoned, but survived. I. M. Vareikis, the NKVD boss in the Far East who was responsible for Rokossovsky's treatment and for the arrests of many other leading Far Eastern military figures, was himself arrested on October 9, 1937, and shot in 1939.[9] G. Lyushkov, NKVD commander of the Far Eastern Frontier Troops, escaped arrest by fleeing across the border into Manchuria on June 13, 1938; he subsequently supplied intelligence to the Japanese.[10] Marshal Blyukher was removed on August 11, 1938, and replaced by G. M. Shtern as head of the Special Far Eastern Army. Blyukher was dead by November 9, 1938.[11] Shtern was shot on October 28, 1941. Despite all these executions and defections, the questions that were raised about the army's battle performance were answered clearly by Zhukov, who together with Konev and Fedyuninsky led the Russians (and some accompanying Mongolian troops) to a decisive victory over the Japanese.

Demid, the Mongolian minister of war and commander in chief of the army, died on August 22, 1937, aboard the Trans-Siberian express en route to Moscow from Ulan Bator. Four quite different explanations have been offered for his death (he was just thirty-six years old). The first and most convincing is that it was related to the purge of Tukhachevsky, and that he was poisoned aboard the train by the NKVD or by his rival Choibalsan. The explanation given officially at the time, and repeated in 1970 in a book by N. S. Sorkin, attributed Demid's death to accidental food poisoning rather than assassination. Yet a third explanation, one that was put forward by G. D. R. Phillips (a British member of Parliament who toured Eastern Siberia) in 1942, was that he was poisoned by a Japanese secret agent. Reports that Choibalsan had attacked Demid in 1938 because he had conspired with the Mongolian military and political leader Gendun against the Mongolian regime were dismissed as "slander" by the *History of the MPR*.[12] The *History* also indicated that Choibalsan:

> committed serious errors . . . in the operations of the Ministry of the Interior which he utilized through his own direct leadership and orders. . . . [C]ruelty and unjust arrests by the Ministry of the Interior became widespread. . . . [T]his led to many people's perishing. . . . [A 1968 source adds] Choibalsan . . . took this special security organization out of the control of the Party and Government and made it possible to defy our revolutionary laws and regulations. . . . Choibalsan removed the security organization from the Party and Government's supervision.[13]

Choibalsan and Demid were rivals in the military and secret-police areas for many years, but Choibalsan seems to have been out of the direct competition from June 1932 to March 1936; the Ninth Party Congress in 1934 was the only one in which he did not take part. He spent most of those years in Moscow. Because of the great importance of the military confrontation with Japan, the other top leaders who had no military background or Soviet military connections were less likely to succeed.

Official interpretations of these events have gone unchallenged in Mongolia and the Soviet Union since there is no independent press or scholarship; thus in searching for the truth outsiders must necessarily rely on speculation and signals that are often murky and ambiguous.

During the period 1936 through 1939, Soviet troops and armor were brought into the MPR, the Japanese threat became increasingly serious, Stalin's personal attention was drawn to the importance of the MPR, and Choibalsan returned to power in Ulan Bator. The direct presence of substantial Soviet armed forces assured that the political outcome in Mongolia would correspond to Moscow's (Stalin's) preference.

IDEOLOGICAL CONSIDERATIONS

The elimination of the Buddhist religion was the most important Communist ideological campaign in the MPR, but the goals of secularization and modernization also had a military-strategic significance. The Japanese attempted to mount a political offensive to accompany and strengthen their military campaign. They tried to use Buddhism and Mongolian traditionalism against both the Chinese and the Russians. Japan presented itself as the defender of the Yellow Faith against the Communists who would destroy it. This made it easier for the Communists in the Soviet Union and the MPR to depict supporters of Buddhism as sympathizers with or agents of Japan; defense of Buddhism implied support of Japan against Russia. Japan attempted to penetrate the MPR and even reach into Buryat Mongolia via the support-for-Buddhism campaign. Thus the religious question had both nationalistic and military-strategic dimensions.

Chinese policy aimed at keeping China's territory from falling into the hands of Japan or Russia involved ambitious plans for the permanent settlement of Han Chinese on Mongolian lands, especially in Hsingan (Manchuria). The Japanese protected the Mongols from this Chinese incursion and won support from the Mongols for so doing. Owen Lattimore wrote in 1933: "The 'Young Mongols' [progressive Bargut and Hsingan Mongols] waver between ideas of union with Outer Mongolia and ideas of treating with Manchukuo and Japan for support." [14]

P. D. Butler, a former British consul-general at Mukden, went to Hsingan in 1935 or 1936; he recorded the following judgment:

> The Japanese in their Mongol policy in Manchukuo are trying to influence the Mongols through their religion, and in the course of the last year or two several lamas either from the Hsingan Province or from Inner Mongolia have been sent to Japan to study in temples and conversely . . . about ten Japanese Buddhist priests have been sent to lamaseries in Mongolia. The Japanese themselves appear to feel more in sympathy with the Mongols than the Chinese. As for the Mongols themselves, the Japanese have rendered them at least one great service, in that they have up to the present checked Chinese penetration into Mongol territory. . . . But the Japanese have one defect in handling a very independent people like the Mongols, and that is they have too great a tendency to paternal government. There is a little too much red tape about it. [15]

In Buryat Mongolia in September 1937, the crimes charged against the political leader Erbanov and his "band of gangsters, bourgeois nationalists . . . diversionists and wreckers" included the allegation that "they tried to separate Buryat Mongolia from the USSR and to put the country under the protectorate of the black fascist Samurai of Japan." In the mid-1930s lamas in Buryat Mongolia were allegedly spreading pro-Japanese propaganda. Lamas of Khori Aimak in 1935–1936 "painted pictures showing the armies of Shambhala as coming from the rising sun, from the east—an indication of Japan. . . ." [16] Bawden pointed out that "the increasing threat from Japan after 1935 . . . undoubtedly created or facilitated the creation of an atmosphere of tension inside Mongolia, in which it was easier to carry out the final work of liquidating the Church. Accusations of treachery and collusion with the Japanese brought against high lamas were more plausible in an ambience of uncertainty. . . ." [17] He also noted that no Japanese coup or sign of one ever occurred in the MPR, but that the allegations of treason with a foreign power served as a justification for severe repressive measures. In judging Choibalsan, the 1969 History of the MPR indicated that he greatly exaggerated infiltration and subversion by Japanese agents in the 1930s, and that this exaggeration caused "unjust perishing of loyal people." [18]

The History also stated that in 1937–1939, "high lamas who had clearly demonstrated that they were irreconcilable . . . were defeated and liquidated by means of revolutionary violence . . ." and then proudly claimed that "the major success of the MPR's ideological work lay in the collapse of the ideological dominance of the Yellow Faith in the MPR."

Differences in ethnicity, race, culture, and nationality belied the ideology of international class solidarity. Everybody was prejudiced and narrow-minded in practice, no matter how generous and liberal he claimed to be. The Chinese were arrogant; the Japanese were intolerant; and the Russians strafed Kazakhs, deported Koreans, imprisoned Chinese, and destroyed the religion of the Mongols. Khalkha Mongols discriminated against Kazakhs and Oirats. Tai Ch'uan-hsien expressed the typical Chinese attitude in November 1930:

> Chinese culture is superior to that of the Mongols. . . . Hence, from now on the Chinese should exert every effort to confer their culture upon the Mongols, who should strive to receive it. . . . Most . . . hesitate to come out frankly for creating a common civilization centered upon the Chinese. This is because they are blind to the historical fact that the Chinese, Manchus, Mongols, and Tibetans have a common ancestry. . . . [19]

The Mongols approved of Japanese measures prohibiting Chinese settlement on their lands and Japanese recognition of the princes and the Buddhist Church, but they were disappointed at the refusal of the Japanese to give them any real autonomy and freedom. The Mongols rapidly became disillusioned with Japanese policy, and Japan seems to have thrown away her initial advantage of Mongolian support by the use of blatant propaganda and a general attitude of racial superiority. [20]

In 1936 "Soviet warplanes strafed the Kazakh horsemen, who were armed only with rifles, and under the withering fire the Kazakhs broke and dispersed." So reported Edmund Clubb about one aspect of Soviet support for the Soviet puppet Sheng Shih-tsai in Sinkiang. [21] Kolarz indicated that "In 1937 the Soviet nationalities policy adopted a new objective . . . the liquidation of the Korean minority in the Soviet Far East." [22] As many as 250,000 Koreans were involuntarily transferred from the Vladivostok area to Tashkent and other Central Asian localities, where they remain in the 1970s. The U.S. State Department's 1943 volume of *Foreign Relations* stated that "several thousand" Chinese prisoners released in 1943 via Tashkent comprised mainly "refugees who had fled from Manchuria to Siberia during the Japanese invasion of 1931–1932. They were arrested, imprisoned, and sentenced to penal servitude of several years for having entered the Soviet Union illegally." [23] The Buryat Mongolian scholars Baradin and Jamtsarano complained that ethnic Russians and not Mongols defined Mongolian culture, and that the enforced use of the Russian language was denationalizing the Buryats, "just like the Mongols who live in China." [24]

Choibalsan's important and comprehensive speech in January 1938 included a reference to trouble in western Mongolia:

> Recently we discovered a serious counter-revolutionary plot in Kobdo and
> Ubsa Nur Aimaks among the Durbets and Altai Mongols, who for a long time
> served the Japanese. . . . This counter-revolutionary organization in the west
> had operated more than ten years and set itself the task of military aid to
> Japanese imperialism to separate from Mongolia the Durbets, Altai Mongols,
> and other minority nationalities, to found an independent State and to attack
> our territory. . . .[25]

Primitive customs allegedly persisted among the Oirats in the 1930s, and they
had built seven new Buddhist temples in 1936–1937. A special joint meeting
of the Central Committee and the Council of Ministers in June 1938
discussed national minorities in the Kobdo District, and set up a Special
Council for Kazakh National Minority Affairs. Close copying of Soviet policy
included adoption of the Latin script that was already being used in the
Kazakh Republic, and invitations to Soviet specialists to come to western
Mongolia to assist in implementing a minority-nationalities policy.[26]

On April 7, 1939, the Buryats officially switched from the Latin to the
Cyrillic alphabet, which was the standard among all the Soviet national
minorities at that time, and Cyrillic finally came into use in the MPR in 1945–
1946. Walter Kolarz suggested that the Latin alphabet had international
connotations and the Cyrillic alphabet had Russian nationalist overtones—
thus the shift had a definite ideological significance.[27]

Development of the working class was aided by the opening of the first
factory in Mongolia in 1933, and of the largest enterprise, the Industrial
Kombinat in Ulan Bator, on March 26, 1934. By 1939 there were approximately 10,000 industrial workers, the "proletariat," in Mongolia, and another
10,000 workers in handicraft-industrial cooperatives. Mongolia had no factory
comparable to the locomotive works in Ulan Ude, which had 6,000 workers
(including 500 Buryats) in 1939. By 1939 Mongols substantially outnumbered
Russian and Chinese among the workers in the MPR (see Table 1).

Trade-union members in 1938 included 8,062 Mongols, 599 Russians, and
1,030 Chinese. More Mongols left the industrial labor force in these years
than joined it, however: for many in the 1930s, factory work was seasonal and
temporary, and they faded back into the steppe. Meanwhile a large number
of ex-lamas were supposed to have been absorbed into productive labor—
more than 30,000 of them in 1936–1938 alone—but there was not enough
industry to employ them, and most of them must have gone back into
livestock herding.[28]

Of approximately 80,000 children of school age in the MPR, 25,000
received some sort of education in the 1930s. Twice as many pupils were in

TABLE 1
NATIONALITIES OF WORKERS IN THE MPR DURING THE 1930s

	1934	1939
Mongols	51%	88%
Russians	39	6
Chinese	10	7

monastery schools, which were based on Tibetan and Buddhist teaching, as were in secular schools, until the monasteries were closed in 1937–1939. In 1940 22,000 pupils were registered in secular schools, and none in religious ones. The army systematically trained its recruits, at least to the point of attaining literacy. While the monastery pupils and the army recruits were all males, the new secular schools included substantial numbers of females: in a specific one visited by Ma Ho-tien in 1927 a third of the 200 pupils were girls. Ma pointed out that "There is not the slightest distinction between the sexes. . . . Chinese women are vastly inferior in that respect."[29] A *rabfak* (a school that prepared people without the necessary educational background) opened in Ulan Ude on February 10, 1930, to prepare Mongols to become regular students at Soviet universities. Four hundred Mongols had completed the course by 1940. Two of its alumni were Tsedenbal, who went on to graduate from the Finance Institute at Irkutsk University, and Shirendyb, who after preparation in the *rabfak* completed a teacher-training course in Irkutsk and eventually became head of the Mongolian Academy of Sciences. Both Tsedenbal and Shirendyb married Russians.

ECONOMIC CONSIDERATIONS

Rapid collectivization of livestock constituted an important part of radical policy in the USSR and in the MPR. Severe losses of animals and widespread revolt and virtual civil war led to abandonment of the program in the MPR in mid-1932; collectivization of Mongolian herds was actually accomplished only twenty-five years later. The fact that the MPR embarked on this radical measure almost simultaneously with the USSR in 1929 but abandoned it in 1932, while the Soviet Union continued the program despite heavy economic losses, throws light on the extent of Mongolian independence and control of its own domestic policy. The official Mongolian and Soviet version is that the Mongols embarked on the program independently, went too far too fast in uncritical adoption of the Soviet model despite Russian cautions and warnings but then reversed themselves when the Russians told them they were pushing too hard, and finally recognized the truth of the Soviet charge only after considerable damage had been done. In fact, the Russians imposed rapid collectivization on the Mongols against their will, pushed it despite violent Mongolian opposition and tremendous loss of livestock, and then reversed themselves and directed the Mongols to abandon the program in mid-1932. The Mongols were happy to do so, and economic improvement resulted almost immediately. The disastrous attempt had originated with a series of Comintern directives which the Mongols had attempted to ignore but finally had to obey. Soviet initiative, example, direction, approval, and even participation accompanied "left deviation" in the MPR.

In December 1927 the Fifteenth Congress of the CPSU adopted the First USSR Five-Year Plan for the years 1928–1932. Collectivization of agriculture, including livestock, was one of its provisions. On May 14, 1929, just a month after he had maneuvered Bukharin out of the leadership of the Comintern, Stalin issued the following instructions: "It is necessary right now—without losing a minute, for time will not wait—to undertake the purging of the Communist Parties of Rightist and conciliatory elements. . . . And this task must be undertaken not in the usual tempo, but in an accelerated tempo. . . ."[30] Dmitry Manuilsky, the secretary of the ECCI from 1928 to 1943, told the tenth plenum of the Comintern in July 1929: "We are conducting an energetic offensive in the USSR against capitalist elements in town and village."[31]

Detailed discussion of the Mongolian "First Five-Year Plan" began in September 1929, including promulgation of a livestock-collectivization program. By the end of 1929, even before the plan had been adopted, 10 percent of Mongolian livestock had become collectivized; the corresponding figure for Buryat livestock was 15 percent. The Eighth Mongolian Party Congress met February–April 1930 and adopted the First Five-Year Plan, to cover the years 1931–1935. By the end of this period the goal of a seven-million-head increase in livestock was to have been reached. A Buryat, I. V. Chenkirov, was sent into the MPR to enforce the Comintern directive demanding collectivization, and with him went "a large group of Party, Soviet, and Komsomol workers, basically from Buryat Party organizations."[32]

On March 2, 1930, however, Stalin delivered his famous "Dizzy with Success" speech, which argued that caution was necessary, and in April the ECCI advised the Mongols that rapid collectivization would be a dangerous course.[33] That warning, in particular, has been cited as an indication that the Russians cautioned the Mongols not to move too fast. The context of Stalin's speech (and the Comintern instruction), however, suggested that it was an attempt to divert public criticism of, and resistance to, confiscation of livestock and property—thus a tactical statement rather than a programmatic and policy one.

Any idea that the Russians were unsuccessfully trying to restrain the ultra-left policies of overzealous Mongols seems disproved by Pavel Mif's speech at the Sixteenth Congress of the CPSU, held June–July 1930 (Mif dealt with China for the Comintern, and served several years as rector of Sun Yat-sen University in Moscow):

> We have seen tremendous successes in the revolutionary movement in Mongolia, where in the past year, under the leadership of the MPRP, there was carried through the confiscation of the cattle and property of feudal and other reactionary elements, where the cooperative and to some extent the kolkhoz movements have been strengthened, where the Left party leadership, which gained power recently, has been conducting ever more systematically and persistently a policy in support of the interests of the poor. As a result of all these revolutionary measures, the way is now opened in Mongolia—one of the most backward countries in the world—to push forward on the road of autonomous development, non-capitalist and independent of international imperialism.[34]

At the Sixteenth CPSU Congress Stalin also delivered his famous "beaten" speech, which insisted on maintaining momentum of radical measures at a radical pace: "It is sometimes asked whether it is not possible to slow down the tempo a bit. . . . No, comrades, it is not possible! . . . We must increase it as much as it is within our powers and possibilities. . . . To slacken the tempo would mean falling behind. And those who fall behind get beaten. . . ."[35]

On September 6, 1930, an RSFSR decree called for permanent settlement of nomads in Russia,[36] and by June 1931 continuing, uninterrupted collectivization in both the MPR and the USSR had affected 32 percent of the animals in the MPR and 40 percent of Buryat livestock. Losses were mounting, however, and by early 1932 the Mongols had lost eight million head of livestock, a third of their total herds. (Five million animals had already died as a result of the policy even before the First Five-Year Plan officially began in 1931). Buryat and Kalmyk losses were similar in scale. Buryats were fleeing by the thousands to the MPR, and Khalkhas were fleeing by the thousands to Inner Mongolia and North China. Thirty thousand Buryats were reported in the MPR in 1931 and some twenty thousand Khalkha refugees were still reported in China in 1934; the actual totals were probably much higher. Widespread revolt raged in the MPR.

On May 29, 1932, the ECCI and the Central Committee of the CPSU issued a directive to the MPRP to reverse course and abandon collectivization. On June 20 the Central Committee of the MPRP formally accepted the recommendation[37] and special Party and government meetings in July scrapped collectivization and abandoned the "First Five-Year Plan," shifting to the right politically and economically in a move called the "New Turn." August 1932 was marked by precipitate disbandment of all the collectives in the MPR, and complete reversal of the former radical policy. On September 22, 1932, the regime in Ulan Bator announced the "complete suppression of the rebellion."[38] All MPR livestock were once again in private ownership by December 1932, but Buryat collectivization continued (by that time 61 percent of Buryat herds were affected). By 1937 the stubborn persistence of the USSR had resulted in the collectivization of 91 percent of Buryat herds and 95 percent of Kalmyk ones.[39]

The USSR-controlled Comintern and the Central Committee of the CPSU had ordered the adoption of concurrent and nearly identical radical policies in the USSR and the MPR in 1928-1929; in mid-1932 they ordered the adoption of separate policies. Stalin met personally with the Buryat prime minister some time in 1932 to discuss how to save the livestock in the Baikal area of the USSR, and limited concessions were made, including toleration of controlled private ownership of some animals. The MPR abandoned the whole program, however, and reversed what had already been done, on the instructions of the ECCI and the CPSU. The immediacy of the Japanese threat and the vulnerability of the MPR, which was being torn by violent dissension, undoubtedly contributed to this decision; but it was also probably easier for the Russians to admit their mistake and abandon their policy in an area that was not formally part of the USSR and thus did not directly involve Stalin's prestige.

The livestock total for the MPR had fallen from twenty-three million head in 1930 to sixteen million in 1932. The abandonment of collectivization dramatically reversed this rapid decline: half the losses had been made up by the end of 1933, and all of them by 1936. The continuation of collectivization among the Buryats caused a continuing decline in the number of their livestock. It was evident that rapid forced collectivization killed animals. The New Turn in the MPR, which lifted the repressive and unpopular measures, led directly to recovery.

This abortive First Five-Year Plan was scrapped in July 1932 and has never been mentioned since: although it was described in detail in Russian-language publications issued in the MPR and Buryat Mongolia from September 1929 to April 1930,[40] it has been ignored since then. The officially recognized First Five-Year Plan ran from 1948 through 1952.

The dismantling of the collectives in 1932 was criticized later as overreaction, and in 1938 Choibalsan tried to make it clear that the policy of collectivization was not discredited by the 1932 dissolution: only the timing had been wrong; the policy had been right.[41]

Conditions became oppressive and violent again in 1937, however, and while reported livestock figures serenely continued to rise, population began to decline. The only five-year period between 1921 and the 1970s to show decreasing population totals was 1935-1940, and 1938-1939 was the only year in which total population showed a net loss (from 747,500 to 725,000). In 1935 deaths from all causes were 12,100 (16.7 per thousand); in 1940 they totalled 15,900 (21.8 per thousand). Bawden pointed out that between 1935 and 1938 the female population rose by 12,500, while the male population declined by 3,200.

There was heavy political pressure to report increasing livestock totals. Stalin had made an offhand remark that Mongolia should support two hundred million head of livestock by 1951–1953, and Choibalsan employed that figure in his report to the Tenth Party Congress in 1940. Tsendenbal told the same congress that a goal of fifty million head must be attained by 1945, and a formal resolution of the congress called for fifty million by 1945 and two hundred million by 1953. The 1969 *History of the MPR* noted that "the above-mentioned slogan was unrealistic."[42] If in fact the total never exceeded twenty-three million head,[43] the drop to twenty-one million in 1945 (the actual total for that year) seems far less extreme, and that change must affect our evaluation of the extent of Soviet exploitation of Mongolia during World War II. It simply does not seem likely that the number of animals increased substantially while the number of people declined due to violent repression and while the Buddhist Church was being finally and brutally destroyed.

Despite propaganda by the Soviets about the importance of forming a proletariat and their requirement that the Mongolians industrialize their country, the Russians did not assist the Mongols in any significant way or encourage them to reach these goals by themselves. The primitive Mongolian economy was left basically unchanged. The MPR was to export raw materials to be processed in Russia. Industrial buildup proceeded in the USSR, but Mongolia was allowed to stagnate. Clearly Mongolia existed to serve Russia's national security, and military-strategic requirements were allowed to prevail over ideological precepts.[44]

ORGANIZATIONAL CONSIDERATIONS

The MPRP was only one among many decision makers and power wielders in Mongolia in the 1930s. Others included individual leaders such as Joseph Stalin and Khorloin Choibalsan; the military—both the Soviet Red Army and the Mongolian People's Army; the secret police—the USSR's NKVD and the Mongolian GVO-MVD; the Comintern, represented by Buryat Mongols and by international Communists such as Shmeral; and the Russian diplomatic representative in Ulan Bator. In general, the Comintern, the Buryat Mongols, and the Revsomols (which were dissolved entirely in 1934) exerted much less power and influence in the 1930s than they did in the 1920s. Choibalsan had been on the periphery of real power ever since 1921, but in the 1930s he became a far more powerful figure than he had ever been before. Stalin, of course, was at the height of his power in the 1930s, and his control was as strong in Mongolia as it was in the Soviet Union itself.

The MPRP was so often and so seriously wracked by major purges and leadership crises that it could not have provided effective administration. Purges and upheavals caused the loss of one third of the party's membership in 1928–1929, three fifths in 1932, and four fifths in 1934. The total membership in 1932 was forty-two thousand; in 1934, eight thousand; and in 1940, thirteen thousand. The top leadership was purged several times: many Presidium members and Party secretaries lost their positions and their lives. Choibalsan was the major survivor, and he credited Stalin with a major role in his success.[45]

The Party was not very effective during these years. The 1969 official *History of the MPR* indicated that "there were certain leading personages of the MPRP who were nationalistically minded, whose education was shallow, who were theoretical and political dogmatists, who had bad backgrounds as small owners, who lacked toughness and endurance, and who had little experience."[46] Fifty-five percent of Party members were illiterate in 1934. Choibalsan complained in January 1938 that even the Party's elite were extremely lackadaisical in their approach to their work, and that "Leaders of the Party and the Government do not themselves go among the arats, do not work with them, do not leave their offices."[47]

Like their Soviet counterparts, Mongolian Party congresses met increasingly infrequently during the 1930s (see Table2). The Seventh Congress lasted forty-eight days and the Eighth, forty-two days, but the Ninth Congress lasted only eight days. The Tenth lasted fifteen days, but since it had 635 delegates, three times the number attending earlier Congresses, free discussion was limited.

A classical Communist dispute on the proper relationship between party and government emerged at the Ninth Congress of 1934. Gendun allegedly spoke of strengthening the government at the expense of the Party in 1933, and the Comintern representatives at the Party congress, Shmeral and

TABLE 2
SOVIET AND MONGOLIAN PARTY CONGRESSES, 1927–1940

Congress	CPSU		MPRP
Fifteenth	Nov. 1927	Seventh	Oct.–Dec. 1928
Sixteenth	June–July 1930	Eighth	Feb.–April 1930
Seventeenth	Jan. 1934	Ninth	Sept.–Oct. 1934
Eighteenth	March 1939	Tenth	March–April 1940

Kolarov,[48] criticized Gendun's view and insisted that the Party must direct the government.[49] The Little Khural, which functioned as the Presidium of the Great Khural, or People's Assembly, from 1924 through 1950 and was often more important than the parent body, included top-level leaders among its members and appeared sometimes to function like the Party's Central Committee, although it was officially part of the government.[50]

The formerly powerful Revsomols, who numbered 23,000 in 1931, were disbanded in 1934. According to Misshima and Goto, the Revsomols had attacked the excessive number and cost of Soviet advisers in November 1933. The Russians had reportedly responded by sending 54 more high military officials for the Mongols to support financially. Revsomol leaders were also arrested, and some of them were executed. The youth organization was recreated in 1935, but it was no longer autonomous, and was completely subject to Party domination. Its membership was just over 6,000 in 1935 and about 17,000 in 1940.

The Mongols experienced a double cult of personality. Its original idol, Stalin, was revered as much in Mongolia as in the Soviet Union, and Choibalsan set himself up as a copy, always acknowledging his debt to Stalin and his own junior position. For example, he praised "the fatherly solicitude of the great Stalin for the destiny and fortunes of our people."[51] Choibalsan emerged in mid-1940 holding concurrently the positions of prime minister, minister of foreign affairs, minister of internal affairs, minister of war, and commander in chief of the army. For years he had led a political minority group that was more radical and more closely connected to the Soviet Union than the regular government and Party were, but most of his rivals had been eliminated during the purges of the 1930s and 1940s.

Choibalsan has often been referred to as "Mongolia's Stalin," and there was indeed a parallel. Both men led their countries practically single-handed for many years, after having gained power through internecine struggle and the elimination of many rivals. Both stressed power and survival with little regard for niceties and subtleties. Both took "their" countries through reigns of terror and destruction, and both consigned their enemies to oblivion, destroying many fine and gifted people. Both also built up what came to be called a "cult of personality," and both were posthumously attacked for having done so. De-Choibalsanization in Mongolia paralleled de-Stalinization in the Soviet Union. Choibalsan copied Stalin, the original.[52]

The Mongolian army, which became much more effective by the end of the decade than it had been earlier, was used domestically to support revolutionary policy; it was, said I. Ya. Zlatkin, "a powerful tool in the struggle with the forces of internal reaction." Sorkin indicated that in the 1920s the Soviet military instructors Kosich and Kangelari actually served as chiefs of staff of the Mongolian army,[53] and he indicated that all the Soviet military instructors were actively involved in Mongolian political developments.

Professor Nicholas Poppe of the University of Washington, a renowned Mongolist who left the USSR during World War II, testified in February 1952 to a Congressional Committee investigating the Institute of Pacific Relations (IPR) that to control the serious rebellion of 1932, "tanks and aircraft were rushed from Russia to Mongolia." Zlatkin publicly denied that statement,[54] but the denial should not be credited. Air Marshal V. A. Sudets practically stated outright that the Russians used planes against troublesome lamas and monasteries.[55] Bawden referred to the destruction obviously wrought at Erdeni Dzu, probably in 1937 or 1938, and noted that the perpetrators of the deed are unknown. Events around the same time in Aga, Buryat Mongolia, suggest that the Red Army had no reluctance about destroying Buddhist monasteries,[56] and that it entered Mongolia in force in 1937. There is no proof that the Russians destroyed Erdeni Dzu, but much speculation that they did so.

The Mongolian army faced resistance by the church in its efforts to get recruits. A decree of February 13, 1936, noted: "Lay people deliberately become lamas for the purpose of avoiding military service." Draft dodging by this route became common, and only the tougher and more strictly enforced laws of the latter part of the decade succeeded in overcoming the church's resistance.[57] In December 1934 it was noted that "We will continue as before to prepare within the Army workers for State offices." In January 1938 Choibalsan noted the army's significant role in supplying cadres. The army also provided training in reading and writing and many skills.[58]

The Soviet MVD undoubtedly entered increasingly into the MPR with the arrival of the Red Army and the military integration of Mongolia with the Soviet Transbaikal and Far East military districts. Bawden concluded that, "the most likely explanation will be that in and after 1936 effective power in Mongolia was in the hands of the NKVD, and so ultimately of Stalin, for some years. . . . Mongolia's purges were being directed from outside the country, and were dictated by the course of events in, and the interests of, the USSR."[59] The 1969 official *History of the MPR* claimed that Gendun appropriated and misused the GVO for his own personal ends in 1932–1936, and "caused quite a few Party and other responsible persons to perish unjustly." It also alleged that by similarly appropriating and misusing the MVD in 1937–1939, Choibalsan committed "crude violations of revolutionary law, and this led to many people's perishing."[60] Plots, counterplots, trials, and executions all too clearly echoed and mirrored the Great Terror of Stalin in the USSR. Choibalsan's terror served political ambition and reflected paranoid exaggeration.

The Buryat-Comintern team that had functioned as a major instrument of

Soviet manipulation of the MPR in the 1920s almost literally died: so many of the leading Buryats were purged and killed by 1937 that the group ceased to exist. The role played by non-Buryat Comintern representatives in Mongolia was never important, and the appearance of Shmeral and Kolarov at the Ninth Mongolian Party Congress in Ulan Bator in 1934 marked the ceremonial end of a relationship that had actually perished many years before. The power of the Comintern in China had also declined,[61] and the organization had generally lost its predominance and importance.

The trial-and-terror method was pursued in Mongolia because: (1) Japan represented a genuine threat, and Mongolia was genuinely vulnerable to that threat; (2) Marxist-Leninist ideology required the elimination of religion and of feudalism; (3) the Russians, the "elder brothers" of the Mongols,[62] operated in that way; and (4) the elimination of rivals and opponents furthered Choibalsan's career. "National security" served as a justification for any and all preventive and punitive measures.

The regime used paranoia, hyperbole, and hysteria in connecting separate acts of resistance or dissent in the church, the army, industry, or other institutions into one Big Plot endangering the country. Acts that might have stemmed from inefficiency or incompetency were interpreted as being deliberate and sinister. The creation of a spectre of a grand united conspiracy suited the regime. Almost any suspicious event could be (and in the 1930s often was) escalated into treasonous support for Japan, which was punishable by death or by a long prison term. To commit such treason required no direct contact with any Japanese anywhere at any time,[63] nor any actual meeting with alleged fellow conspirators. In a story that was widely circulated for many years, Gendun, Demid, and General J. Yondon plotted together, turning away from Russia and toward Japan.[64] Subsequent de-Stalinization, de-Choibalsanization, and rehabilitation have cleared up some of these politically motivated false charges. Demid has been cleared, but Gendun has not. In 1938 Choibalsan needed a Big Plot to correspond to Stalin's Big Plot in the USSR at the time.[65] The situation resembled the one Solzhenitsyn described among the administrative personnel of the Jida camp (just a few hundred miles from Ulan Bator) in 1937. He quoted them as saying, "We've fallen behind! Everyone else has plots, and we have fallen behind! We do have a major plot of course, but what kind?"[66]

SUMMARY

The military-strategic aim of the coordinated Russian-Mongolian program was to provide a united defense against the threat of Japan. The Mongolian border was closed and impermeable. Mongolia was militarily integrated with the Soviet Transbaikal and Far East military districts.

The major ideological goal was the destruction of the Buddhist Church. Although only a minority of Mongols favored that policy, judicious Soviet backing of certain anti-church Mongols against the others, plus the presence of Red Army troops in the later 1930s and the use of such instruments as the NKVD, facilitated its accomplishment.

One economic goal, that of shifting Mongolia's trade from China to Russia and excluding any substantial Chinese presence in Mongolia, was accomplished, but the livestock-collectivization attempt failed. The political goals were attained, but only after traumatic struggle and the elimination by force and execution of many people who were unacceptable to the Russians and/or the Mongols.

There were distinct shifts in the political climate during the 1930s from left to right and back to left; in the end, Choibalsan and a leftist philosophy prevailed.[67] Much of Mongolian politics derived, in both substance and form, from Russian originals.

The military-strategic requirement was basic; all else was built on that. The destruction of the church involved two separate elements: a change from the backwardness and superstition the Soviet and Mongolian regimes talked about so much, and the elimination of a rival power base. Stalin's ubiquitous drive for unalloyed control penetrated to Mongolia, too: he would permit no independent and autonomous structure to survive very long.

The insistence on bypassing capitalism was manipulated to require the exclusion of the Chinese, even if the Russians were not really prepared to replace them. The isolation of Mongolia and the sealing of its borders were justified by the threat of Japan, but these measures were also used to separate Mongolia from China, even though the military-strategic requirement was supposed to have been Soviet-Chinese cooperation against Japan. Stalin actually preferred isolation and sealed borders, and simply justified his psychological preference by citing military-strategic motives for it.

The enforced collectivization of livestock was ideologically justified, but in this case too the drive for power and control was a significant element. The attempt was abandoned, however, when it appeared to endanger the military security of the USSR.

Although the Soviets provided practically no industrial development or investment in Mongolia despite the ideological imperatives to supply them—military-strategic requirements overrode ideological ones—Mongolia in 1940 was not the same as Mongolia in 1921. Their positive contributions in providing education offset the negative one of destroying the church. The "new Mongols" had broader horizons and less constricted minds; much restrictive and superstitious debris was cleared away. Thus the Russian influence in Mongolia was in many ways a progressive one, enabling the Mongols to emerge from feudalism while bypassing capitalism.

5. World War II and the Death of Choibalsan: 1940–1952

MILITARY-STRATEGIC CONSIDERATIONS

Following their defeat at Nomonkhan in 1939, the Japanese concluded a neutrality pact with the USSR on April 13, 1941. In the Mongolian-Soviet version of events, which ignores or deemphasizes the war between Japan and the United States in the Pacific, the Japanese prepared a massive offensive against Mongolia and the USSR despite the neutrality pact, but the German defeat at Stalingrad and surrender there in January 1943 caused Japan to abandon that offensive plan.[1]

Control of Mongolia provided the Russians with a valuable base for operations in Manchuria, and half the Soviet force that participated in the lightning campaign against Japan from August 8 through 20, 1945, went into Manchuria and Inner Mongolia from bases in the MPR. The Mongolians and Soviets insist that this offensive played the "decisive role" in the defeat of Japan in World War II. The 1969 *History of the MPR* says of the part the United States played in ending the war:

> Without any need whatsoever for using them in the Anti-Japanese War, the American imperialists dropped atomic bombs over the Japanese cities of Hiroshima and Nagasaki on August 6 and 9, inhumanly killing many hundreds of thousands of ordinary people and committing a crime before mankind. . . . [T]hey considered that this was the main reason for Japan's defeat in the War and attempted to deny the decisive role of the Soviet Army as well as to frighten the world with the atomic bomb.[2]

Actually, Japan was already defeated before the joint Mongolian-Soviet operations in Manchuria began, so the main military question had already been decided. The Mongolian-Soviet action was a huge maneuver, a great war game that tested equipment and transport capacity. The buildup in the Far East that began in February 1945 was undertaken seriously, but the offensive itself only confirmed an outcome that was already known. A. M. Vasil'evsky commanded 1.5 million men of the "Special High Command of Soviet Forces in the Far East" in August 1945; under him were three army groups. The largest of these, the Transbaikal army group, was commanded by

Roman Malinovsky. A great part of that force was in eastern Mongolia, much of it in a joint Soviet-Mongolian horse cavalry-mechanized group (KMG) under the command of I. A. Pliev, with Choibalsan leading the Mongolian elements. Pliev's group included four Mongolian cavalry divisions and three Mongolian tank regiments, which moved southeast to Dolon-Nor (and occupied it on August 17), and a smaller Mongolian contingent consisting of one motorized brigade and one artillery regiment, which moved with much larger Soviet forces to Kalgan (and occupied it on August 20). There were no more than 80,000 Mongolian troops in all, and their total casualties were 675.[3]

The careers of the longtime (1959–1969) minister of defense and commander of the Mongolian army, Jamyangiin Lkhagvasuren, and his successor, B. Dorj, were connected with those of the Red Army generals Pliev and A. I. Danilov in a way that illustrates very important aspects of the Mongolian-Soviet relationship. J. Lkhagvasuren went to the Soviet Union in 1935, where he attended the Lenin Military-Political Academy, and returned to Mongolia in January 1939. Pliev arrived in the MPR in 1936, when 110 Soviet military instructors were sent to that country to help build up its defenses against Japan; he left the MPR in the spring of 1938 for Belorussia and a distinguished career on the European front during World War II. Both Lkhagvasuren, who was then deputy chief of staff of the Mongolian army, and Colonel B. Tsog, a division commander,[4] served under Zhukov at Nomonkhan in August 1939.

In 1945 the buildup of the Soviet forces to attack the Japanese included the establishment of a Far Eastern front, which was divided into three parts: the Transbaikal, the First Far Eastern, and the Second Far Eastern. Included in the Transbaikal front was the KMG, including Mongolian cavalry and Soviet tank and armor units, under General Pliev's command.[5] Another part of that Transbaikal front was the Seventeenth Red Army, commanded by General A. I. Danilov. Pliev's deputy from the Mongolian contingent was Lkhagvasuren, and one of the cavalry-division commanders was Dorj. Pliev's KMG occupied Kalgan, Dolon-Nor, and Jehol City in August 1945. Pliev later left Mongolia; Lkhagvasuren came to be army commander in chief and minister of defense; and Dorj attended the Frunze Military Academy in the USSR. In 1963 General Danilov was sent to Ulan Bator as senior adviser to the Mongolian forces that were being built up against China. In 1969 Dorj replaced Lkhagvasuren as commander in chief and minister of defense. Pliev accompanied or headed several Soviet military delegations to the MPR for such occasions as the fortieth and forty-third anniversaries of the establishment of the Mongolian army and the celebration in Ulan Bator of the fiftieth anniversary of the establishment of the Soviet army.[6]

The presence of Soviet and Mongolian military units in Inner Mongolia and Manchuria raised the possibility of uniting Inner Mongolia with the MPR. A Soviet book published in 1975 offered this assessment:

> The defeat of the Japanese aggressors in 1945 and liberation of the territory of Inner Mongolia by soldiers of the Soviet Union and the MPR established favorable conditions for responding to the needs of the people for national regeneration.

> In August 1945 in the liberated regions there spread a wide movement for national self-determination. The Mongolian arats demonstrated massively for self-determination and the union of Inner Mongolia with the MPR. At numerous meetings and gatherings in all hoshuns and aimaks unanimous resolutions were adopted on this question. An uninterrupted stream of letters was addressed to the Government of the MPR.[7]

United States diplomats and foreign-service officers on the scene reported a strong possibility of a Soviet takeover in Inner Mongolia, especially in July and August 1947.[8] Meanwhile the Kuomintang appeared to be going out of its way to antagonize and discourage Mongols; the house arrest of Teh Wang in Peking during most of the crucial period 1945–1948 meant that the most authentic, gifted, and popular non-Communist leader of the Mongols was precluded from participation in the struggle against Communist domination.[9]

Ulanfu, supporting Mao at all times, effectively negotiated with and fought the Soviets, and sometimes deceived them; he ultimately emerged as the top CCP political figure in Inner Mongolia, while the Kuomintang was totally defeated and the Russians and the Mongols of the MPR returned to Ulan Bator. At several places and on numerous occasions it appeared that the Russians and the MPR did intend to pursue an active and forward policy, but they always withdrew before any serious confrontation occurred. For a time in the latter part of 1947 it seemed that the MPR might support the Barga leader, Hafengge, against Ulanfu, but in January 1948 Hafengge decided to change sides rather than fight: Barga was incorporated into Ulanfu's Inner Mongolian Autonomous Region (IMAR) and Hafengge became a deputy chairman of the region.

In what Dreyer called "a belated burst of creative thinking," Teh Wang was released by the KMT and appeared at Alashan in the spring of 1949; by then, however, Fu Tso-yi, a veteran Kuomintang army officer and commander in chief of the North China Bandit Suppression Headquarters in 1949, had already surrendered Kalgan to the Chinese Communists' People's Liberation Army (PLA). Before the end of the year, the governor of Suiyuan (Tung Chi-wu), who flanked Teh Wang on the west, defected to the Communists, thereby placing the Mongol in a hopeless situation. Teh Wang fled—to the MPR.[10]

In Sinkiang, the defection of Sheng Shih-tsai from the Russians in 1942 led to significantly modified border relationships with the MPR. Osman Bator, a Kazakh who had been struggling against Sheng Shih-tsai since February 1940,[11] became a desirable Soviet-Mongolian ally as a result of the shift in Sheng's loyalties; beginning in 1942, Osman occasionally took refuge from his Chinese pursuers in the MPR, usually north of his headquarters at Barkol. His hiding place was a mountain called Baitik Bogdo near the border town of Peitashan, northeast of Urumchi and several hundred miles east of Shara Sume. Chinese and Mongols disagreed about the location of the border in that area, and many incidents occurred involving claims that China invaded MPR territory in pursuit of Osman Bator. The scale and political significance of these clashes escalated substantially in March 1944, when the Chinese (no longer Sheng Shih-tsai, but the KMT) claimed that Soviet planes had attacked Chinese troops on Chinese soil. The Soviet-Mongolian story was that the Chinese troops had invaded Mongolia, and that the Mongolian Air Force had helped to repel them. Averell Harriman reported a talk on the subject that he had with Stalin on June 10, 1944:

> I asked whether Soviet planes had participated in the border skirmishes. The Marshal [Stalin] replied that several squadrons of Soviet planes had been turned over to their Mongolian ally. Some of these planes had participated. They were piloted by Mongolian fliers, however. The Marshal added that Soviet armed forces would be sent to the assistance of Mongolia if Sinkiang troops endeavored to invade it. . . .[12]

Henry Wallace, who was then on a special fact-finding mission in Asia, reported to President Franklin Roosevelt on July 10, 1944, that "[The difficulties . . . in the early spring on the Sinkiang, Outer Mongolian border were caused by Chinese attempts to resettle Kazakh nomads who fled into Outer Mongolia, [and] were followed by Chinese troops who were driven back by Mongols."[13]

A large-scale Uighur rebellion broke out late in 1944, and on the anniversary of the Bolshevik Revolution that year, the East Turkestan Republic (ETR) was proclaimed. It included the three northwestern districts of Sinkiang: Ili, Chuguchak, and Altai. In September 1945 a 6,000-man army, including Osman Bator and his Kazakhs, arrived in Shara Sume; the whole province was seething. In a remarkable and incompletely explained development, between November 10, 1945, and June 20, 1946, 120,000 Kazakhs, Uighurs, and Russians living in the ETR area of northwest Sinkiang were granted citizenship in the USSR and given Soviet passports with Soviet visas. It certainly looked like the Soviets were preparing to annex the ETR, especially since Tuva had been incorporated into the USSR in October 1944,[14] but no annexation occurred.

Uighurs quarreled with Kazakhs, and nationalists of many stripes opposed Soviet interference, so that tensions and rivalry never let up. Osman and his Kazakhs broke with the others, and ultimately the Soviet Russians. The fighting around Peitashan in June 1947 became an excuse for the KMT and China to condemn the MPR in the United Nations.[15] Osman opposed the Chinese Communists when they entered the province: in March 1950, 16,000 Kazakhs began to leave Sinkiang permanently, but the Chinese Communists slaughtered 7,000 of them, and Osman himself was caught and executed in April 1951. Only 350 Kazakh survivors ultimately reached Srinagar, Kashmir.[16]

In the 1940s—World War II and its immediate aftermath—a quinquennium of war plus a quinquennium of adjustment to the new postwar conditions diverted attention from Mongolia. That small country was for everybody a peripheral matter: China was absorbed in civil war, the USSR was concerned with Europe and busy with domestic reconstruction, and Japan was licking the wounds of defeat and limiting itself to the Pacific off the mainland. Yet the war had subjected the whole of Central Asia to forces that could have led to fundamental reorientation, and the postwar years might have significantly altered its political and strategic patterns. The USSR might have extended its predominant influence to Manchuria, Inner Mongolia, and Sinkiang. Although many events in 1944–1947 indicated that such Soviet expansion was indeed occurring or at least being attempted, in the end no such shift in orientation occurred: New China controls Manchuria, Inner Mongolia, and Sinkiang more completely than did old China.

IDEOLOGICAL CONSIDERATIONS

The Constitution of 1940 marked the end of feudalism in Mongolia and the elimination of the influence and power of the Buddhist Church. The Communist regime considered Buddhism the main force of feudalism, and the principal enemy to be destroyed in the process of the development of socialism. The regime in Ulan Bator presented the campaign to eliminate Buddhism in the MPR as "a historical accomplishment of the Mongolian people on their non-capitalist path of development,"[17] and as a policy of international significance that should constitute a basic part of the model of the evolution of feudal societies to socialism. Replacing Buddhism with Communism in Mongolia was a violent process, and considerable blood was spilled. The Communists "succeeded," in that they virtually destroyed the church by 1940, while they were eliminating feudalism and bypassing capitalism, but they were not at that time building socialism. The 1940s were a decade that lacked vigorous movement—a presocialist limbo.

Ivan Maisky wrote in 1950 that "the Mongolian people have made an astounding leap from Feudalism to People's Democracy bypassing the Capitalist stage. In world history nothing like this has ever previously occurred."[18] Certainly much had been done toward eliminating the identity of the Mongols. The most important elements of that identity had been the Buddhist religion (in a Tibetan, lamaist version); the nomadic livestock herding of most Mongols outside the church; the Turkic language of the Mongols, unrelated to Chinese or Russian; their literature, which was largely folkloric and epic in form and content; and their history, which could be summed up in the name of Chinggis Khan and in the idea of pan-Mongolism. By 1940 Buddhism had essentially been eliminated, but the nomadic way of life continued much as before. The traditional language was retained and even encouraged, but the Russian influence was felt in the adoption of the Cyrillic script instead of the old form and in the content of education—the regime manipulated investigation and scholarship to discredit Chinggis Khan and pan-Mongolism and thus the old "nationalistic" version of Mongolian history.

Secular education absorbed the young boys who had formerly gone into monasteries, and it also served girls—a revolutionary change. Another of the many areas that had formerly been dominated by lamas was medicine; the provision of medical care had been an important service of the church, and the new regime quickly found that until it could provide a substitute, the total elimination of the church would have to be delayed. That this would take some time was evident from the slow growth in number of Western-trained— that is, Russian-trained—doctors: there were only 108 in all Mongolia in 1940, 134 in 1947, and 180 in 1952.

Secular education was carried on in the Mongolian tongue, whereas the church had stressed the Tibetan. Literacy greatly increased (in 1935, only 6 percent of the population could read and write, but by the end of 1940 the figure was 20 percent, and in 1950 it was more than 60 percent), and within the literate population, the use of the Tibetan language almost disappeared. The official MPR decree adopting the new alphabet was dated March 25, 1941, but it included an interesting note that decrees of July 26, 1940, and February 21, 1941, providing for Latinization, were cancelled and superseded by the new regulation. Use of the Russian script began seriously in 1946, but publications printed in the old script continued to appear for several years after that. The official provision for the use of Arabic numerals was dated September 20, 1940.[19]

The university in Ulan Bator was established under Soviet supervision and with indispensable direct participation by Russians; on October 5, 1942, the first class of 89 students entered for what was then a one-year course. The 11 Russians who formed the first faculty included professors and instructors in various fields: one each in general chemistry, analytical chemistry, physics, mathematics, botany, and the Russian language, two in zoology (one in general zoology and one "zoo-technician"), and three in medicine (one each in anatomy, surgery, and physical therapy). Courses were taught in Russian. By the fall of 1944 there were 355 students and 25 professors, including several Mongols; the rector of the university then was Shirendyb, who later became president of the Academy of Sciences of the MPR. One of the students who delivered a report at the university's first scientific conference in November 1944 was D. Tsevegmid, who was later to serve as rector of the university, president of the Academy of Sciences, and then deputy prime minister and chairman of the State Committee on Higher and Special Middle Education.[20]

One of the highly qualified Soviet scholars who devoted years to study in the MPR and shaped an important part of the work of the Mongolian Committee of Sciences was the geographer E. M. Murzaev. He was in Mongolia as an adviser and expedition leader in 1940–1944, and he was a key figure in the Russian contribution to, and influence on, Mongolian studies and Mongols.[21] A high degree of professional competence and an impressive dedication to knowledge characterized at least some of the Russians in Mongolia, even though ideological restrictions and enforced conformity hampered others. Many examples of unconscionable manipulation occurred, however, and certain fields and subjects were obviously far more vulnerable than others.[22]

Russian influence was expressed in many ways. For example, the equestrian statue of Sukhe Bator in Ulan Bator's central square was dedicated in 1946. It was the product of a Mongolian sculptor, S. Choimbol, who had learned his craft in the USSR from 1943 through 1946 under the guidance of a Soviet artist, S. D. Merkulov. S. Gonchigsumla, who was to become the chairman of the Union of Mongolian Composers, began his schooling in Ulan Bator, but in 1934, at the age of nineteen, he enrolled at the Irkutsk Veterinary Technical Institute and became acquainted with European classical music. He played briefly as an accordionist with the orchestra of the state circus, and then in 1943 began to attend the Moscow Conservatory. The titles of his compositions usually reflected the socialist-realism theme: "Song of the Party"; "Glory to Sukhe Bator"; "Twenty Years of Socialist Mongolia"; and "Ulan Bator Waltz."[23]

In 1941 Tsedenbal made a complaint that would be repeated many times even in the 1970s: "We continue to find passiveness, fatalism, contemplation, submissiveness, and humility."[24] Mongols were supposed to become eager, active, supportive, positive, forward-looking, and future-oriented. There was to be no passive submission to fate, no blind acceptance of what existed, no uncritical bowing to forces beyond human understanding. Mongols were to see themselves as masters of their fate, but real Mongols were not like that.

ECONOMIC CONSIDERATIONS

The key economic indicator in Mongolia, the number of livestock, declined throughout the war and recovered very slowly in the immediate postwar years. The official First Five-Year Plan (for the period 1948–1952) was supposed to have increased the number of animals from twenty-one million head to thirty-one million, but in 1952 the actual total was less than twenty-three million. Taxes during the period of the plan were levied according to these theoretical livestock totals, not the actual number of animals owned. The totals were impossible to reach; the taxes were outrageous; the incentives were nonexistent; and the results were disastrous.[25]

During the war, exports of livestock and wool from the MPR to the USSR doubled, while the quantity of clothing shipped from the USSR to the MPR declined from a value of 13 million rubles in 1940 to 1.8 million in 1942 and 2.2 million in 1944. It was a period of Soviet exploitation of Mongolia.[26] The number of industrial workers, though still very small (less than thirty thousand), doubled during the decade 1940–1950, and more than one-fourth of these workers were women. A draconian labor law was enacted, and registration and labor books were required, but nevertheless severe labor shortages and poor attitudes continued to be the subject of many official speeches and pronouncements. Fifteen thousand Japanese prisoners of war in Ulan Bator from 1945 through 1947 impressed the Mongols with their hard work, which included considerable major construction in the capital city.[27]

The Russians added 225 miles of railroad—from the border to Ulan Bator—to the 150 miles that had been built before the war (from the Trans-Siberian Railroad at Ulan Ude to the Mongolian border). The first train ran officially on November 1, 1949, but full service may have begun only a year later.[28] In 1952 Murzaev noted that the rail service supplanted hundreds of trucks and thousands of camels and horses on the main route between Mongolia and the USSR, and that whereas it took a packhorse twelve to fifteen days to travel the Ulan Ude–Ulan Bator route, the train could cross it in less than a day. He cited S. S. Demidov's estimate that a single freight train could carry a load equivalent to that borne by seven thousand camels.[29] Solzhenitsyn reported that the railroad was entirely an NKVD, forced-labor project.[30]

ORGANIZATIONAL CONSIDERATIONS

The party congresses of the MPR, like those of the USSR, became even fewer and farther between during the 1940s and 1950s than they had been during the late 1920s and 1930s (compare Tables 2 and 3). Meetings of the full Central Committee were held semi-annually throughout this period. The last (thirty-second) Little Khural met in February 1950. Party membership more

TABLE 3
SOVIET AND MONGOLIAN PARTY CONGRESSES, 1939–1954

	CPSU		MPRP
Eighteenth	March 1939	Tenth	March–April 1940
		Eleventh	December 1947
Nineteenth	October 1952	Twelfth	November 1954

than doubled between 1940 and 1947, to a total of twenty-eight thousand (3 percent of the total population). Between 1947 and 1954, the percentage of workers among Party members increased markedly, the number of intellectuals increased slightly, and the number of livestock-herding arats decreased considerably (in 1954 15 percent of party members were workers, 39 percent were arats; and 46 percent were intellectuals). Sixty-eight percent of army officers were Party members or candidate-members in 1944.

Until the plebiscite of 1945 and the proclamation of independence in early 1946, the top official Russian in Ulan Bator was called a representative. In 1946 this representative, I. A. Ivanov, who had filled that position since 1939 and was a foreign-service professional, assumed the title of minister. His successor, Yu. K. Prikhodov, was minister from 1948 to 1950, and ambassador to Mongolia in 1950–1951.[31]

SUMMARY

World War II ended with Soviet-Mongolian troops in Manchuria and Inner Mongolia, and a confused situation in Sinkiang. Major territorial shifts were forecast, and the impression that the Russians had expansionist ambitions was widespread. The Kuomintang was criticized for its purported mishandling of minorities, and this area of Central Asia was judged to be an easy one for the Communists to exploit politically.[32]

Various powers were active in Inner Mongolia: the Soviet Union appeared to be trying to annex all or some of the region, the Kuomintang was mishandling a potentially valuable asset in Teh Wang, and Ulanfu was imaginatively and effectively maneuvering on behalf of the CCP.

In Sinkiang two separate developments in different parts of the province also suggested aggressive expansionism, but the situation was far from clear. The East Turkestan Republic (Ili) appeared to be preparing a maneuver of incorporation similar to that used in Tuva in 1944. At Peitashan, Osman Bator and his troops had used Mongolian territory as a sanctuary, and western Mongolia (and perhaps the USSR) was significantly involved in minor clashes with Chinese.

Although considerable jockeying took place, the end result differed little from the situation before the Communist takeover in Peking: all Sinkiang, including the "East Turkestan Republic," was incorporated into the Chinese People's Republic (CPR), and Ulanfu led a united IMAR that lost no territory to the MPR. Osman Bator was killed, and Teh Wang was placed under arrest in Peking. Peitashan continued to be a point of disagreement, but no further armed clashes with international complications took place.

PART THREE

THE AGE OF TSEDENBAL

6. China—Cooperation and Competition: 1952–1962

Choibalsan and Tsedenbal span the whole Communist period in Mongolia. Both were educated in Russia and both spoke Russian fluently; both spent long periods of time in the USSR; and both served as important instruments of Soviet control of the MPR—Soviet puppets. Choibalsan was the key Khalkha long before he emerged publicly as leader; he was a founding father of the MPRP, participating in the earliest events that marked its establishment and development. Throughout the dozen years he served as prime minister and was openly identified as the top political leader (1940–1952), Tsedenbal was his protégé and heir apparent. Nonetheless the two men differed considerably in background and style.

Choibalsan was far more like Stalin, whereas Tsedenbal resembled Brezhnev. Thus Mongolia, like the USSR, went from a cult of personality to control by bureaucracy. Choibalsan was a soldier; Tsedenbal, a civilian. Choibalsan spent much of his career as revolutionary fighter and wartime leader; Tsedenbal has been an economist. The cultivated official image for decades was that of Marshal Choibalsan in a Russian-style military uniform; Tsedenbal in a Russian business suit represents Mongolia now as he has since Choibalsan's death in 1952.

The Age of Choibalsan was the Age of Stalin, and Choibalsan copied the style of the Soviet leader. The changes in the USSR following the death of Stalin were mirrored in the MPR. Purges, violence, and ruthless suppression gave way to smoother, less primitive, and less deadly forms of control. Economic development began to be emphasized in place of the policies of destruction and elimination favored by Stalin. The curtain isolating Mongolia from the rest of the world was lifted.

The Age of Choibalsan and of Stalin was also the age of the Japanese threat. Overtly or covertly, much of the period was occupied in maneuvering and sometimes fighting in a Russo-Japanese war in which Mongolia was an active ally of Russia and a target of Japan. The Age of Tsedenbal has been the age of the new China, of Mao, and for Mongolia, of the predominant influence of Sino-Soviet relations.[1] In Mongolia the decade following Choibalsan's death in January 1952 began with about five years of Sino-Soviet cooperation, followed by three years of competition between the two nations, and then a period of confrontation. Since it was an exceptionally important ten years, each of these three periods should be examined separately.

January 28, 1952–May 15, 1957
FROM THE DEATH OF CHOIBALSAN TO THE
BULGANIN-TSEDENBAL JOINT STATEMENT

Military-Strategic Considerations

The victory of Mao in October 1949 and the establishment of a new relationship between the USSR and China caused a major change in the position of the MPR. Now it was to become a connecting link, a bridge, in a larger Russian-Chinese cooperative alliance.[2] Tsedenbal met with Stalin on September 5, 1952, and with Mao on September 29; provision for the construction of the Trans-Mongolian Railroad was a major new aspect of these negotiations. That railroad, which included 337 kilometers of wide-gauge track on Chinese territory, extended to Ulan Bator and then on to a connection with the Trans-Siberian Railroad at Ulan Ude; it was to become a principal conduit for Sino-Soviet trade and an important link in the passenger route from Peking to Moscow. The Red Army withdrew from Mongolia, and even though Mao apparently did not gain everything he wanted, a new situation much more favorable to China had at least begun to develop.[3] The closing out of joint Soviet-Chinese projects in Sinkiang, and the Soviet withdrawal from Manchuria in 1955, plus the elimination of the Soviet monopoly in the MPR, seemed to offer China a substantial change from the situation in past decades.

Ideological Considerations

Some unconnected events of these years all stemmed from or affected Mongolian nationalistic sentiments. One was the celebration in Inner

Mongolia in 1954 of the 727th anniversary of the death of Chinggis Khan. Ulanfu, the powerful Mongol who belonged to the CCP, publicly praised the wisdom and tolerance of Mao for permitting the reinterment of what were supposed to be the bones of Chinggis Khan in their traditional hallowed place, Ejen Khoro in the Ordos.[4] The Chinese Buddhist Association issued a book in 1956 that indicated the tolerance of the Peking regime for minority-nationality religions and its cooperation with them.[5] In the Soviet Union, a Buddhist temple was constructed for the Buryat Mongols at Ivol'ginsk (near Ulan Ude) in 1956, and in the same year the Kalmyk Mongols who had been proscribed by Stalin during World War II were rehabilitated.[6] The small national minorities lying between the Chinese and Russian giants seemed to be tolerated at least temporarily.

The new Chinese regime appeared ready to adopt the Cyrillic alphabet for minority languages in 1955–1956, and at a meeting at Küke Khoto in May 1956 involving Russia, China, and Mongolia, this policy was discussed in some detail. At that time there was praise for the ease of communication that it would provide between China's minorities and those of the USSR and MPR.[7] A joint Russian-Chinese-Mongolian history project was discussed at a tripartite meeting in Ulan Bator in November 1956, and an official and scholar of the MPR, Shirendyb, was selected as its general editor. Further joint meetings were held to work out details. One of the first international gatherings in which Mongols went abroad to participate was a meeting of the Congress for Peace in Asia and the Pacific, held in Peking.

Economic Considerations

Russians began to leave Mongolia, and the first "new" Chinese laborers arrived in May 1955. By 1956 there were ten thousand of them in the MPR, and only about sixteen thousand Russians. These Chinese were mainly construction workers who erected various buildings in Mongolia as well as many small bridges and similar projects. The small and scattered population in the MPR was never able to provide sufficient manpower, especially workers equipped with even simple skills, so the practical Chinese labor force was extremely useful.[8]

Ninety-seven percent of the livestock in the MPR were still privately owned in 1953, and the Second Five-Year Plan, which covered the period 1953–1957, made little progress toward collectivization. A similar program for herdsmen in Inner Mongolia was not much more advanced.[9] The number of industrial workers in the MPR increased from about thirty thousand in 1952 to forty-six thousand in 1955.

Organizational Considerations

Choibalsan died of cancer in Moscow on January 28, 1952. Ulanfu attended his funeral in Ulan Bator early in February, and a special memorial service was held for the deceased Mongolian leader in Kalgan. Ulanfu and a high-level Chinese delegation attended the Twelfth Party Congress in November 1954. Ulanfu cut the ribbon inaugurating service on the Trans-Mongolian Railroad on January 1, 1956, and one of his deputy chairmen in the MPR, Chi Ya-t'ai, served from July 1950 through September 1954 as the Chinese ambassador in Ulan Bator (Ho Ying succeeded Chi Ya-t'ai).

An unexplained interregnum followed Choibalsan's death: Tsedenbal's succession was not announced until May 28, 1952. Stalin died on March 5, 1953, and Dashiin Damba took over as first secretary of the Mongolian Party—leaving Tsedenbal still as prime minister—on April 6, 1954. Shirendyb was at this time the first deputy prime minister and a full member of the Politburo. It is not clear what was going on at that time, but Damba and Shirendyb certainly occupied very high posts at the time when China was most vigorously reentering the MPR, and both lost their high positions soon after the Russians called a halt to the Chinese "incursions" in May 1957. Another event that was undoubtedly relevant but was not explained was the removal of the Communist official Kao Kang from his high post in Manchuria in December 1953.[10] The territory assigned to the IMAR in China grew steadily in 1952–1954: parts of Chahar were added in 1952, of Suiyuan in 1954, and of Ninghsia in 1955.

May 1957–May 1960
FROM THE BULGANIN-TSEDENBAL JOINT STATEMENT TO CHOU EN-LAI'S VISIT TO ULAN BATOR

Military-Strategic Considerations

The Bulganin-Tsedenbal joint statement of May 15, 1957, was essentially a "Stop China" document, wielding economic weapons.[11] The former policy of cooperation between the USSR and China, with Mongolia as a bridge joining comradely Communist brothers, changed to one of competition. This rivalry was limited to the fields of trade and aid, but Russia's intent was to win in Mongolia by use of economic weapons, which China did not really have at its disposal.

There was one minor incident between 1957 and 1960 that was never satisfactorily explained, but probably had nothing to do with China. A border incident occurred in 1958 involving Tuva and the MPR; it required the services of a Soviet border expert, Zaikin,[12] and appears to have caused the removal of a Mongolian minister of foreign affairs, Avarzed. It was several months before his replacement, Shagdarsuren, was named; thus at a very critical time in Sino-Soviet and Mongolian relations, the MPR had no minister of foreign affairs in office.

In these years, large-scale migrations of Han Chinese continued into

Sinkiang, Inner Mongolia, and Manchuria;[13] this influx undoubtedly added considerably to the Soviet Union's apprehension about China's active role in Mongolia, and strengthened its determination to stop China there. Farther afield, Sino-Indian clashes occurring at the time also required Soviet assessment and decisions, and may also have influenced Soviet conclusions about Chinese intentions in the MPR.

Ideological and Educational Considerations

When George Roerich returned to the USSR in 1957 it was arranged that the Buddhist temple in Leningrad would be turned over to him as a Buddhist Institute in the Academy of Sciences of the USSR. Critics such as Rinchen, who was, until his death in 1977, the leading unorthodox literary and intellectual figure in the MPR, had often complained that the study of Buddhism in the USSR had been allowed to die with the famous Shcherbatskoi, who had been killed in the purges of the 1930s. The hope that Tibetan studies would flourish again did not last long, however, for Roerich died in 1960 and the temple was once again used for unrelated purposes.[14]

Decrees in 1958 and 1960 reversed the earlier commitment to the Cyrillic script for national minorities in China, and Latinization was adopted instead.[15] Just as the political purpose earlier had been to encourage cross-border contacts, the new policy was aimed at discouraging them. The Russian-Mongolian-Chinese joint-history group met a second time in Moscow in 1957, but cancelled the meeting scheduled for 1958. Events in Tibet, including the Dalai Lama's flight to India in March 1959, dealt a savage blow to Buddhist and Tibetan life in China.

The Soviet-Mongolian Friendship Association founded in May 1958 was dedicated to attracting Mongols to the USSR and to alienating them from China; that policy was deliberately fortified in September through the formation of Buryat Mongol, Kazakh, and Kirghiz sections of the association. One thousand Mongols were studying in the USSR at this time, compared with only thirty in China. Of fifty-one dissertations written by Mongols from the MPR in the USSR between 1951 and 1961, nineteen were submitted between 1951 and 1958, and thirty-two between 1959 and 1961;[16] thus there was a sharp escalation in the later years. Almost all these developments worked against the earlier policy of cooperation and rapprochement. Mongolia was becoming a competitive battleground instead of a cooperative meeting place.

Economic Considerations

The extension of aid provided in the Bulganin-Tsedenbal statement and the Three-Year Plan governing the economy for the years 1958–1960 provided for the collectivization of livestock and, beginning in 1959, the opening of New Lands for grain farming. The percentage of privately owned livestock declined from 75 in 1957 to 25 in August 1959. The so-called MZhS (Machine Livestock Stations) supplied the political muscle to enforce collectivization in the MPR just as the MTS had done in the USSR.[17] The New-Lands program followed the Soviet example, and two hundred Soviet agricultural specialists came into the country to help. The joint statement called for "gradual transference of the arat population to a settled form of life."

Meanwhile the Great Leap Forward in China had enforced rapid changes in Inner Mongolia, with communes being formed in the minority areas in just a few days during August 1958.[18] Tolerance and gradualism had been abandoned, and this change caused widespread resentment. Ulanfu warned against emphasizing agriculture over herding. There was a definite parallel between the policies adopted in Inner Mongolia and the MPR, and their timing was remarkably similar. Nevertheless, there were always far more Han Chinese active in Inner Mongolia than there were Russians in the MPR.[19]

Harrison Salisbury observed in 1959 that "From 1921 forward Mongolia was the forgotten stepchild of the Communist world. I could see no evidence that the Communists had made any effort to start the country down the path toward any kind of modern economy. . . . For years Mongolia was left to its own devices. . . . Even after World War II, Mongolia slumbered on. . . ."[20] Steel production was begun at Paotow in Inner Mongolia in 1959, but no comparable industry was developed in the MPR. The Chinese laborers in the MPR built apartment buildings in 1958–1960 (mostly in Ulan Bator) that enabled 13,500 families to change drastically their formerly yurt-based way of life.

Organizational Considerations

When Damba was purged, between November 1958 and March 1959, four Politburo members and two candidate-members were also removed; thus Tsedenbal was not simply reuniting the positions of prime minister and first secretary, but conducting a more radical reorganization. The Mongolian ambassador to Moscow served 1956–1959, the Mongolian ambassador to Peking, 1957–1959, and the Soviet ambassador to Ulan Bator, 1957–1960. There was plainly a unique and powerful strain in those years, although it is not clear whether it could be called pro-Chinese or anti-Chinese. International relations—the sensitive and growing Sino-Soviet rift—certainly affected Mongolian domestic politics. The fact that one of Khrushchev's principal victims, the veteran Bolshevik V. M. Molotov, was banished to Ulan Bator seemed to bring Soviet domestic politics into Mongolia. Tension and strain must have been considerable. With the limited evidence available, however, it is difficult to clarify who supported whom and what implications can properly be drawn from the events.

May 1960–January 1963
FROM THE VISIT OF CHOU EN-LAI TO THE VISIT OF IL'ICHEV

Military-Strategic Considerations

The formation in 1961 of the Society for Support of the Army, with nearly a hundred thousand members between the ages of eighteen and thirty-five, focussed attention on the military. In mid-March 1961, Malinovsky and Pliev received medals for their service to Mongolia in Ulan Bator in a ceremony witnessed by the Chinese general Hu Kuang-te. From May to August 1962 a major reorganization of the military was undertaken, with much shifting of personnel. Military delegations to Moscow were received by some of the highest civil and military officials of the USSR, including Khrushchev himself. General Danilov went to Ulan Bator as senior military adviser in 1963.[21]

When Chou En-lai was carrying on discussions with Tsedenbal at the end of May 1960, his goal seemed to be separation of the MPR from the Soviet Union rather than a cooperative three-way deal. Widespread revolts in Sinkiang, and a resulting mass flight of refugees into the USSR (seventy thousand to the Kazakh Republic in 1962), aggravated tensions and problems.[22] The Sino-Indian border war and Peking's resultant unhappiness with Moscow increased them yet more. In gaining entrance to the United Nations on October 28, 1961, and joining CMEA (or Comecon, the Council for Mutual Economic Assistance) on June 7, 1962, the MPR was in effect making anti-Chinese moves—allying itself even more closely with the USSR. Only the Mongolian-Chinese border treaty of December 1962 broke this unrelieved pattern of pro-Soviet actions.[23]

Ideological Considerations

Celebrations in Inner Mongolia and the MPR in May–June 1962 of the eight hundredth anniversary of the birth of Chinggis Khan led to important political repercussions involving many complications and implications that were not readily evident. Russian sensitivity to China's symbolic manipulation of memory of Chinggis Khan was plain; indeed any suggestion of a personality cult at that time was delicate, since it might suggest a need for reassessments of Stalin and Choibalsan, as well as of the reputations and power of Mao Tse-tung and Liu Shao-ch'i. Careers and reputations of Maisky, Rinchen, Jamtsarano, Ulanfu, and S. V. Kiselev (the Russian archaeologist) affected the celebration and were affected by it. A Mongolian Politburo member, Tomor-Ochir, lost his position because of this matter, and Kiselev may have lost his life as a result of it.

Bones and relics purported to be those of Chinggis Khan were traditionally kept and guarded at Ejen Khoro, in the Ordos section of Inner

Mongolia. The Chinese Communist regime encouraged celebration of the octocentennial at the elaborate mausoleum there, and the Mongolian Communist regime made its own plans for marking the occasion at the actual birthplace of Chinggis on the Kerulen River in the eastern MPR, at Delun Boldog. The Russians seem to have suspected some sort of dangerous collusion between the Khalkhas and the Inner Mongols, or perhaps a Chinese plot, and they stifled the ceremonies held in the MPR. A monument was erected, special commemorative stamps were issued, and some speeches were given, but the Russians suppressed as much of the celebration as possible.

The fact that attacking Stalin was already controversial, and that Mao did not condemn Stalin as Khrushchev did, increased the significance of the Chinggis Khan celebrations. The Russians were also sensitive to an inescapable ambiguity about Chinggis: was he a quintessential Mongol and an authentic Mongolian hero, or was he an emperor of China firmly implanted in the mainstream of Chinese history? And was he not a barbarian conqueror who had ravaged Russia and significantly delayed its development?

A nationalities meeting held in Peking in April–May 1962, just before the Ejen Khoro anniversary celebration, was attended by Liu Shao-ch'i, Chou En-lai, and Teng Hsiao-ping; Ulanfu delivered a major speech. Then the celebrations took place, with much fanfare and publicity. When Mao returned personally to active participation in the government, beginning in September 1962, minorities were instructed to pursue the class struggle, and soon Chinggis Khan faded away, almost never to be mentioned again.[24]

S. V. Kiselev's attention to Kara Korum and other remains from the distant past inevitably encouraged nationalism. Suspicion and sometimes condemnation of archaeological investigation has arisen many times in Mongolia. Kara Korum had some connection with the Chinggis Khan mystique, and Chinggis was out of favor. The strong attack of September 1962 on Tomor-Ochir for having encouraged the Chinggis Khan celebrations was repeated by *Pravda* on November 1. On November 8, Kiselev died, allegedly of natural causes.[25]

With the completion of collectivization, a new constitution of 1960 proclaimed the full attainment of socialism.[26] In 1961 Nyamyn Jagvaral, who was already a Politburo member at the time, presented the classic formulation of the necessity for settling the nomadic population, a formulation still cited fifteen years later as binding policy for the regime. S. K. Roshchin, the highly competent Russian economist who served as an adviser in the MPR from 1959 to 1961, added that such a settlement could occur only with far-reaching changes in the pattern of the economy.[27]

In May 1961 the Mongolian Scientific Committee became the Academy of Sciences, with Shirendyb its first, and thus far its only, president. The academy is closely modelled on the Soviet one, and maintains direct ties with it. Shirendyb followed Soviet advice and worked intimately with Russians in establishing it.[28]

Il'ichev's speech in Ulan Bator in January 1963 followed the one he delivered in Moscow in December 1962 insisting on a narrow orthodoxy, and those who were hoping for liberalization and further thawing were grievously disappointed. The second de-Choibalsanization in January 1962 was as limited in application and restricted in effect as the second de-Stalinization in the USSR.[29] The MPR joined in the open polemics that raged between the USSR and China in 1963, fully supporting all the Soviet positions against the Chinese. There was no sign of an independent Mongolian stance.

Economic Considerations

In 1960 Chou En-lai offered the MPR a steel mill and a three-hundred-thousand-man labor force in a proposal that was clearly aimed at separating the MPR from the USSR and orienting it toward China. "Like Albania" was the Chinese slogan. The proposal represented China's last and most important attempt to regain influence in Mongolia. There was a last-chance aura about this final effort to reverse the trend of events since 1921. It was perhaps too desperate a move. The idea of three hundred thousand Chinese probably boggled the minds of the Mongols. The Mongols needed manpower, but such a massive amount would swamp and overwhelm them. The likelihood that the Mongols would have responded independently to any initiative by the Chinese or by anyone else was not very great, in any case. They were bound to consult the Russians, and the Russians naturally told them to have nothing to do with the offer. There was also an aura of bravura surrounding the proposal. Could Chou En-lai really commit the Chinese government to such an investment in May 1960; was his own position in Peking that firm and assured?

In any case, the Russians were able to obtain the outcome they wanted—Mongolian refusal of the Chinese offer—without the use of armed force, although the political turbulence in 1962 may have resulted in part from differences of opinion among the Mongolian leadership. An article in *Trud* by the chairman of the Mongolian Trade Unions in September 1974 stated:

> Beginning with 1960, the Chinese leadership started to exert open political and economic pressure on Mongolia in an attempt to undermine the traditional fraternal friendship of the Mongolian people with the Soviet people and the peoples of other socialist countries, to put the Mongolian people under the influence of Mao Tse-tung's ideas, and to compel Mongolia to pursue a pro-Maoist policy.[30]

Tsedenbal indicated that "[T]he Chinese leaders attempted to exert pressure on the party and state leadership of the MPR. . . ."

The Chinese project would have been at Darkhan, and the Russians took it over, minus the steel mill. The official announcement came in August 1961, and construction began on October 17. A "Collective for Construction of Darkhan" was announced, consisting of four Mongols, five Russians, one Czech, and one Pole. The last Chinese laborers arrived in the MPR on May 5, 1961, and the first large-scale departure, which was highly publicized as a media event, occurred in May 1962. No Chinese ever worked on the Darkhan project.

The Chinese proposal had obviously been based on Paotow as a model. The steel mill there had just started production, and a large Han Chinese labor force operated it. Iron and coal were available near Darkhan, so the project was feasible, but the Russians were not prepared to make a commitment of that scope and scale, at least in 1960, and their plans for the Darkhan project were far more modest. Of course they had no three-hundred-thousand-man labor force to throw into it. The Russian project at Darkhan grew very slowly; its progress fell far behind official projections and plans. It functioned as a center for handling the grain harvest of the New Lands, supplying bread instead of steel. Undoubtedly the Mongols would have been more impressed by steel.

The military-strategic implications of the threat of Chinese-controlled heavy industry and a Chinese population of several hundred thousand so close to the Russian border had been disturbing for the USSR. Darkhan is on the main line of the railroad north of Ulan Bator; thus it had the potential to separate the Mongolian capital from the Soviet Union. The surrounding area in the Selenga Valley is suited for agriculture, and Chinese farmers might have developed it intensively. The Trans-Mongolian Railroad provided transit through the desert barrier that had formerly limited Chinese population movement northward. Thus by adopting and adapting the Darkhan project and pushing the New Lands program, the Russians were trying to eliminate a credible Chinese threat.

This threat may have changed Russia's plans and raised the priority of Darkhan and also of farming in that area. It may have delayed development of the city of Choibalsan in eastern Mongolia. The Sino-Soviet split in Mongolia meant that the new railroad was very little used, and Tsedenbal complained in 1975 that ever since 1962 "the MPR is finding it very expensive even to maintain the railroad, since only 7% to 8% of its carrying capacity has actually been used."[31]

The number of Mongolian industrial workers increased from 66,200 in 1960 to 72,400 in 1961, and 75,200 in 1962. The peak year for Chinese trade was 1961; at that point it reached one-fifth the volume of Soviet trade with Mongolia. The number of Russians in the MPR continued to decrease: in 1963, the low point, there were only 8,900.

Organizational Considerations

Between 1958 and 1962 unstable and volatile membership on the Politburo and in high positions was typical. (During that period Tomor-Ochir was on the Politburo for two years, off for one-and-a-half years, on for another nine months, and finally off for good.)[32] An extended period of stability began in 1963 and lasted at least fifteen years. The Party alleged that the source of the earlier instability had been the attitude of Tomor-Ochir and other officials toward Choibalsan and toward Chinggis Khan, but the pressure on Mongolia of Sino-Soviet tension was probably the real cause.

7. China—Threat and Confrontation: 1963–1973

MILITARY-STRATEGIC CONSIDERATIONS

In the decade 1963–1973, four main factors dominated the military-strategic situation affecting Mongolia:

1. The number of Russians in the MPR increased and the number of Chinese decreased. Whereas in 1963 there were twice as many Chinese as Russians in the MPR, by 1969 there were three times as many Russians as Chinese.[1]

2. The general Soviet military buildup in the Far East included the movement of substantial Red Army units into Mongolia, and construction of a barrier of modern weapons along the Mongolian-Chinese border.

3. Political instability in China—the excesses of the Cultural Revolution—included the removal of Ulanfu and the detachment of major territories from the IMAR. The Cultural Revolution increased the political power of the Han Chinese over national minorities.

4. Demographic trends continued to threaten the USSR: in 1974 the Chinese population in Inner Mongolia and Manchuria was about seven times greater than the total Russian population in East Siberia and the Soviet Far East, and it was increasing annually ten times as fast as the ethnic Russian population in those areas of the USSR.

The visit of Brezhnev, the signing of a new Mutual Defense Treaty between the USSR and Mongolia, and the reentry of the Red Army into the MPR all occurred in 1966, before the excesses of the Cultural Revolution and Red Guards late in 1966 and in 1967 and 1968, and obviously well before the Damansky Island incident of 1969. The fears or expectations in and around 1960 that the Chinese would inevitably force the Russians out of Mongolia and that the Russians would be unable to control Chinese expansion there proved unfounded.[2] The Russians reasserted their dominance and eliminated the Chinese influence with little difficulty.

The Mongolian army is inevitably small, while the size of the territory it must defend is immense; thus foreign military force is required for security.

The Soviet Red Army provides that force: it moves out from its Transbaikal and Far East military districts into Mongolia whenever the Russians decide it is needed, but is not always stationed there.

Indeed, the more the Russians come in and take over as they have in recent years, the less significant is the Mongolian military itself. The role of the Mongolian army is only supportive; Russians make the important decisions in military matters. The Soviet military establishment does not entrust the Mongols with the military security of the USSR against China. In any case, most of the Mongolian military elites were trained in the USSR and gained their military experience fighting or training to fight alongside Russians.

The Chinese military scare beginning in 1966, particularly the Russian-Chinese hostilities at Damansky Island in 1969, colored the military situation in Mongolia and thrust military concerns even more into the foreground. Such concerns never disappear, but they do fade in and out of prominence at various times; they were very prominent in 1966 and thereafter. The Russians did not hesitate at that time to move in the Red Army and to make use of Mongolia as a strategic shield for the USSR. Military-strategic concerns were the determining factors in Soviet policy, and once again the USSR made it quite clear that the MPR was of vital interest to the Soviet Union. They regarded an attack against the MPR as an attack against the USSR, and would vigorously defend Mongolia against any threat or aggression.

The extent of direct Soviet participation and interference in the MPR is closely related to the degree of tension and the immediacy of threat in the Sino-Soviet relationship. The growing split between the two giants reversed an apparent trend toward a reduced Soviet presence in Mongolia, and the Damansky Island incident in 1969 raised the cold war to a warm one: it quickly led to substantial military reinforcement and reorganization that were rapidly reflected in the MPR. Increasing attention was directed in Soviet military publications to the nature of possible hostilities. The large numbers of men (half a million to a million) and tanks (more than ten thousand) assigned to the Transbaikal and Far East commands since 1969, the kinds of force commanders assigned to them, and military literature highlighted,[3] all suggest that the 1945 operation against the Japanese in Manchuria and Inner Mongolia was viewed as something of a model for future confrontations.[4]

As cooperation turned into competition and then confrontation, Chinese concern about Soviet control of the MPR increased. The threat worked both ways: Mongolia might be a platform for Soviet aggression in China as well as for Chinese aggression aimed at the USSR.[5] Chinese vital interests, even more than Soviet ones, were involved: the safety of Peking itself; the possibility that the Soviets would insert a wedge to split off Manchuria; and the vulnerability of new towns and industrial facilities in Inner Mongolia and North China and of the nuclear installations at Lop Nor in Sinkiang.[6]

During the Cultural Revolution, in 1967, a government-inspired mob in Peking "broke through into the Mongolian Embassy grounds, attacked the diplomatic cars, damaging or burning them. They demanded that the leaders of the MPR should be similarly dealt with and that its government should be overthrown." Chinese diplomats allegedly committed "acts of hooliganism" then.[7] Apparently several other scattered incidents occurred in 1967. On January 31 Chinese students returning from Moscow held an "anti-Mongolian and anti-Soviet" meeting in the Ulan Bator railroad station, and the Chinese embassy distributed anti-Soviet propaganda. On May 21, departing Chinese held a "provocation meeting" in the Mongolian capital, and Chinese workers walked off construction jobs and deliberately harassed and slowed transit on the Trans-Mongolian Railroad. Meanwhile in May and August, Red Guards demonstrated at the Mongolian embassy in Peking, broke into it twice, and turned over the ambassador's car.[8]

In a move that appears to have been motivated principally by the desire of the Chinese to improve defenses against the USSR, a restructuring of the IMAR in August 1969 removed huge chunks of territory and a substantial indigenous Mongolian population from the region, incorporating them into regular provinces. Soon after that the Inner Mongolian military region was reduced to a military district directly subordinate to Peking. No known protest demonstration or riots accompanied or followed this drastic action.[9]

IDEOLOGICAL AND EDUCATIONAL CONSIDERATIONS

The Cultural Revolution began in Peking in August 1966 and quickly spread to Inner Mongolia, where Red Guards were active in Küke Khoto, and Ulanfu was attacked in September. Ulanfu's public appearance in Peking on October 1 was his last for many years. Kuei Pi, Chi Ya-t'ai, and Wang To, some of his close colleagues, were among the victims of a purge and mass demonstration in November 1967. They were all ancient fighters in political, and sometimes military, battles: Ulanfu, Kuei Pi, and Chi Ya-t'ai had attended the Mongol-Tibetan School in Peking in the early 1920s; Ulanfu had attended Sun Yat-sen University in Moscow 1927–1930 and Kuei Pi had attended the Higher Party School in Ulan Bator during those same years. Chi Ya-t'ai had been first ambassador of the new China to the MPR from 1950 through 1954, and Wang To had been secretary of the Ulanchap League Party Committee and a member of the Inner Mongolian provisional government under Ulanfu in 1949. The discrediting of all these Mongols, combined with the breaking up of the IMAR in 1969, emasculated the already weak autonomous movement of the Mongols in China. Ulanfu did surface in Peking in August 1973 as an honored member of the CCP, but political blows by Han Chinese have seriously weakened the identity and integrity of Mongols in China.[10]

Mongols in the USSR also came under attack. The arrest in 1972 of the religious leader Bidya Dandaron in Buryat Mongolia for practicing and propagating his Buddhist faith and attempting to maintain Buddhist studies as a discipline was an example of the Russian desire to stifle Mongolian identity there. Dandaron died at age sixty, two years after his arrest and incarceration: he had spent twenty-two years of his life in prison. Four pupils studying Buddhism with him were committed to psychiatric hospitals. The *stupas* (memorials) he erected to honor his father and his teacher (Tsedenov, a famous Buryat lama) were destroyed by the authorities.[11]

In June 1970 a meeting in Ulan Bator included Buddhist representatives from North Vietnam, South Vietnam-NLF, India, Malaysia, Nepal, Pakistan, Singapore, the USSR, Japan, and the MPR (the host). The head of the MPR Buddhists and the director of the Gandang monastery in Ulan Bator were the conveners and hosts of what was planned as a "forum for Buddhists of Asia." The USSR representatives included the "Khambo Lama" of the Buryat Mongolian Buddhist Church (which was officially sanctioned by the Soviet regime), and S. D. Dylykov, the Buryat specialist in the Institute of Oriental Studies of the USSR Academy of Sciences. An extra anti-Chinese twist was added at that meeting when Tibet and the fate of the Dalai Lama and Panchen Lama were discussed.[12]

Education of Mongols in the USSR has been an important factor in the political as well as the cultural relations of the two countries. The official Soviet listing indicates that thirty Mongols received advanced academic degrees in the USSR between 1971 and 1973.[13] Of these, twenty-six attended schools in Moscow and Leningrad, the largest single group at the Academy of Social Sciences, Central Committee, CPSU, Moscow. Several worked at the Institute of Oriental Studies (IVAN) in Moscow or Leningrad: one worked in the School of Journalism at Moscow State University (MGU). One received a degree at Irkutsk University; one at the Siberian Academy of Sciences at Novosibirsk; one (on the subject of Tuva) in the Academy's Far Eastern branch at Vladivostok; and a Kazakh at Alma Ata completed a dissertation on language and literature among the Kazakhs of the MPR.

Some of the dissertations dealt with ideological subjects, for example, "Forming New Man" and "Forming Socialist Attitudes Among Youth." One discussed the MPR as an example of the building of socialism, bypassing capitalism, and another examined the relationship between internationalism and nationalism. Half a dozen were on early Mongolian history. A Russian, Dubinin, submitted a dissertation on the Comintern in Mongolia, 1919–1928, at the Institute of International Relations in Moscow. Despite the great importance of military-strategic matters in Mongolian-Chinese, Mongolian-Soviet, and Sino-Soviet relations, none of the dissertations were on military subjects.

Many of the Mongols who are currently doing advanced academic work in the Soviet Union have participated in joint expeditions in Mongolia for many years. For example, an elaborate five-year paleontology expedition (1969–1973) that included seventy Russians and several Mongols has prepared extensive publications and supplied dinosaur remains and related specimens for a special museum built in Ulan Bator.[14] A geological expedition composed of a hundred Russians and forty Mongols pursued the more practical aim of locating mineral resources from 1967 through 1971.[15] These activities have helped to bind a Mongolian intellectual elite very closely to the USSR.

ECONOMIC CONSIDERATIONS

In 1973 D. Zagasbaldan, chairman of the Mongolian Statistical Administration, presented essential facts about Mongolian economic development:

> There is special interest . . . in establishing and strengthening economic relations with the borderpoints and areas of Siberia closest to the MPR which share common economic, ethnographic, and climatic relations. Intensive development of the eastern districts of the USSR, industrializing more rapidly, and particularly the establishment of a unified energy system and scientific centers broaden the possibility for setting up close productive relations.[16]

Projects most likely to be undertaken in the future are those most directly connected with the USSR. Likewise, the development of Mongolia will depend on, and be directly related to, the USSR's development of Eastern Siberia. Lieutenant G. C. Binsteed, a British army officer who travelled extensively in Mongolia and Manchuria, noted the interconnection in 1914: "Russia would like it [Outer Mongolia] kept free from development by anyone else, or at any rate by the Chinese, so that it shall remain a potential field for the employment of such commercial and industrial energy which is or may become superfluous in Siberia. . . ."[17] When China threatened to move in, the Soviet Union was spurred to begin Mongolian development earlier than it would have otherwise. The Soviet Union regards Mongolia as most valuable from the military-strategic viewpoint—as a means of protecting the Trans-Siberian Railroad and the Transbaikal territory—but it also views Mongolia as an economic extension of Eastern Siberia. Indeed, the country's economic development serves, and is inseparable from, its military-strategic function.

The Darkhan project was reluctantly undertaken, limited in scope, and much delayed in execution. The population of forty thousand that was scheduled to be reached in 1965 was not attained until November 1974. In fact, the cornerstone for the town was laid on October 17, 1961, and a grain elevator opened only in 1964, and a bakery (commercial, for bread) not until 1970. The Mongols suffered from a chronic labor shortage and a chronic aversion to construction work, the Russians had no surplus manpower in Siberia to divert to Mongolia, and the Chinese were leaving. The 1969 *History of the MPR* noted:

> Because of the stoppage of aid rendered to our country by the PRC during the Third Five Year Plan [1961–1965] in consequence of the splittist, great-power chauvinism of Mao Tse-tung and his group, it was not possible to complete fully certain projects of our large-scale construction plan. Indeed, because of such factors certain changes were made in the Third Five Year Plan during 1964.[18]

The prevailing mixture of economic and ideological motivation and the conflict of practical economic need with ideological preference are both illustrated by the Darkhan project. The town was established in the middle of the New-Lands program; its principal functions were raising grain and milling flour to decrease imports from the USSR into the MPR, thus helping to reduce the prevailing trade imbalance. It was also useful in settlement of the rural population, and development of an urban proletariat. The town and its light industry provided workers; the Soviet and Mongolian regimes preferred settled grain-farming and Goskhozes to livestock cooperatives (SKhOs) and nomadism, which they wanted to limit.[19] The import substitution worked reasonably well. In 1960, the USSR sent 34,000 tons of flour to the MPR, and 26,000 tons were processed in Mongolia. In 1969, 18,000 tons of flour went from Russia to Mongolia, while 102,000 tons were processed in Mongolia—much of it at Darkhan.[20] The trade imbalance increased nonetheless: from 24 million rubles in 1960, to 125 million by 1970, to 163 million in 1973.

Official policy was not always straightforward, however. While praising and encouraging urban and industrial development as the wave of the future, the regime was at the same time sending new graduates to rural areas and announcing limitations on urban populations.[21]

A satellite open-pit coal mine at Sharyn-gol was connected to Darkhan by a forty-five-mile rail line that was opened in November 1963. Production began there in 1965. Coal has been supplied to Ulan Bator from the nearby mines at Nalaikha for many years, and in 1969 an open-pit mine began production at Adun-Chulun, to supply the eastern Mongolian city of Choibalsan.[22]

Attempts in the 1950s and 1960s to establish Mongolian oil production and refining failed: the considerable investment in prospecting, well-drilling, and construction of a refinery all came to nothing by 1970. Drilling and production of oil had begun in 1948 at Dzun-Bayan, sixty kilometers east of Sain Shanda in the East Gobi Aimak; by 1951 the refinery had been built, and production reached a peak of 28,600 tons in 1960. At that time two thousand workers were employed in the oil industry. Production fell to 14,200 tons in 1965, however, and then to 4,500 tons in 1969 when the refinery was closed down. Meanwhile, the influx of Soviet petroleum exports to the MPR increased steadily, even during the few years when Mongolia was producing some of its own oil. This attempt at import substitution ultimately failed.[23]

The Chinese completed only twelve out of ninety-two projects in the MPR, and some of those required reconstruction or repair. In 1965, seven Chinese-built enterprises were operating, four were unfinished, and twelve had not been started at all. Discussions in December 1972 raised the possibility that the Chinese would complete the unfinished projects, but instead the last seven uncompleted buildings were transferred to Mongolian ownership in May 1973.[24]

ORGANIZATIONAL CONSIDERATIONS

Political stability marked the period 1963–1973. The membership of the Politburo continued unchanged throughout those years[25]—the turbulence and volatility of the preceding decade were entirely absent. The period of violent upheaval that included the Great People's Cultural Revolution in China, a substantial Soviet military buildup, and the Damansky Island incident found no political reflection in Ulan Bator. The 1960s paralleled the 1930s in many ways (in the later decade the Chinese, not the Japanese, were the enemy), but the purges and domestic violence that marked the earlier period were not repeated.[26]

Procedure settled into routine: a Soviet party congress that adopted a new Five-Year Plan for the USSR was followed by a Mongolian party congress and its Five-Year Plan. Thus the Twenty-Third CPSU Congress (March–April 1966) adopting the Eighth Soviet Five-Year Plan was followed by the Fifteenth MPRP Congress (June 1966) producing the Fourth MPR Five-Year Plan, and the Twenty-Fourth CPSU Congress (March–April 1971) enacting the Ninth Soviet Five-Year Plan was followed by the Sixteenth MPRP Congress (June 1971) and the Fifth MPR Five-Year Plan. In June 1971, four of the Mongolian Politburo members were former chairmen of the State Planning Commission.[27] Tsedenbal the economist had replaced Choibalsan the soldier, and the career of civilian economist was the road to political success in Mongolia.[28]

The Party increased in size by one third, to fifty-nine thousand members and candidate-members in 1971. In the period 1961–1971, the number of women in the Party doubled, from seven thousand to fourteen thousand. The one political surprise was that when the veteran Sambu died on May 21, 1972, no successor to him was named chairman of the Presidium of the Great Khural—"President" of the MPR. The position was to remain vacant for more than two years, with no known explanation.[29]

A sign of Russian uneasiness about fiscal matters was the call by the Soviet-Mongolian Intergovernmental Commission in July 1968 for a more rational and sensible Mongolian allocation of Soviet aid and assistance to the various branches of the economy.[30] Russian concern about the "wasting" of Russian money by Mongolians was an old and familiar story, going back to St. Petersburg's unhappiness with the spending habits of the Jebtsun Damba Khutukhtu in 1915.[31]

The rural Party organization is described approvingly by Daniel Rosenberg, who spent July 1972–October 1973 in the MPR observing it in operation:

> The Party is effective on the *negdel* [SKhO or livestock-cooperative] because the best workers are asked to join the Party, and thus it is the most experienced and hard-working people who are providing leadership in the community. . . . Because the Party leadership of the community comes from within (one out of fifteen *negdel* members are members of the MPRP), the Party is an effective force in introducing new ideas and techniques and in encouraging the herders. Party members become agents of change in the community, mostly by the example they set, and they play a leading role in decision-making on the *negdel* through their participation, as a Party responsibility, in varied aspects of *negdel* life.[32]

8. Developing Erdenet: 1974–1978

MILITARY-STRATEGIC CONSIDERATIONS

The function of the MPRP is to provide a reliable and supportive socialist-Communist environment for the Soviet Red Army at minimum cost. Military-strategic considerations are the dominant ones in Soviet policy toward Mongolia: the principal need is to form a defensive shield for the vulnerable choke point where the Trans-Siberian Railway is forced by the geographic situation to run south of Lake Baikal and close to the Mongolian border. Protection for this key point, which is partly provided by the huge mining project developed by the Russians at Erdenet, affects the defense of the vital Soviet interest in the vast Transbaikal territory (extending all the way to the Pacific Ocean) and its population. In order to play any significant role in Asia, the Soviet Union must control and protect this Baikal corridor.

On November 26, 1974, Brezhnev was in Ulan Bator following his meeting with President Ford in Vladivostok. On that occasion Tsedenbal and Brezhnev expressed their common assessment of China. Tsedenbal charged that China had the chauvinistic outlook of a great power and that it aimed at hegemony in Asia. He expressed "resolute opposition to the expansionist policy of China in regard to the sovereign independent socialist Mongolian state." Brezhnev emphasized Soviet-Mongolian friendship and cooperation and criticized China for its aspirations to Soviet territory and its allegations about "disputed areas." The Soviet Union, said Brezhnev, made no territorial claims and recognized no disputed areas.[1]

While much of the MPR's polemical press campaign against China from 1974 through 1977 (with a brief hiatus after Mao's death in September 1976) simply repeated the Soviet accusations, the Mongols have repeatedly made ten specific claims relating directly to Mongolia:

1. Chinggis Khan was not "progressive" and the Mongolian Empire was not Chinese. The Mongols have claimed that overall the Chinggis Khan period was a tragedy, and they have vigorously attacked China's alleged glorification of Chinggis. This question has engendered controversy in the MPR and USSR and caused tensions in Mongolian-Chinese relations in 1962.

2. Nomads in Central Asia through the ages were essentially independent of China. The Mongols have asserted that thirteen years of joint Soviet-Mongolian archaeological work has proved that the nomads were basically separate from China and that their culture was in no way derived from Chinese culture.

3. The eighth-century Turkic prince Kul-tegun was not related to any emperor of China. Famous Russian and Danish archaeological studies conducted in 1889 and 1893 identified a "Kul-tegun" monument dating from 732 A.D. According to the Soviets and Mongols, the Chinese inscription on it was added later, but the Chinese have claimed that the inscription was an integral part of the monument and proved the Chinese connections of the prince.

4. The Manchu (Ch'ing) dynasty (1644–1911) was not Chinese, and in any case the Manchus did not completely dominate the Mongols. The MPR has insisted that Manchu-Mongol relations were not the same as Chinese-Mongol relations, and that the Mongols always retained some degree of economic and cultural integrity separate from the Manchus and/or the Chinese. It has also claimed that the Chinese idealized the role of the Manchus, who were in fact "reactionary-exploitative."[2]

5. Western Mongols (Oirats) were different from other Mongols; thus Manchu-Chinese domination of the Oirats was not the same as their domination of the other Mongols. The Mongols have argued that the "Jungarian Khanate" of the western Mongols in the seventeenth and early eighteenth centuries was independent and sovereign, never subject to the Manchus or the Chinese. "To speak of some sort of dependence of the Jungarian Khanate on the Ch'ing Empire is wrong." Chinese claims that the Oirats were subject to the Manchus just as much as the other Mongols are "absurd" and "unscientific."[3]

6. The Mongol break with the Manchus and Chinese in 1911–1912 was a progressive liberation and freedom movement. The Mongols claimed that the Chinese were in grievous error when they characterized these events as "separatist and reactionary."

7. The period of Mongolian autonomy from 1911 to 1919 was also a progressive development. The Mongols could have supported their claim by citing the exchange between the Jebtsun Damba Khutukhtu and Yuan Shih-k'ai in which the Mongolian theocratic ruler argued that the Chinese leader's attempt to assume control of Mongolia as a right of full succession to Manchu sovereignty over the area was not defensible. He told Yuan that the Mongols had sworn fealty to the Manchus, not to the Chinese; that the relationship had been one of suzerainty and not of sovereignty; and that

the fall of the Manchu dynasty had dissolved any Mongolian obligation. Thus the Chinese could not legitimately assume Manchu rights over Mongols.[4]

8. The Mongolian Revolution was a true revolution establishing an independent state, and was an expression of legitimate and genuine Mongolian self-determination. The Mongols have alleged that the Chinese joined "reactionary bourgeois ideologues" in characterizing the Mongolian Revolution as "accidental" and a perversion of history.[5]

9. The events involving Japan in the 1930s, culminating in the Nomonkhan incident of 1939, compromised an important part of Mongolian self-justification and legitimacy. They also represented a further step away from China and toward the USSR.

10. The USSR was primarily responsible for the Allied victory over both Germany and Japan in World War II. The Mongols have asserted that China has denigrated the Soviet role in the war, and commemorated the thirtieth anniversary of its end in 1975 in the same way as the West did, not as the USSR did. The Mongols have said further that Hitler's attack on the Soviet Union was greeted with joy by Mao, and that it would have suited Mao if the Russians had abandoned Moscow, Leningrad, and Stalingrad, and waited for the Allied invasion in the West. Despite the fact that the USSR and the MPR actively participated in the war in the Far East only for a week, the Mongols have endorsed the Soviets' claim that they had played the decisive role in the victory over Japan.

Obviously the political thrust of this sustained outbreak of Mongolian-Chinese polemics was that the Mongols had never really been subjects of China and that Mongolia had never in fact belonged to China. In each instance, the Chinese interpretation of the historical events supported the opposite conclusion: that a long-term direct and close relationship had existed between China and Mongolia in which China had established de-facto and de-jure sovereignty over Mongolia.

A small Chinese community, a Chinese-language newspaper, a small embassy of the Chinese People's Republic (CPR), and an insignificant amount of trade represent the tag end of the Chinese presence and influence in Mongolia—a presence and influence that once were predominant and powerful. Small, low-level official receptions and perfunctory protocol greetings are still exchanged, and chilly but more-or-less correct mutual official relations continue. The Mongols, however, have charged China with border violations, unbridled aggressiveness, dogmatic Maoist leadership, and ideological misrepresentation and manipulation. They claim specifically that the Chinese want to control and even annex the MPR. Tsedenbal charged in 1974: "Mao intends that the MPR become attached to China. The present

Chinese leaders have no wish to acquiesce in the independence of the MPR."[6]

Reports especially in 1974 and 1975 claimed that China was concentrating large military contingents near the Mongolian border, and that Chinese troops often violated the frontier, killing animals and chopping down trees. Tsedenbal claimed that "there are fairly frequent cases of the Chinese releasing on Mongolian territory domestic and other animals carrying highly infectious diseases." On December 20, 1975, a Chinese who lived in Mongolia and "worked on the so-called Council of Chinese Citizens" was expelled from the MPR for anti-Mongolian activity (which was not further defined).[7]

The question often arises whether Inner and Outer Mongolia are essentially unified or significantly different. The various forces maintaining a division between the two regions include:

1. Geography: The Gobi Desert imposes a natural separation, and the distance from Peking to Outer Mongolia is greater than the distance from Peking to Inner Mongolia.[8]

2. History: The Manchus defeated the two areas at different times, exercised different kinds of control over them, and were more successful in excluding Chinese settlers from Outer Mongolia. The fact that large numbers of Chinese farmers permanently settled in Inner Mongolia while few migrated to Outer Mongolia increasingly became an important mark of distinction.

3. Culture: The closer contact of Inner Mongolia with the Han Chinese and with Peking intensified and accelerated the influence of Chinese culture there, in contrast to the limited Chinese cultural impact on Outer Mongolia.

4. Culture: In contrast, the Russians exerted much greater influence in Outer Mongolia than in Inner Mongolia, increasing the differences between the two areas.

5. Political Factors: Soviet ideological and material assistance was more important to the Chinese revolutionary movement than regaining Outer Mongolia, so for a long time the CCP made little effort to assert a claim there.[9]

6. Political Factors: The Sino-Soviet dispute has tended to fix the differences between the two Mongolias, with China focussing its efforts on Inner Mongolia and the USSR concentrating its influence in Outer Mongolia (the MPR).

7. Military-political Factors: Japan in effect excluded Russia from Inner Mongolia for decades, contributing to Russia's lack of influence there.

8. Military-political Factors: The military weakness of the Chinese in

relation to Russia and later the USSR has meant that the Chinese have been unable to defend by arms the Outer Mongolian territory they have claimed to rule, and that overt or implied Russian/Soviet duress has prohibited China from exercising its sovereignty over that territory.

There were and are genuine differences between the Mongols of Inner Mongolia and of the MPR, but the two peoples differ from one another much less than they do from the Russians and the Chinese.[10] A distinct Mongolian culture unites all Mongols and differentiates them from all non-Mongols. The essential difference between Inner Mongolia and the MPR is the fact that China exercises political control in one and the Soviet Union does the same in the other.

The journalist Ross Munro sent dispatches from Inner Mongolia during August and September 1975 that provide a basis for comparison between the IMAR and the MPR: "China seems to have found a formula for dealing with minorities, at least here in Inner Mongolia. The key is a sort of quota system that gives preferential treatment in schooling, employment and entry into administrative positions in government and industry."[11] The native Mongolian population in the IMAR numbered 440,000 in 1975, only 5 percent of the region's total population of 8 million. All China contained somewhat more than 1.5 million Mongols at that time, so a substantial portion were living outside "their" autonomous region. Wherever they live now, however, they are outnumbered by Han Chinese, and intermarriage is apparently common in the cities and towns, further diluting the purely Mongolian element. Even the Silingol League, the area that has the highest percentage of Mongols, has a population that is only 25 percent native and 75 percent Han Chinese. Throughout the MPR, on the other hand, the overwhelming majority is Mongolian; no significant foreign immigration has occurred.

The birthrate is higher among Mongols than among Chinese, and the number of Mongols in China is almost certainly increasing, even though it cannot keep up with the pace of Chinese immigration into the region. Thus there is no danger of the physical disappearance of Mongols in China, as there might have been before 1949. The Chinese Communist regime specifically and officially encourages a high birthrate among the Mongols and other national minorities.

The biggest single blow to the identity and integrity of the Mongols as a separate and distinct group in China probably was the already mentioned reduction in the size of the IMAR by administrative decree in 1969: a large number of Mongols and much of the former territory were shifted to other provinces. While the physical survival of Mongols in China is assured, and their continued administration of their own territory is probably at least partially assured, the survival of a Mongolian cultural identity there is less certain.

Although some Mongols in the IMAR remain nomads, a clear trend to semi-settlement has been evidenced by the large numbers of permanent winter huts and dwellings. Cultivation of fodder and drilling of wells has enabled them to make fewer moves of shorter distances. Fodder and wells are common in the MPR, too, but in Inner Mongolia it is the Chinese who usually pursue agriculture, and the Mongols who normally herd the animals. The nomads apparently have fewer possessions than their brethren in the MPR, but watches, radios, and clocks seem to be fairly common. No mention was made in Munro's report of motorcycles in Inner Mongolia, whereas there are many of them in the MPR. Private plots for growing vegetables exist, but there is no private ownership of animals.

"The Inner Mongols are deprived of the most elementary rights, not even having the right to speak Mongolian in the presence of the Chinese," charged the MPR's Tsedenbal in 1974. Ross Munro reported in 1975 that few Chinese spoke Mongolian, and that conversation in mixed groups was nearly always in Chinese. The elementary schools in Inner Mongolia used Mongolian as a first language, and added Chinese in the third grade. Classes in middle schools were already predominantly conducted in the Chinese language, with only limited instruction in Mongolian. Schooling at the university level was entirely in Chinese, except for a few specialized Mongolian history and literature courses. The Inner Mongolian University served 525 students in 1975, of whom 220 (42 percent) were Mongols. In the MPR, of course, schooling at all levels was in the Mongolian language, except for a few specialized university courses in Russian, and the MPR university served 2,500 students, practically all of them Mongols. The Mongolian language is still written in the traditional vertical script in Inner Mongolia. Newspapers and publications commonly include both traditional-script Mongolian and Chinese. The Chinese language undoubtedly dominates in Inner Mongolia far more than the Russian language does in the MPR.

In many ways, Inner Mongolia in China is far more similar to Buryat Mongolia in the USSR than it is to the MPR. The Buryat Republic has absorbed a large amount of Russian immigration and settlement and has suffered administrative manipulation (for example, the separation of the Ust-Ordya and Aga Districts), and the Russian language is probably as dominant there as the Chinese language is in Inner Mongolia.

"Lamaism is dead, temples are no longer open and the prayers are no longer heard," stated Munro's 1975 report on the situation in Inner Mongolia. The religion had been destroyed. A major Silingol temple had been padlocked and marked off-limits to visitors. Some of the buildings were being used for storage. An official told Munro that "God is not reliable; he is a reactionary." While atheism is the general rule in the MPR, and many temples are closed and rotting, there are still a few functioning lamas; and an official church still exists there. Tolerance is limited, but lamaism is not entirely dead; prayers are sometimes heard.

The announced goal of the Chinese is the protection and preservation of Mongolian culture, but Munro's report of songs and dances and various performances in Inner Mongolia suggests that in 1975 culture in the IMAR was largely synthetic and manipulated—"national in form, socialist in content." Apparently, however, more of the traditional brick tea was available in Inner Mongolia than in the MPR, along with *kumiss* (fermented mare's milk) and many new, nontraditional baked goods. The official line in Inner Mongolia seems as Pollyannaish as it often is in the MPR: "Racial chauvinism has ceased to exist; there is no more Han chauvinism." The past, of course, was all bad: "To be Mongol before the Communist takeover was to be discriminated against." Although Mongols constituted only about 5 percent of the total population of the IMAR in 1975, they filled 12 percent of ordinary positions and more than 16 percent of the region's top-level government posts.

Mongolian modernization, industrialization, and technology are probably more advanced in the MPR than in the IMAR. The impressive examples of Inner Mongolian industrialization—the steel mill at Paotow is the outstanding example—are overwhelmingly Chinese in management and labor force. There is some Mongolian light industry, related to food and other livestock products, as well as a Scientific Research Institute of Animal Husbandry and Veterinary Science, and probably some Mongolian studies at the university. Still, there is no scholarly and intellectual apparatus for the Inner Mongols that is at all comparable to the MPR's Academy of Sciences. [12]

Damdinjavyn Maidar, a member of the Politburo of the MPR, spoke in September 1975 of "developing the process of political and economic consolidation of Mongolia with the Soviet Union." He provided numerous examples of close and direct connection, and although few were entirely new, their cumulative and aggregate impact meant significant change. Soviet influence is penetrating the MPR at more levels than ever before in the 1970s, and the infrastructural web is growing ever stronger and tighter. Concern about China has undoubtedly accelerated and intensified a trend that has been clearly evident for a long time.

The close connections between the MPR and East Siberia tend to soften the border separating Mongolia from the USSR and add to the factors encouraging ultimate political integration. Before his official arrival in Ulan Bator on November 30, 1973, the present Soviet ambassador to the MPR, A. I. Smirnov, had served more than thirty years as an oblast-level Party secretary, the last twenty years of that time in Chita Oblast on the Mongolian frontier. His predecessor, Shchetinin, who was ambassador from 1968 to 1973, had been with the Irkutsk Oblast Party committee for seventeen years, eleven of them as first secretary. Political power thus connects across the border, just as electrical power does. The Selenga Valley and the new Erdenet mining project are to be tied in with the "GRES" East Siberian high-voltage and long-distance power-transmission station now under construction at Gusinoe in the Buryat Autonomous Republic of the USSR. This kind of development in Siberia and its direct connection with the MPR fortifies the northward orientation of the MPR and separates it ever more thoroughly from China. The Baikal Amur Mainline Railroad (BAM) which is presently under construction, is another example of this process.

Fitzroy Maclean, a well-known author and extensive traveler, raised a question of potential importance: "One is bound to ask oneself to what extent the native population in these frontier regions . . . might prove a liability to the Russians in the event of serious trouble between the two countries or of an attempt by China to mobilize the peoples of Asia against the Russian interlopers." Referring specifically to the Kazakhs in the USSR, he stated his belief that their trouble-making days are over: "It is true that the forced disruption of their tribal and nomad way of life after the Revolution and the collectivization of their livestock caused trouble at the time, but over the years they have been thoroughly Sovietized and brought into line." [13]

Sixty-three thousand Kazakhs live in the MPR—in Bayan-Ulegei Aimak in the western MRP, close to the Soviet-Central Asian border. The USSR may be trying to encourage a closer connection between Mongolian Kazakhs and Soviet Kazakhs. In 1975 the Russian-language press in Mongolia went out of its way to stress that "Khalkha" is the name for the basic population of the MPR and does not refer to Kazakhs; on another occasion it stated that Manchu domination of Khalkha Mongols never extended to the Oirats of western Mongolia (and thus not to the Kazakhs). Furthermore, at least two Kazakhs in Alma Ata have recently submitted dissertations concerning MPR Kazakhs and Bayan-Ulegei Aimak. [14] Kazakhs seem to be discriminated against in filling Party and Central Committee positions in the MPR; for example, the former first secretary of Kazakh Aimak, who was a Kazakh, was recently replaced by a Khalkha. In addition, few Kazakh names ever crop up in the press, and only rare media features mention them at all. [15]

These national-minorities questions may become increasingly important since shifts in ethnic populations have resulted in a rising percentage of natives and a declining percentage of ethnic Russians in the border areas of the MPR. Meanwhile, the percentage of Han Chinese on the Chinese side of the Mongolian border has been increasing rapidly, so an increasingly concentrated Han population on the borders faces a population that is becoming less and less Russian. The ethnic minorities will not gladly turn to ethnic Chinese for help, however; Maclean's point was that although there are indeed growing numbers of non-Russian peoples in the border regions of the USSR, their ideological orientation is still more Soviet than traditional. Maclean concluded in another book, about the Caucasus:

> Their rulers in Moscow feel far more secure in their control over them [peoples of the Caucasus] than they did thirty or forty years ago and far readier to face competition with the outside world. As each fresh generation grows up, the process . . . of ideological assimilation, of Sovietization, is carried a stage further. . . . Everywhere in the Union millions and millions of young Soviet citizens, whatever their nationality, are being taught in identical schools, are reading identical books and newspapers, are listening to identical broadcasts and speeches and sucking in identical propaganda. Everywhere distinctive national usages are dying out and national differences becoming less marked than they were. . . .[16]

IDEOLOGY, INDOCTRINATION, AND EDUCATION

The ideal is the New Man; the reality is the New Class. The ideal is rule by arat and proletariat; the reality is rule by bureaucrat. The Mongolian regime wants orthodox enthusiasm, conformist commitment, and participatory dogmatism; it proscribes dissidence, dissonance, and nonconformity, and it scorns alienation and passivity. The regime claims that the society has been energized and equalized; it has in fact been stratified, certified, and specialized.

The New Man corresponds to, and derives from, the Soviet version. He is a devoted and unselfish collectivist who works with great efficiency at a rapid pace to fulfill and overfulfill the plan.[17] The New Class is actually an educated elite whose members hold key jobs and are well rewarded for doing so. "Arat" is an ambiguous term that is used in several different ways; some are derogatory and some laudatory. The arat as the simple nomad living in a yurt and tending livestock is both idealized as pure in heart and clear of vision, and held in contempt and treated with arrogance. Although he represents "the masses" in whose name the regime rules, he also represents the feudal past and many of the things that are to be eliminated forever. "Arat" is used as shorthand sometimes for any member of a livestock-cooperative (SKhO; *negdel*), and sometimes for all the population—"the people."

Nomads living in yurts are gradually disappearing from the scene. More and more of the rural people who tend livestock live in permanent dwellings now. The economic plan for 1978 that was announced in December 1977, however, included specific reference to the manufacture of frames for yurts (and also to the manufacture of *dels*, the traditional Mongolian robes that were once the costume for all Mongols).[18]

The number of workers in the MPR—the industrial proletariat—increased from 15,000 in 1940 to 28,000 in 1950; 66,000 in 1960; 88,000 in 1966; and 110,000 in 1973. A major ideological imperative required the formation of an indigenous proletariat where none had existed before: The Party in Mongolia had to create a working class. That industrial work force developed rather slowly, but its strength among Party members was deliberately overrepresented. The number of workers in the Party increased by 13,000 between 1958 and 1976, to a total of 21,000 (31 percent of the total Party membership). The number of arats (as SKhO members) increased by 12,000 to 13,000 in the same period (they made up 19 percent of Party members in 1976), and those in the category of intelligentsia and employees increased by 11,000—from 22,000 to 33,000 (50 percent of total Party membership in 1976). In terms of percentages, however, the workers in the Party increased, the arats decreased, and the intelligentsia and employees stayed about the same between 1958 and 1976.

The Central Committee of the Party and the elites that run the country are essentially all intelligentsia—not workers or arats. Official propaganda describes two friendly and nonantagonistic classes—the workers and the cooperative arats—plus a supplementary "working intelligentsia," but that intelligentsia is not just a group of supernumeraries. Its members are bureaucrats, officials, and professionals who have elite status and tell workers and arats what to do. In contrast to the ideological dictates of the Party, it is the bureaucracy, the intelligentsia, and the semi-parasitic urban population that have developed impressively, not the industrial proletariat. The urban proportion of the population increased from 28 percent in 1956 to 46 percent in 1973 (641,000 people out of the total population of 1.4 million in 1973).

"Intelligentsia," as the term is now commonly used in Mongolia, designates an officially endorsed segment of the nonantagonistic Communist class system. Tsedenbal often uses the term "intelligentsia" interchangeably with "employees" (in the statistical category "workers and employees"). In that sense the intelligentsia may include even many poorly educated and inarticulate people. Even if the term is limited to Mongols who have completed their higher education, however, there can be no doubt that the class is much larger now than it ever was before.

A bourgeois-style critical intelligentsia, however, is another matter. There was such a thing in Mongolia and it included many remarkable and gifted individuals, but most of them perished in the purges of the 1930s. Speaking of the USSR, Solzhenitsyn said that "there is no longer an intelligentsia in our country. . . . It has all disintegrated into a collection of smatterers,"[19] and the same could be said about Mongolia. Rinchen, who died in March 1977, was in a sense the last survivor of the Mongolian intelligentsia. He had been listed as one of nine distinguished members of the Mongolian Academy of Sciences in 1971, but on March 26, 1976, he was mercilessly attacked, with the justification that he was a liar and a bourgeois nationalist. It is ironic to find Soviet publications attacking Mao and the Chinese People's Republic for their intolerant treatment of the population and the traditions of Tibet and Sinkiang,[20] since Rinchen had unhesitatingly equated the destruction Mao carried out during the Cultural Revolution with Stalin's rampages in the 1930s, and he had found little difference between Soviet suppression and Chinese suppression.[21] His death received no official mention, good or bad.

Special middle schools, technicums, and professional-technical schools all offer two years of vocational training to many of the graduates of the universal eight-year general schooling. Separate technicums specialize in, for example, teachers' training, pre-school teaching and operation, trade and marketing, finance and economics, para-medical training, law, construction, communications, railroad operation, agriculture (livestock and grain farming; SKhO and Goskhoz training), veterinary medicine, irrigation and water management, and music and choreography.[22] Half of these technicums are located in Ulan Bator, the other half in a wide variety of places all over the country. Plans to form new Goskhozes and open up more farmland in 1976–1980 include provision for the establishment of special professional-technical schools (PTU) to train the necessary cadres and personnel.

Extensive and systematic on-the-job training is also conducted at big projects such as those at Darkhan and Erdenet, and most university students spend so-called "third semesters" working on SKhOs or Goskhozes or at construction sites. Practical and vocational courses in the general schools include those in machine shop, electricity, agronomy, veterinary medicine, and the like. The educational system is basically oriented toward the economy and jobs; it is overwhelmingly technical and practical.

In 1975 university-level students totalled about 13,000; the entering class that fall contained 6,000 of these. Requirements for admission to a university included ten years of schooling, which may be eight years of general schooling and two years at a technicum or PTU, or ten years at a full middle school. The total number of students in higher education has increased steadily since the Mongolian State University opened in Ulan Bator in October 1942 (see Table 4).[23]

In October 1975 it was announced that 22,600 students had completed courses of study at Mongolian institutions of higher education. Faculties and departments have split off from the state university to form six additional institutes. The university has departments of mathematics, physics, technology,[24] construction, biology, communications-engineering, and social sciences, and there are separate institutes of education, agriculture, finance and economics, physical culture, and medicine, plus the Higher Party School (which has been classified as a "VUZ"—a higher educational institution—

TABLE 4
STUDENTS IN HIGHER EDUCATION IN THE MPR

Year	Number of Students
1942–	95
1950–	1,500
1960–	6,900
1967–	9,500
1975–	12,800

since 1962).[25] At the twenty-eighth graduation of the Mongolian State University in January 1974, representatives of the six hundred graduates told the local reporter that during their time as students they had worked in the summers harvesting grain, digging wells, and building cattle sheds, and that one had worked in construction at Bratsk, in Eastern Siberia, USSR.

Higher education in Mongolia is conducted by 780 professors and instructors, of whom 140 held advanced degrees in 1975. At that time, a total of 480 Mongols had earned *kandidat* degrees (roughly equivalent to M.A.s) and 44 held doctorates (roughly the same as Russian Ph. D.s). Most of these degrees were granted by Soviet institutions.[26] Six doctorates and seventeen other advanced degrees were earned by Mongols in 1974 and 1975 in the USSR. These theses and dissertations were about equally divided between ideological and economic subjects. One concerned political work in the Mongolian army. Twenty-one of these degrees were awarded by schools in Moscow or Leningrad, one in Irkutsk, and one in Novosibirsk. Three were earned at the Academy of Social Sciences, two at the Institute of Marxism-Leninism, and one at the Higher Party School (all of these institutions come under the authority of the Central Committee of the CPSU). One student completed a course of study at the Lenin Military-Political Academy.

The Central Committee of the Party, the Presidium of the Great Khural, and the Council of Ministers jointly issued a statement of guidance to the teachers of the country at the Fourth Teachers' Congress in August 1975. That statement constituted a six-point summation of educational philosophy:[27]

1. Pupils should receive scientific-theoretical knowledge along with vocational and polytechnical training. The schools should produce qualified cadres and specialists who are thoroughly acquainted with contemporary science and technology. The levels of knowledge in both general and technical subjects should be improved, and the young people ought to be instilled with the idea that knowledge and culture are everyday requirements, not exotic and unusual luxuries.

2. Teachers should inculcate students with the Communist world view, the ideas of Marxism-Leninism, and the principles of proletarian internationalism. They should imbue the pupils with a flaming patriotism and arm them thoroughly against the influence of bourgeois ideology, nationalism, and chauvinism. Class consciousness and a party spirit are important requirements for teachers and pupils. As active builders of socialism, both the young people and the teachers have a serious responsibility. They should honor the revolutionary tradition of the older generation, and develop the Mongolian people's eternal and unbroken friendship with, and fraternal class feelings toward, the great Soviet people and the countries of the socialist commonwealth. Marxism-Leninism should be their guide.

3. Ethical training of the younger generation is important. Class lectures should be supplemented by individual work and other work outside class every day. A spirit of honor and truth, frankness and modesty, and collectivism and comradeship should be instilled. Students should be encouraged to become political activists, to appreciate the importance of organization and discipline, to take a socialist attitude toward work, and to recognize their social responsibility. Any sign of antisocial behavior must be suppressed.

4. Scientific knowledge and high moral quality are necessary attributes for teachers and pupils. Teachers should provide an example of the scientific spirit, strive to raise their own political and scientific knowledge, serve as models of highly cultured behavior, and learn from the rich experience of the educational authorities of the USSR. For Mongolian teachers, the Russian language is one of the necessities for increasing their knowledge and improving their qualifications, and the teaching of Russian should be improved at all levels.

5. There must always be a united front of school, family, and society in educating youth. The Party, the state, voluntary organizations, industrial and agricultural enterprises, and all economic organizations must provide concrete assistance to schools and teachers. Scientific establishments and scientists, higher educational institutions and their professors, and the intelligentsia in general should all work to improve the quality of teaching in the general schools of the country.

6. The effectiveness of teaching should be increased. The learning process should be made more relevant to life and practical economic construction and production, and it should strengthen the material base of education.

Newspaper listings for the last month of 1977 indicate that Ulan Bator television presented programs six to seven hours daily five days a week, and for about twelve hours on weekends. Most of the programming on the single local channel derived from the USSR, and there was also a satellite transmission ("Orbit") from Moscow.[28] Ten or fifteen minutes of nightly news, late movies, and a great deal of sports made up most of the viewing schedule. There was no evidence of regular and systematic educational programs on television. During the month several programs, including locally originated ones, were presented in the Russian language. The programming included a great deal of music, some films from Eastern Europe and Cuba, one-time presentations of programs from Japan and Finland, and a special on Panama featuring a speech by the general secretary of the People's Party of Panama. At least two original television plays by Mongolian authors (one a woman) in the Mongolian language and two Mongolian-made films were shown during the month, and about once a week a short documentary focussed on one aimak. There were no programs dealing with China.

Visual evidence of Soviet influence in Ulan Bator includes much of the recent architecture, including the House of Culture of the Mongolian Trade Unions, the Palace of Science and Technology for Youth, the Lenin Museum, and the Palace of Weddings. A new project for a House of Culture, Science, and Technology is to be the largest building complex in the city: it will include a twenty-story building, a two-thousand-seat amphitheater, a library, an exhibition hall, and a cafe, all interconnected under one roof. Moscow architects submitted proposals for the complex and one of them, Yu. L. Shvartsbreim of the Mezentsev Building Institute, was chosen. When he was in Ulan Bator in 1976 he pointed out that the Soviet architect Mezentsev had designed the Sukhe Bator-Choibalsan Mausoleum in Ulan Bator's central square.[29] The Russians built and operate the House of Science and Culture (DSNK), a kind of "Soviet House" established to encourage interest in the USSR.[30]

ECONOMIC CONSIDERATIONS

The mining operation now under construction at Erdenet is the largest and most dramatic economic enterprise ever undertaken in Mongolia: the copper and molybdenum produced there should contribute significantly to the equalization of Mongolian-Russian trade. Erdenet has added a whole new dimension to Soviet-Mongolian relations. It has deepened and intensified Mongolia's dependent symbiotic relationship with Russia, integrated Mongolia with Eastern Siberia more intimately than ever before, brought Russians and all the appurtenances of a large-scale operation into Mongolia for the first time. Russians dominate the project's planning and operation, and the USSR is to receive all of the mineral product, but many Mongols are working there and the political, social, and economic impact is already considerable. The Chinese and all other outside parties are being totally and irreversibly excluded from any meaningful role in Mongolia.

The showpiece of the Erdenet project will be one of the ten largest copper mines in the world. Besides the mine it includes a 164-kilometer railroad to Salkhit and a 180-kilometer asphalt highway to Darkhan; substantial bridges over the Orkhon River (one of them 200 meters long); a high-voltage electric power line from Darkhan and ultimately from the Gusinoe power complex in the USSR; a dam in the Selenga River to assure an annual supply of 60 million cubic meters of water; and a 64-kilometer pipeline (1 meter in diameter) to carry that water to the mine. All these components were under construction and partially completed by mid-1975. The railroad opened on October 4, 1975, and the first passenger train on the line ran on June 6, 1977. The water pipeline began operation in February 1977. Erdenet's population reached thirty-two thousand by November 1977.[31]

The USSR provided the initial impetus for the project, decided where and when to undertake it, and will be its principal beneficiary. The role of the MPRP is to commit Mongolian economic planning to the project, organize and supply Mongolian manpower to assist in its operation, see that Mongolian training and education are adapted to its needs, and assure the realization of its goals, including the exportation of its product to the USSR. The economic purpose of the project is to reduce the Soviet subsidy to Mongolia, but it has a military-strategic function as well. Erdenet itself, the rail line to Salkhit (near Darkhan), the increasing populations of both Erdenet and Darkhan, the increase in permanent settlement and farming in the surrounding area, and the new coal mines with their branch rail lines to the main railroad all in effect fortify the shield protecting Baikal. Darkhan and the first New Lands program in 1960 made up an earlier phase of the effort to defend Baikal, and Erdenet and the second New-Lands expansion beginning in 1976 carry the process much further.

Erdenet is much larger and more revolutionary than Darkhan; there is an important conceptual difference between the two projects. Darkhan's product was destined for Mongols; the project benefitted Russians only indirectly by increasing Mongolian self-sufficiency. Darkhan thus helped the Mongols to help themselves. Erdenet's product is destined for Russia, and the project helps the Mongols to help the Russians; it is an example of neocolonialism. Erdenet is also such a major and probably irreversible commitment that it practically eliminates the Russian option to withdraw from Mongolia. The intention of the Russians to remain seems unmistakable in view of the permanency and elaborateness of their construction in Mongolia in recent years.

Erdenet's molybdenum may be more important than its copper. There has been a global surplus of copper in the 1970s, and the Soviets have many domestic sources of it as well: the gigantic Udokan development in Eastern Siberia, related to the new Baikal Aimur railroad construction in Siberia, assures future supplies without reliance on Erdenet.

Fluorspar became a politically significant item of Mongolian export to the USSR when the amount sent to Russia by China fell off substantially in 1960. Not until 1973–1974, however, did the Mongolian supply increase by a large amount: in 1974 the USSR imported 250 tons of fluorspar from Mongolia and 85 tons from China. Mongolia maintained the same level of supply to Russia in subsequent years, but China increased its share from 25 percent of the Mongolian-Chinese combined export in 1975 to 38 percent in 1976. Fluorspar appears to be the only commodity involving Mongolia directly in Sino-Soviet affairs.

The New-Lands-II program was adopted by the Eleventh Party Central Committee plenum of January 29, 1976. It called for adding 230,000 hectares by 1979 to the half-million already sown in Mongolia. The additions required by the annual schedule have thus far been met and exceeded (see Table 5). Targets for sown areas have proved easier to meet, however, than those for harvest. A substantial shortfall occurred in the grain crop in 1976: the total crop (340,000 tons) was less than the harvest before the new areas were added. The USSR had to double its exports of grain to the MPR, exceeding the amount sent sixteen years earlier. It was a disappointing performance for an import-substitution program. The 1977 harvest of 407,000 tons fell short by 100,000 tons. The target for 1978 is 547,000 tons.

Seventy-five percent of the land to be added for grain farming is in Selenga and the Central Aimaks, north of Ulan Bator in the Darkhan area. In 1975, 40 percent of the total sown area, and 33 percent of the total grain harvest, were accounted for by Selenga Aimak alone. Selenga and the Central Aimaks dominate grain farming, and most of the large state farms (Goskhozes) are found there. This area not only offers the best soil and climate conditions for grain, but it is closest to and most accessible from the USSR. For example, Soviet combine operators from Eastern Siberia were able to enter the MPR with their machinery and collected 35 percent of Selenga Aimak's 1975 crop.

Erosion through dust storms is a clear and present danger.[32] The fact that more grain is being sown and less is being harvested suggests the possibility of

TABLE 5
LAND SOWN UNDER THE NEW LANDS II PROGRAM
(in thousand hectares)

	Scheduled	Actual
1976	38	40
1977	77	90
1978	61	(Annual plan – 71)
1979	54	—

serious trouble. The pollution that Erdenet is likely to produce may cause even greater problems: copper mining is a dirty business,[33] and Erdenet's watershed feeds Baikal. A joint Mongolian-Russian commission has been established to monitor pollution and protect the environment, but its effectiveness and its political power have not been tested. The landscape of northern Mongolia is obviously undergoing massive alteration, and the effects could spread northward across the border.

There are seven key indicators of the Mongolian economic situation:

1. Because there are very few Mongols, a critical and chronic manpower shortage affects all plans and projects in the MPR. In addition, the pace of development in Mongolia depends on development in Eastern Siberia where a similar shortage exists. The situation is further aggravated by the fact that very close by are millions of Chinese who are available and willing to help.

2. Adding to the problems caused by the labor shortage are widespread apathy and significant motivational and attitudinal problems. The regime blames these on feudalism and Buddhism, but they may actually be the results of the traditional nomadic life-style of the Mongols, of Communist economic forms and organization, and of the laborers' lack of interest in working hard to satisfy Mongolia's debts to the USSR.[34]

3. For more than twenty years the USSR has been sending more goods to Mongolia than it has gotten back in return: the Soviet Union has been subsidizing the MPR, and the trade imbalance has grown no smaller with the passage of time. A large part of Mongolian economic development is aimed at reducing that imbalance, and attempts at import substitution have accounted for much of the economic change that has occurred.

4. The basic livestock economy has not improved despite decades of exhortations, numerous reorganizations, and establishment of a plethora of rules and regulations. In 1978 Mongolia's herds contained fewer than twenty-five million animals, but this total has not grown appreciably over the past forty years. Each successive Five-Year Plan has set the same goal, which has never been attained.[35]

5. Despite heavy ideological emphasis on industry and the proletariat, actual development in those fields has been slight—largely limited to light industry and the processing of livestock products.

6. Until the substantial mining operation now under development at Erdenet begins production (that event is scheduled for 1979) mining and mineral production will remain of limited importance. Neither critical materials nor large quantities of the more common minerals are mined. Although the Erdenet copper-molybdenum mining complex is the largest economic enterprise ever announced for Mongolia, it is destined to send

100 percent of its product to the USSR, thus minimizing its relevance to the Mongolian economy.

7. The most important changes and developments in Mongolia occur in the northern third of the country, the part closest to the USSR, especially in the Selenga Valley, which has for more than a century been the principal Mongolian-Russian trade route north from Ulan Bator.

In a statement of December 3, 1975, Tsedenbal was very specific about the interrelation of the Party and the economy:

> Higher committees of the Party must infuse into the basic Party units—the Primary Party Organizations—the importance of securing and improving Plan-fulfillment in the basic working collectives—the SKhO's, Goskhozes, the brigades, the teams—because that is the level which determines whether the economic goals of the Party are reached or not. One of the ways of doing this is for Party members to fulfill their own personal Plan-goals. If the Party member fails to meet his target, Party discipline suffers, and the force of the Party member's example is seriously weakened. That in fact does often happen: in 1975 nearly 2,000 Party members failed to meet their own individual Plan goals; they failed in their socialist duty.

> Party committees at all levels, including the basic Primary Party Organizations, should devote their meetings to questions of practical production, of fulfillment of Plan goals. Discussion should be direct and practical, related to specific jobs and problems. The Party must work directly with SKhO and Goskhoz chairmen, factory directors, and technical specialists, to maintain unceasing control. Party control must operate at all levels: the Central Committee must control the Ministries and Commissions of the Government; Aimak and City Party Committees must control the Government administration at their levels; and Primary Party Organizations must control SKhO's, Goskhozes, and factories.

> The Party in addition to inspiring work and assuring fulfillment of the Plan, must also instill a responsible attitude toward State property. Damage, theft, ignorance, and simple neglect result in loss and destruction of machinery and equipment. Socialist discipline must insure dedicated work and care of property. The slightest infraction must be severely punished.[36]

ORGANIZATIONAL CONSIDERATIONS

The sudden rise of Batmunkh to prominence as Tsedenbal's replacement in the position of prime minister on June 10, 1974, was the most surprising political development in recent years.[37] Batmunkh was not a Politburo member before his appointment; he rose from obscurity—a position far down in the elite hierarchy. His biography, however, is entirely orthodox for current

Mongolian leaders: a background in economics, advanced study in Moscow, career movement from Party to government and from government to Party and even simultaneous positions in both—a characteristic of most top-level Mongolian officials. Batmunkh studied economics in Ulan Bator, at the Mongolian State University; for several years (1952–1958) he worked at the Higher Party School, first teaching the history of the CPSU and then occupying the number two leadership position at the school. He attended the Academy of Social Sciences of the Central Committee of the CPSU (Sector of Political Economy) in Moscow, where in 1961 he submitted his dissertation entitled "The Law of Planned, Proportional Development of the Economy, and Economic Planning in the MPR." He became director of the Economics Institute in Ulan Bator, and in 1967, deputy director and then director of the Mongolian State University. He served about a year (1973–1974) as head of the science and education sector of the Central Committee of the MPRP, and was appointed a deputy prime minister in the government on May 9, 1974. On June 10, 1974, he replaced Tsedenbal as prime minister and was made a full member of the Politburo.

When Tsedenbal surrendered the position of prime minister to Batmunkh, he assumed the position of president (chairman of the Presidium of the Great Khural) and continued in his role as first secretary of the party. The former president, Sambu, had died on May 21, 1972, but no successor had been announced. The position of chairman of the Presidium of the Great Khural was simply left vacant for more than two years, until Tsedenbal was appointed to it in June 1974.[38]

Tsedenbal is ten years older than Batmunkh, who might be either his protégé or his rival. Early signs of rivalry include a press photograph showing Batmunkh squeezed between Tsedenbal and Brezhnev at the Ulan Bator airport on November 26, 1974, and a photograph taken on July 5, 1974, showing Batmunkh at center stage signing an agreement, with Tsedenbal hovering in the background. In late 1974 and early 1975, Politburo listings in the press were uncharacteristically presented in alphabetical order; thus Batmunkh was placed first, several places ahead of Tsedenbal. Batmunkh was given priority in listings for the last time, however, on April 22, 1975. An official photograph taken on July 5, 1975, returned Tsedenbal to center stage and relegated Batmunkh to the background, and by November, Tsedenbal's name was again appearing first in all press accounts. Tsedenbal dominated the tenth plenum of the Party's Central Committee in December 1975, and in his speech there he argued forcefully that the Politburo and the Central Committee must dominate the Council of Ministers and that Party organizations at all levels must lead government offices and officials. (Major parts of this speech were quoted earlier in this chapter.) In September 1976, a bust of Tsedenbal was unveiled in his hometown in a tribute that obviously copied the Soviet unveiling of the bust of Brezhnev in *his* hometown. Throughout

1977 it was clear that Tsedenbal was regarded as the senior official and Batmunkh as the junior. Tsedenbal's election district was in Ulan Bator and Batmunkh's was in a western aimak (province); Brezhnev sent congratulations to Tsedenbal and Kosygin sent congratulations to Batmunkh.

Tsedenbal criticized the Party for "massive inadequacies" in December 1975. He complained of widespread failure to assume responsibility, lack of initiative, bureaucratic formalism instead of pragmatic activism, and the production of more paper reports than material goods. He charged that Party mobilizers too often failed to mobilize the members, and that instead of taking the initiative, Party members frequently sat back and remained silent. The one out of ten adults who was a member of the Party, he said, should be a living example for the other nine: when the Party member was not active and effective, his bad example influenced the attitudes and actions of nine—and this happened all too often. He charged that the evils of bureaucracy plagued the Party; far too many meetings and discussions dragged on much too long, and too much of the Party's apparat produced far too many reports. According to Tsedenbal, production was inefficiently organized: sitters, bustlers, and bumblers never got around to setting concrete and specific tasks, with concrete and specific deadlines, and reports, investigations, and more reports continued to deal with the same problems, without any discernible improvement. The plan was always overfulfilled on paper, but underfulfilled in reality.

Tsendenbal then pointed out that:

> There are many celebrations and parties to honor old comrades, for their fiftieth birthday, their sixtieth birthday, and other occasions. Such celebrations with family, close friends, and acquaintances, are fine, and the Party does not oppose them. But such parties have gotten quite out of hand in recent years. They have come to exceed all limits which ought to govern a socialist society and style of life. They exceed the boundaries of Communist morality, and must be curtailed.[39]

He claimed that irresponsibility surrounded and suffused government-sponsored trips to the USSR (22,800 Mongols participated in such official travel during the period 1970–1975—852,000 workdays by Tsedenbal's calculation—and all too often no concrete economic results were ever achieved). Damage, theft, ignorance, and neglect, in addition to endless meetings and discussions, also caused immense losses.

CHANNELS OF SOVIET INFLUENCE

Soviet influence is exerted on Mongolia through:

1. Political organizations in both the USSR and Mongolia in which party and government form parallel structures that overlap, and so are not

clearly differentiated. Thus Soviet influence can flow from the CPSU to the MPRP and through it to the Mongolian government, or from the Soviet government to the Mongolian government and thence to the MPRP.

2. Direct relations—between the CPSU and the MPRP.

3. Direct relations between the Soviet government and the Mongolian government, with intergovernmental commissions and special-purpose groups supplementing the regular governmental and diplomatic connections.

4. Direct relations between Soviet ministries and their Mongolian counterparts.

5. Direct ties between Soviet and Mongolian subgovernmental units: for example, between a Soviet oblast and a Mongolian aimak, between a Soviet factory and a Mongolian factory, or between a Soviet state farm and a Mongolian one.

6. Connections between scholarly and scientific organizations in the two nations, such as direct ties between the Soviet and the Mongolian academies of sciences.

7. Connections between other societies and organizations, such as the Mongolian-Soviet Friendship Association, and Soviet-Mongolian competitions, such as contests with prizes that are testaments to friendship.

8. Transportation, communications, and the media: Soviet-built railroads, for example, constitute principal links with, and within, Mongolia.

In each of these cases, Soviet institutions have inspired Mongolian copies. The personnel of these institutions, both Russians and Mongols, also maintain both direct and indirect connections. Not only do Soviet delegations of all sorts go to Mongolia, and Mongolian counterparts to the USSR, but Russians also work directly with Mongolian representatives, and many Mongols are trained in the Soviet Union or in Soviet-inspired Mongolian vocational and educational institutions. The result is a complex relationship in which Soviet influence is expressed through ideology, institutional models, and personnel—through substance, form, and people. The Party is far from the only channel used by the USSR to control the MPR; in fact, the Soviets have lines of influence at every level and in every facet of Mongolian life, and many of the direct contacts have nothing to do with the Party. Influence is exerted through back channels as well as direct ones.

In September 1975, Damdinjavyn Maidar, a Politburo member, spoke of "developing the process of political and economic consolidation of Mongolia with the Soviet Union," and provided many examples of close and direct connections. These included: direct economic relations between the two countries over the past fifty years; joint Mongolian-Soviet enterprises in the

MPR such as Erdenet; direct connections between thirteen governmental ministries and commissions of the MPR and twenty ministries and commissions of the Soviet Union; a joint commission, "Mongol'sovtsvetmet" to control mining of nonferrous metals; direct connection between forty Mongolian research institutes or laboratories and eighty Soviet counterparts; joint investigation of resources in Mongolia; joint preparation and coordination of the 1976-1980 Mongolian Five-Year Plan; and direct connection between Soviet oblasts and Mongolian aimaks, bypassing normal central government channels. Although few of the channels of influence were entirely new in 1975, most of them have become more important because they are being developed more systematically and extensively than before; their cumulative impact is becoming so great that it constitutes a qualitative and substantive change. Soviet influence penetrates the MPR at more levels than ever before and a complex infrastructure undergirds the more orthodox government-to-government and party-to-party relations.

THE MONGOLIAN ELITE

In Mongolia as in the USSR, equality is far from a reality. Economic and social inequality characterizes the society, with well-developed trends toward stratification, professionalization, specialization, and differentiation. There is a New Class—a privileged elite—and above all there is the New Bureaucracy. The society is one of credentials—the university degree separates the "washed" from the "unwashed" (those familiar with traditional Mongolia will recognize the literal sense in which this describes the situation). Holders of university degrees are subdivided into those with Russian degrees and those with Mongolian degrees, and many Mongols return from study in Moscow or Leningrad with a Russian wife. The members of the Mongolian elite generally live, eat, and play Russian-style; they have been socialized into Soviet society, into the Communist world. Their status and their comforts derive from the USSR. They like to travel, and that is a major perquisite of official position. They also prefer to live in Ulan Bator: Tsedenbal once complained that most of Mongolia's trained agricultural specialists never left the city.[40]

The considerable stratification in Mongolian society is sometimes publicly admitted.[41] The population is divided in various ways: the urban population from the rural; agricultural from industrial workers; the university-educated (intelligentsia) from the relatively uneducated; generalists from specialists; workers from administrators and officials; and the inhabitants of Ulan Bator from the rest of the country. University-educated and urban people, industrial workers, specialists and professionals, officials, and intelligentsia are all increasing in number, while rural livestock-herding nomads are decreasing.

Something very like the Soviet pattern of inequality prevails in the MPR. There are a technological elite, an intelligentsia, an urban elite, and an influential group of toadies and sycophants, both inside and outside the Party organization. Bureaucrats are plentiful, and the military has an elite group. There are even a few Buddhist lamas, but clerks are more numerous than clerics.

Most of the important people, even when their importance derives primarily from non-Party positions, are included in the Central Committee of the MPRP, and those who are not members of the Central Committee are at least Party members. Of the influential people, most are males, inhabitants of the capital city of Ulan Bator, and Khalkhas. Most speak Russian, and many have received at least part of their education in the USSR. A high proportion hold university degrees. Most of them live in apartments rather than yurts and wear Russian-style clothing rather than the Mongolian *del*. Most enjoy the use of chauffeur-driven official cars, or own private cars. Many of them vacation every year in the USSR, and many send their children to school in the Soviet Union. The elites tend to travel extensively—to New York for United Nations meetings, to Moscow for Party and other gatherings, and to East European capitals for CMEA meetings or other types of consultation, discussion, and negotiation. Most of them work in offices and are quintessential bureaucrats.

The Mongolian Military Elite

The Mongolian military establishment accounts for forty members of a national elite that numbers about five hundred.[42] The forty include ten members of the Central Committee of the Party and six candidate-members. The key person is probably Sanjiin Bata, head of what is in fact the Defense Department of the Central Committee, although its official title is Administrative Organization Department. No Politburo member deals directly and primarily with defense matters, but Bata greets the many visiting Soviet military delegations and appears to be present whenever military matters are involved. He served as ambassador to Moscow from 1956 through 1959 and was a deputy minister of defense in the 1960s. The current minister of defense of the MPR is Lieutenant-General Jarantain Avkhia (b. 1923), who succeeded General Batyn Dorj (b. 1914) in September 1978. Major-General Gendenpil is First Deputy Chief of the Army General Staff. Construction troops come under Major General D. Babuu, a deputy minister of defense who headed the Darkhan military construction project in the 1960s. Major General S. Sanjmatav serves as chairman of the administration for civil aviation. A first deputy minister of defense, Major General Ch. Tumendemberel, serves as chairman of the civil defense administration. Major General Ts. Sodnomdarja serves as military attaché at the MPR embassy in Moscow.

Head of the important political administration of the army is Lieutenant General D. Yondonduichir, who was state prosecutor from 1960 through 1964. The political administration includes a military history section, which is headed by Major General B. Tsedev. The foreign affairs department of the defense ministry is headed by Lieutenant General J. Jam'yan, who was a prominent figure in the early 1960s, but was in obscurity for many years. In October 1974 he reappeared as chairman of a Committee to Aid the Vietnamese People, and then for a time was chairman of civil defense. Major-General J. Yadma has been chief editor of the Mongolian army newspaper (*Ulaan Od* or "Red Star") for more than fifteen years; that paper slavishly copies the soviet *Krasnaya Zvezda*. Major-General S. Dorj is Chief of the Political Department, Internal and Border Troops.

The commandant of the Sukhe Bator War College is Lieutenant General J. Yondon, former first deputy minister of defense and chief of the army's general staff. General S. Ravdan, who died recently, was a former head of the political administration and the minister of foreign affairs in 1955 and 1956; he served with General Pliev in Inner Mongolia in 1945.[43] An Association of Alumni of Soviet Military Academies is headed by Major General Sanjmatav, the civil aviation chief, and a graduate of the Moscow Military-Political Academy, Colonel L. Dambinyam, heads the Department of Social Sciences at the Sukhe Bator War College. A first deputy minister of defense, Colonel General B. Tsog, who was at Nomonkhan in 1939, is head of the MPR Society for Promotion of Defense.

The Departments of Security and Justice, the Supreme Court, and the office of the state prosecutor are all closely related to the military of the MPR; high-ranking officers fill many of the top posts in these segments of the government. Lieutenant General B. Dejid is minister of security. A first deputy minister of public security, Major General S. Budragcha, serves concurrently as chief of militia, and a deputy minister, Major General Sh. Arvai, heads the Border Guards. Gonchigyn Ish (b. 1924) has been Chairman of the Supreme Court since April 1978, succeeding Major-General R. Gunsen. Ish was first deputy state prosecutor, 1969–1978. Major-General Ravdangiin Gunsen (b. 1923) succeeded Lieutenant-General Avkhia as state prosecutor April 1, 1978, when Avkhia became first deputy minister of defense (since September 1978 Avkhia serves as minister of defense). The former minister of justice, D. Purev, who completed an advanced degree in the USSR in 1971, stated in April 1977 that the system of justice in the MPR was specifically based on the legal code of the USSR. J. Avkhia had been state prosecutor since 1970.[44] In 1977 a first deputy minister of public security, P. Dechin, was named chairman of a civil defense directorate. It has already been noted that a first deputy minister of defense, Major General Tumendemberel, served as Chairman of the Civil Defense Administration. Either,

Dechin succeeded Tumendemberel or two civil-defense bureaucracies exist.[45]

High-ranking Soviet officers visit the MPR fairly regularly. A recent ministry of defense delegation, in March 1977, was led by S. V. Vanyagin. Marshal of Aviation Sudets (retired), who founded the Mongolian Air Force in the 1930s, often appears in Ulan Bator for various ceremonies, most recently in July 1977. General of the army Fedyuninsky, a major Soviet leader at Nomonkhan in 1939, published an article in the Ulan Bator newspaper on August 18, 1977, just before his death. General of the army P. I. Batov was honored in Ulan Bator in July 1977 for his "merit in strengthening the defense capability of the MPR." In October 1977 *Krasnaya Zvezda* published an article by a Soviet lieutenant-colonel about a sentimental visit to former comrades in the Mongolian army. In December 1976 a street in Ulan Bator was renamed after Marshal Zhukov, and a Zhukov museum and memorial are under construction in the Mongolian capital.

There is undoubtedly no area of Soviet-Mongolian relations in which the Mongols are more completely dominated by the Russians than military affairs. Since 1966, and especially since the Damansky Island incident of 1969, the MPR has in effect been completely incorporated into the Trans-baikal and Far East military districts of the USSR, and Soviet divisions have been stationed on the Mongolian-Chinese border for more than a decade. Thus the real chiefs of the Mongolian army are the commanders of the Far East military district (General V. A. Petrov in July 1975) and the Transbaikal military district (General I. Tretyak in October 1977). It is not known if the Soviet military attaché in Ulan Bator, Major General V. V. Fedotov, plays a role of particular importance.

The Ideological and Instructional Elite

Occupations involving ideology, indoctrination, information, and education account for about 150 of the 500 members of the Mongolian elite, including 12 full members and 9 candidate-members of the Central Committee, but no Politburo members.[46] The highest-ranking person in this group is the secretary of the party's Central Committee, who serves concurrently as the minister of culture (S. Sosorbaram). The Ideology Department of the Central Committee and the Revsomols are of major importance for indoctrination. Writing, the arts, and journalism are important weapons in the Communist arsenal of indoctrination; they are used not only to spread the doctrine of Marxism-Leninism, but also to educate the people about the indispensable contribution of the USSR to Mongolia and the importance of maintaining the very closest and most friendly relations with the Soviets. "Follow the Soviet Union and Marxism-Leninism will take care of itself" is part of the message conveyed. The Russian language is considered an important part of Mongolian "right thinking," and the pursuit of fluency in Russian is in itself evidence of a proper attitude. The Mongolian-Soviet Friendship Association is the major mass organization that engages in indoctrination.

A large apparatus has been established for education and training that is generally independent of and separate from the ideological apparatus, although the two occasionally overlap. Three separate aspects of the propaganda process can be identified: the propaganda line and its ideological basis and explanation are provided by the Soviet Union; the ideological apparatus in the MPR receives and transmits the Soviet line to the Mongols; and the Mongolian educational and training apparatus takes its ideology from that apparatus but carries on its own professional or technical pedagogical programs. No Mongols are theoreticians, or "propagandists" in the Soviet sense; they are only "agitators." They do not establish the line, but merely transmit it.

The Ideology Department of the Central Committee, and the secretary of the Central Committee, who is concurrently minister of culture, unite party and government in ideological matters. The unions of writers, journalists, and artists, and the Revsomols, are the main organizational arms for this sort of activity. One deputy prime minister (Tsevegmid) serves as chairman of the State Committee for Higher, Secondary Specialized, and Vocational and Technical Institutions; through the Academy of Sciences and the state university he controls much of education and training. The ministry of education, which was headed by D. Ishtseren from December 1965 until his death on March 25, 1978, is responsible for elementary and standard-secondary education. R. Sanjaasuren succeeded Ishtseren. The Higher Party School and the Institute for Party History are directly available only to Party members, not the general population. In Mongolia as in Russia, "culture" includes museums, the circus, radio, television, films, encyclopedias,[47] and architecture; all of these are administered by agencies of the state bureaucracy.

An agency in the Soviet pattern that is especially important as a result of the extraordinary past predominance of Buddhism in Mongolia is the government's Council for Religious Affairs, headed by an atheist, Baljinyam. The tame official Buddhists have been integrated into the propaganda apparatus as "agents of peace" to other countries, especially Buddhist ones. The apparatus also includes several "Peace Committees" and Afro-Asian Solidarity Groups that fortify Soviet policy in those areas of the world.

The fact that some Mongols—Buryats, Oirats, Kalmyks, and the closely related Tuvans—live in the USSR unquestionably makes the Mongols regard the USSR more favorably. The Soviet government appoints and exploits for propaganda purposes a head of Buryat Buddhism who works with and supports the official Buddhist Church in the MPR.

One of the most important Soviet influences in Mongolia has always been Russian scientific and academic or scholarly interest in Mongolia and its people. Extensive Russian publication on Mongolian topics, much of it nonpolitical and some of it objective and unbiased, flatters the Mongols and leads them to regard the Soviets far more favorably than the Chinese, who have shown little interest in writing about Mongolia. The Institute of Oriental Studies of the USSR Academy of Sciences (IVAN) worked intimately with Mongolian scholars, authors, and professors for decades; some of those involved have maintained close personal friendships dating back as much as fifty years. Many of the Mongols originally embarked on scholarly and academic careers with the sponsorship and assistance of Soviet Mongolian specialists.

The recently established House of Science and Culture (DSNK) places a direct and overt USSR propaganda office in the middle of Ulan Bator. It stresses friendship with the Soviet Union and encourages Mongols to learn the Russian language.

Thirty-four members of the Mongolian ideological and instructional elite—including eleven full members of the Central Committee and five candidate-members—have been promoted, demoted, or threatened with some kind of change in their status since 1974. The preceding decade had been one of comparative stability and calm, but the period 1974–1976 has been marked by far greater activity, and more changes are likely to follow.

Twenty of these thirty-four elite-members have been active leaders in the field of ideology since before 1964. At least half of them hold Soviet advanced academic degrees. They have held positions in many different areas of the Party and government: seven each in the Ideology Department of the Central Committee; the Revsomols; the ministry of culture; the Union of Writers; and the Union of Journalists. Three of them have worked in the Academy of Sciences; two (politically the most potent members of the group) have held the position of secretary of the Central Committee. Two have been members of the State Commission for Women. The group also included three editors of *Unen*, the Party newspaper, and two of *Namyn Amdral*, the Party journal. (Because some members of the group have held more than one position, the jobs listed above total more than thirty-four.)

Although the changes that occurred during these three years resulted partly from events and rivalries in Mongolia, they surely reflect developments in the USSR as well. Rumors of Brezhnev's illness and speculation on his successor have undoubtedly affected the MPR, and the trouble in which Mme. Furtseva found herself in mid-1974 and her death the following October probably also had an effect on Mongolian ideological politics.[48]

The Economics Elite

In a very conservative classification, 140 of the 500 Mongolian elite-members would be considered to be primarily occupied with economic affairs. Most top-level officials are veterans of Gosplan, which formulates the Five-Year

Plans, and/or of CMEA, which negotiates foreign-trade matters, mainly with the USSR. Six of the eight full members of the Politburo, including both Tsedenbal and Batmunkh, have backgrounds, educations, and experience predominantly in the field of economics, as do both Politburo candidate-members. Thirty-five of the ninety-one Central Committee members and eleven of the sixty-one Central Committee candidate-members also fit into this category. Economics accounts for about as many members of the 500 elites as ideology, but they include three times as many Central Committee members, and they completely dominate the Politburo. Most of the government ministries and special commissions are economic in nature.

The third plenum of the Central Committee of the Party met on December 21, 1977, and heard reports on the economy from D. Sodnom, chairman of the State Planning Commission, and Ts. Molom, minister of finance. Sodnom was himself minister of finance in 1964; he has been a deputy prime minister since June 1975. It was announced in 1977 that the Soviet ministry of finance would send a representative directly to the Mongolian finance ministry;[49] this may be related to the call of the Soviet-Mongolian Intergovernmental Commission in July 1968 for a more rational use of Soviet aid by Mongolia.[50]

In December 1977 a Mongolian-Soviet seminar in Tashkent dealt with the participation of women in labor and social life; several Mongols took part. The Women's Council of the Soviet Central Asian Republics hosted the meeting, and of course the locale was an interesting one for a focus on the rights of women. Women were never veiled nor sequestered in Mongolia as they were among the Muslims of Central Asia, but two simple statistics attest to their traditionally low status: out of 1190 pupils in Mongolian schools in 1926, only 48 were girls, and the literacy rate in 1928 was 9.2 percent for males and 0.26 percent for females. In August 1965 a United Nations meeting in Ulan Bator dealt with women's roles. A new preschool complex was opened in Ulan Bator in November 1977 in a ceremony presided over by Anastasia Ivanovna Filatova-Tsedenbal, the Russian wife of the Mongolian leader and chairperson of the Mongolian Children's Fund. She had begun to get press attention at the time she accompanied her husband on a visit to Tito in Yugoslavia in September 1974, and she continued to receive it as head of the Children's Fund. Thus women have been receiving more official public attention, which may have provided them with some improvement in status.

Health and the medical profession appear to be low on the scale of political priorities in Mongolia. The long-time minister of health, D. Nyam-Osor, a candidate-member of the Central Committee, seems to be the only one in his field or any remotely related field who is on the committee at all. Nevertheless, health has been one of the major success stories of the Communist period. The number of physicians and health personnel has increased tremendously.[51] Within the last few years attitudes toward traditional Tibetan medicine seem to have become more tolerant. For a long time it was derided as simple superstition and part of the deceit of the masses practiced by the Buddhist Church, but recently it has received public praise on several occasions.

Most of the Russian civilian officials in Mongolia are engaged in economic matters; they deal either directly with the domestic economy of the country or with factors affecting foreign trade—that is, trade with the USSR. At least five of the advisers in the Soviet embassy in Ulan Bator are specifically designated as economic counsellors. A Soviet trade representative is permanently stationed in Ulan Bator, and the Soviets have also sent to Mongolia representatives of the Joint Soviet-Mongolian Intergovernmental Commission; Russian construction crews with Soviet bosses; teams of combine operators to assist in the Mongolian grain harvest; several key personnel of the Trans-Mongolian Railroad; and many Russians in all sorts of positions connected with construction and operation of the giant Erdenet project.[52]

Organizational Elite

Seventy-four of the five hundred Mongolian elite-members fulfill duties that are primarily organizational, although many of them, such as the large group of Aimak Party secretaries, obviously bear heavy economic responsibilities. The seventy-four include seventeen full members and thirteen candidate-members of the Central Committee; members of Party control groups and Aimak Party organizations; and People's Control and Aimak Khural personnel (both government agencies). Most of the Central Committee members and candidate-members are Aimak Party first secretaries. The long-time Politburo member N. Luvsanravdan is chairman of the Central Committee's Commission on Party Control. G. Ad'yaa is head of the Central Committee's Department of Party Organization. The local administration in the MPR includes 17 aimaks, three "republic cities" of aimak rank; and the Railroad Administration and an army Party organization that are probably equal in rank to the aimaks. Of the first Party secretaries for these units, those who control ten of the aimaks and the city of Erdenet are full Central Committee members, and a Politburo candidate-member (Altangerel) heads the capital city of Ulan Bator's party organization. Five aimaks and the Railroad Administration are led by Central Committee candidate-members. The Party heads for one aimak (Ara Khangai) and one city (Darkhan) are not on the Central Committee at all, and the status of the first secretary for Khubsugul Aimak and for the army are not known.

The government structure includes few Central Committee members or candidate-members. N. Luvsanchultem, chairman of the Great Khural, and N. Tsedenpil, deputy chairman of the Great Khural, are also full members. The deputy chairman of the Commission on People's Control, D. Namsrai, and B. Jadamba, chief of a department under the Council of Ministers, are candidate-members. The only Aimak Khural chairman to be a candidate-member of the Central Committee (there are no full members) is Ts. Dalai of Sukhe Bator Aimak.

Among all the Russians in Mongolia, the Soviet ambassador, Aleksandr Ivanovich Smirnov, has the most to do with organization since he served for decades as Party Secretary for Chita Oblast and since he deals with the MPR in many ways as if it were an East Siberian oblast. Konstantin Viktorovich Rusakov, the most recent appointee as secretary to the Central Committee of the CPSU, served as ambassador to the MPR from March 1962 to November 1963. He then joined the apparat of the CPSU's Central Committee. In November 1974 he was in Ulan Bator alongside Brezhnev. This example shows that there is a man with considerable personal experience in Mongolia at the very top of the Soviet political structure.

Foreign-Affairs Elite

The thirty-nine foreign-affairs personnel among the Mongolian elite include as full members of the Central Committee the minister and the first deputy minister of foreign affairs and the ambassadors to the USSR, East Germany, and the United Nations. Candidate-members of the Central Committee include a deputy minister of foreign affairs, the head of a ministry department, and the ambassadors to China, Cuba, Yugoslavia, Bulgaria, and Rumania.[53]

In summary, the Mongolian elite includes all the members of the Central Committee, the government ministers and chairmen of commissions, the top military figures, the top leaders in the aimaks, and many economists and technical specialists. Its members lead the official organizations for writers and artists and the youth movement and they make up much of the country's foreign-affairs establishment. Most of them have university educations and a knowledge of the Russian language, and many owe their opportunities and their careers to Russian sponsors. They constitute a New Class, a bureaucracy, a kind of neobourgeois group. Most of them have abandoned their pasts, and those who have not done so find barriers in their paths. Although most of the highest-placed members of the elite belong to the Party's Central Committee, some powerful individuals have non-Party connections instead. Service to the Russians counts heavily and is well rewarded, but defiance of or disservice to them can still be dangerous.

SUMMARY: 1974–1978

The Soviet Red Army continues to be stationed on the Mongolian-Chinese border, and firm separation is maintained between the MPR and Inner

Mongolia.[54] Meanwhile the border in the north between the MPR and Eastern Siberia is in effect softening; more contacts and more kinds of connections unite the two areas ever more closely. As the American scholar George A. Cheney has reminded us:

> Murzaev points out that northern Mongolia, drained by the Selenga and Onon Rivers, is a continuation of the eastern Siberian landscape. The assignment of this region to Central Asia . . . is purely arbitrary . . . The southern two-thirds of the country, on the other hand, separated by a continental divide from the Selenga-Onon drainage system, belongs to Central Asia.[55]

Siberian developments, including the new Baikal Amur Mainline (BAM)—a railroad combined with Mongolian development north of Ulan Bator, including Erdenet, tend to strengthen the northward orientation of Mongolia and to deepen its separation from China.

Even the rural population is abandoning yurt living and nomadism, although the continued manufacture of frames for yurts indicates the persistence of that way of life. There are fewer nomads all the time. The proletariat, whose growth is required in Communist ideology, does continue to increase, but bureaucrats and nonproletarian urban dwellers are increasing even more rapidly.

Erdenet is a very impressive project and should act as a major corrective to the long-term Mongolian-Soviet trade imbalance. Its construction is proceeding rapidly; many of its constituent parts have already been completed and are in operation. Erdenet is a much larger project than Darkhan, and in its implications far more revolutionary, but the claims made thirty-five years ago for a very similar project at Jida-Zakamensk, 175 kilometers north of Erdenet on the Soviet side of the border, were just as grandiose: "One of the tremendous potential industrial bases of the world . . . a self-sufficient huge industrial center . . ."[56] That does not mean, of course, that Erdenet will necessarily fade into insignificance as Jida did, but it does suggest the need for skepticism about possibly inflated claims until the actual results can be evaluated.

9. Conclusions

Russian and then Soviet concern about the vulnerability of the Baikal area and the danger that the vast Transbaikal territory might be separated from the rest of Russia motivated action to guarantee that no foreign threat could be built up in Mongolia. The shakiness and instability of the Chinese regime both frightened the Russians and provided them with opportunity. For many years Japan posed a direct military danger to the USSR, while the threat of China was far more vague and indefinite (although never absent). The vulnerability of the Russians was the result of distance and manpower—too much distance and too little manpower. A weak and divided China was never able to put together a sustained movement for the recovery of Outer Mongolia, however; once the Soviet Communists became ensconced in Mongolia in 1921, they were able to maintain their predominant position with comparative ease. Japan proved to be a more serious challenge, but the Soviet military victory at Nomonkhan in 1939 turned away that threat.

With Japan defeated and a Communist regime installed in Peking in 1949, the way seemed open for Sino-Soviet cooperation. As it began to develop, the whole geopolitical position of Mongolia started to change; but that significant change was so short-lived that its ultimate consequences never became clear. A Sino-Soviet confrontation and a resultant split between the two countries caused a reversion of the MPR to the status of a buffer; the tentative beginnings of China's return to Mongolia were eliminated. Soviet monopoly was reimposed. By the 1970s the Soviet Union had in effect enclosed the MPR completely within its own defense system and extended the de-facto strategic border of the USSR southward to the border between the MPR and China.

A greatly expanded role for ideology under the new regime was one of the significant differences between tsarist Russian and Soviet Russian policies in Mongolia. The destruction of the old and traditional—most dramatically expressed in the crushing of the Buddhist Church—was another Soviet innovation. The extension of secular education and the formation of an army absorbed the young males who had formerly devoted their lives to the church. Ideologically inspired promises of industrialization and development, and of the formation of a proletariat, were not fulfilled; the Soviets really made little investment in Mongolia until the challenge of China surfaced in the latter 1950s.

Economics in the service of military-strategic policy—with ideology providing the justification but not really the reason—describes much of what happened in the MPR. Military-strategic requirements formed the real bases of Soviet policy; economic and organizational aspects were simply adapted to them. Exclusion of the Chinese was an early goal, and a noncapitalist monopoly served to attain it; by the end of the 1920s the USSR had its monopoly. Ideology had been used to exert economic pressure to obtain a military-strategic goal.

An ideological-economic disaster then occurred, however—the abortive collectivization program of 1929-1932. The Comintern and Joseph Stalin bore responsibility for its failure. The Mongols had tried to reject the idea, but the pressure from Moscow had been inexorable. When the collectivization policy failed, the Soviets of course created scapegoats and used all kinds of excuses, including an attempt to ascribe the program to overzealous Mongols. Direction from Moscow had initiated it, however, and manpower from Buryat Mongolia had helped to implement it.

Economic change was limited in the 1930s, and livestock-herding nomadism continued, as did the practice of living in yurts. The pressures of World War II led the Russians to exploit Mongolia even more, and to contribute even less to its development. Rationing resulted, and continued for many years.

The brief period of Sino-Soviet cooperation and the return of China to Mongolia resulted in an influx of several thousand laborers and the completion of the Trans-Mongolian Railroad, but the flow of laborers stopped and then was reversed, and soon the railroad was hardly used. Sino-Soviet collaboration had turned to competition, and then became confrontation. Earlier Chinese offers made in the context of cooperation with the USSR had involved true joint-development projects, but by 1960 Chinese offers were clearly aimed at separating Mongolia from Russia. The USSR forestalled the Chinese moves, however, and effectively reasserted its monopoly over Mongolia.

As the Soviet Union moved more aggressively and generously to outmaneuver the Chinese, a pattern of concentration of development in the Baikal Corridor began to take shape. The construction of Darkhan and the development of the New Lands were early steps to fill in the territory between Ulan Bator and the Soviet border. Communications were established on several levels: national (USSR to MPR), city (Moscow to Ulan Bator), and regional (Eastern Siberia to the northern Mongolian lands across the border). The regional integration, which was especially direct and intense, was furthered in the 1970s by the creation of Erdenet, the building of additional railroad spurs from the Trans-Mongolian main line, direct electric-power transmission from Eastern Siberia, and the New Lands II program.

At the same time, direct contacts began between Soviet and Mongolian ministries, as well as between Soviet oblasts and Mongolian aimaks; thus direct subgovernmental ministerial connections were added to the official USSR-MPR relationship and the local East Siberian-Northern Mongolia ties. The scale and intensity of Russian involvement in Mongolia had escalated, and the Soviet investment was becoming substantial. The long period of minimum commitment and the maintenance of open options was coming to an end, and an irreversible and multifarious network of cross-boundary connections was erasing the border between the USSR and the MPR.

The organizational weapon of the MPRP was an instrument unknown to tsarist Russia; along with Marxist-Leninist ideology, it constituted a radical new factor. For many years, however, the Mongolian Party was unorthodox and "un-Communist," allowing many non-Communists and even lamas and princes to become members. The Soviets often relied heavily on the Revsomols and the Comintern to maintain control in Mongolia, bypassing the Party; in fact, extensive and massive purges in the 1930s practically eliminated the MPRP. Only after that did it become a reliable instrument for the Stalinist regime. Later the primacy of military matters in World War II also tended to push the Party aside. Many alternatives for direct connection of Russians and Mongols are presently used, so that the Party is only one of several tools or channels of Soviet control—often not even the preferred one. Economic and military organizations have more power. The most important strand in the web connecting the USSR and the MPR has been the Red Army, and military-strategic considerations rather than Marxism explain the most important developments in Mongolia.

The Party's secondary role may be traced to the fact that it was a late addition to Russia's arsenal of influence in Mongolia; a significant Russian role in the country antedated the Bolshevik Revolution and the establishment of the MPRP in 1920. Pre-Communist "weapons" included Russian officials, including consuls-general and special diplomatic representatives; trade; permanent settlers; loans of money and provision of technical advisers; the establishment, arming, and training of a Mongolian military force; education; assistance by scholars and specialists; and the use of Buryat Mongols in Mongolia.

Special diplomatic representatives from Russia to Mongolia before the Communist era exerted great power in Urga, as did their Communist successors in Ulan Bator. Trade was a significant motivation for many Russians before the revolution, and competition with Chinese merchants was the name of the game, but the Communists succeeded in forcing out the Chinese and establishing a trade monopoly. Permanent Russian settlers in Mongolia were few both before and after 1921, and the continuing manpower shortage has limited Russia's development of Siberia as well as its presence in Mongolia. The tsarist government extended loans to the autonomous Mongolian government in 1912 and 1913, and the Communist government did the same in 1957 and for many years thereafter. Both tsarist and Communist governments complained that the Mongols misused the money, and both insisted on establishing their own representatives as financial watchdogs in the Mongolian ministry of finance. Some technical advisers were provided by the Russians before 1921, but nowhere near the number and variety they sent in the Communist period: the tiny trickle became a flood. Attempts to establish and train a Mongolian army began in 1912–1913, but they were unsuccessful. A very small number of Mongols, including the illustrious Sukhe Bator, received some Russian military training, but the opposition of the Buddhist Church in particular hampered recruiting and general operations. Until the mid-1930s Communist attempts to establish a Mongolian army continued to produce only frustration: great efforts yielded infinitesimal results. When the church was really destroyed, however, and the Japanese threat became evident, organized Mongolian fighting forces finally came into being, and by 1939 a Mongolian army actually existed.

Secular education began under Russian auspices in Urga in 1913, and in the following year the Russians chose a few Mongols to go to Irkutsk to continue their studies. This was education on a very small scale, however; most of the population remained unschooled and ignored, or at best received Buddhist instruction in monasteries. The literacy rate was scandalously low, and the restricted Russian effort did not improve it noticeably. At first secular education under the Communists was hardly more successful, but by the 1930s many obstacles had been overcome and serious mass education had commenced. The literacy rate began to climb. The Communists included girls in their education program, so social revolution was significantly furthered. The number of people who received schooling became incomparably greater than it had been in the tsarist period, and the number of Mongols sent to Irkutsk for Russian education multiplied many times.

Communist-inspired education in Mongolia included a new element, however: the teaching of Communist ideology in effect converted education into propagandistic indoctrination. The number of schools, teachers, and pupils unquestionably increased, but this substantial expansion was accompanied by a qualitative transformation. The school Jamtsarano ran in Urga in 1913 had served few pupils; the number of Mongols sent to Western Europe to study in the 1920s had been very small; and the Mongolian Scientific Committee of the first decade of Communist rule had not been impressively influential. Nevertheless, all these endeavors had been characterized by an integrity and a respect for both truth and diversity that were later lost.

Communist ideology began to dominate culture, art, and literature; it manipulated history and destroyed tradition; it silenced judgments passed by those with critical intelligence.

Scholarship was one of the weapons the Russians used to increase their influence in Mongolia, and it represented one of Russia's competitive advantages over the Chinese. Although the tradition of scholarship continued after 1921, its essence died with Stalin and the purges. The mass murder and massive physical devastation practiced by the Communists in the purges introduced a kind of violence and destruction never practiced by the Russians in Mongolia before 1921.

Buryat Mongols provided an important communications link between Russians and Khalkha Mongols in Outer Mongolia. Many Buryats had been educated in Russian universities, and many were already political activists and experienced political participants by 1911. A surprising amount of liberal thought was permitted free expression in Eastern Siberia at that time, and collaborative-scholarship teams of Russian exiles and Buryats were not uncommon in Outer Mongolia. After 1921 the role of Buryats in Mongolia was greatly expanded. The Comintern-Buryat connection was very close, and a Buryat clique dominated Outer Mongolia in the 1920s. In 1926–1927 Ma Ho-tien referred to a journey from Inner Mongolia to Outer Mongolia to Buryat Mongolia as a historical progression from backwardness and obscurantism to enlightenment and modernity. The purges and the other massive revolutionary changes of the 1930s in the MPR ended that special Buryat role, however, and the Khalkhas then came into their own. During the transitional period of Buryat domination, the Khalkhas had begun to receive education and experience that had previously been unavailable to them.

Since the Mongolian Party was not monolithic and unchanging, the importance of its role, the degree of its independence, and the vigor of its activity varied. Several times purges depleted the Party and necessitated its subsequent reconstruction as practically a new organization. Other groups, including Soviet counterpart organizations, affected the Party. The Comintern exercised great power for many years, for example, but then faded away, and for a long time the Revsomols wielded greater power than the Party itself.

The Party was much smaller in the 1920s, but it was both more representative and more pluralistic than it was to become later. Party congresses had been long and full of substantive discussion and real debate in the early years; later, Party membership increased and Party congresses were attended by many more delegates, but they did not last nearly as long, and dissent and variety in opinion were eliminated through discipline and the encouragement of uniformity.

Russian Communist theory and practice were and are imposed on the

Mongols through education, indoctrination, culture, and propaganda, via Mongols who are in effect Russian protégés forming a New Class. Service to the Russians wins promotions and fluency in the Russian language and conformity to Russian ways of doing things are a Mongol's surest passports to success. The so-called superstructure is staffed by an educated elite that transmits and interprets Russian manners, directives, and thought. The Mongolian political structure and conceptual framework derive from and copy the Russian original; Russian precedents determine Mongolian decisions.

The interplay of strategic and ethnic concerns largely determines Mongolian policy, but the MPRP gives Soviet strategic interests priority over problems involving Mongolian national identity. The Mongols are willing and even eager to follow the Soviet lead for three principal reasons: (1) Russian strategic interests and Mongolian national interests coincide in one important respect—opposition to China; (2) improved health and education assure physical survival and greater career choices for Mongols; and (3) the Russians have paid well for services rendered by Mongols—in extending generous support to a Mongolian elite that does the USSR's bidding and in supplying goods without requiring direct repayment.

The negative content of nationalism is always important: nationalism is almost always anti-something, or rather, anti-someone. Both Russians and Mongols fear the Chinese simply because there are so many of them. Many Mongols also fear Russians, but the Russian threat is less direct; the Soviets are unlikely to move in on, dominate, and assimilate the Mongols as the Chinese have shown through their takeover of Inner Mongolia that they are willing to do. In dealing with the Mongols, the Russians have actually benefitted from their own greatest weakness: inadequate numbers. It is the very impossibility of massive Russian settlement in Mongolia that makes the Mongols prefer the Soviets to the Chinese. The fact that the Russians fear and oppose China as much as the Mongols do makes it harder for the Mongols to realize the full extent of the Russian "occupation" of Mongolia—a spiritual, ideological, and adminstrative and organizational domination rather than a physical presence. Uniquely Mongolian culture and true Mongolian freedom and independence have been casualties of that occupation.

The Mongolian regime's sensitivity to criticism and the virulence of its reaction to the slightest sign of resistance to Soviet and Communist domination is a good indicator of the actual state of affairs. The fact that the regime with all its weight and authority felt compelled to attack the seventy-year-old Rinchen yet again in March 1976 suggests its lingering insecurity. The term "totalitarian" is still relevant, despite the undeniable improvements and changes that have occurred since Stalin and Choibalsan. The insistence on orthodoxy persists, though the Mongols perhaps suffer from it less than many other victims of Communism and the USSR. Mongols are not physically disappearing, and they have always shown a considerable spirit of independence, but as a people with a unique culture and identity they are still the victims of Soviet domination. Some traditional Mongolian life continues, and there are still a few Mongols who resist effectively all the indoctrination and pressure. It is to be hoped that there will always be such Mongols.

Mongolia is really ruled by a Communist regime modelled very closely on the system and apparatus that control the USSR. The MPRP is an important instrument of control, which functions both as an agent of Soviet domination and as a domestic ruling group, but many other important instruments also transmit Soviet direction. The military—specifically the commanders of the Transbaikal and Far Eastern military districts of the Red Army and the central Soviet military command in Moscow—occupies a leading role, and military-strategic requirements override ideological or nonmilitary political considerations. Planning and construction for Eastern Siberian regional development tends increasingly to incorporate northern Mongolia. Several government ministries in Moscow deal directly with their Mongolian counterparts, bypassing Tsedenbal and the central Mongolian Party and government. The MPR is thus a dual polity, partly integrated into the USSR and partly independent and organizationally autonomous.

APPENDIXES

1. Ninety Principal Participants in the Mongolian Revolution of 1921

Of ninety individuals important in the 1921 Mongolian Revolution,* the eight most important included three Russians (Lenin, Shumyatsky, and von Ungern-Sternberg); one Buryat Mongol (Rinchino); one Altai Oirat (Borisov); two Khalkha Mongols (Sukhe Bator and Choibalsan); and one Chinese (Chang Tso-lin). Thirty less important but nonetheless significantly involved people included eleven of Russian or Baltic nationality; eight Buryat Mongols; four Kalmyks; five Khalkha Mongols; and two Chinese. Fifty-two other participants, who were of less crucial importance to events, included thirty-seven Russians; ten Buryats; one Khalkha, one Altai Oirat, one Chinese, one Czech, and one American. The ninety are listed here, with a brief characterization of each. Many of them later played important roles in Mongolia or related areas, and many of them were killed in the purges of Stalin in the 1930s; some of course died in 1921.

THE PRINCIPAL PARTICIPANTS

LENIN indicated interest in and plans for Mongolia as early as June 1919 (A. N. Kheifets, *Sovetskaya diplomatiya i narody Vostoka, 1921–1927,* p. 19). From the very

---

*The basic story of the revolution appears in Chapter 3 of this book. Consult Maps No. 3 through 7 in *History of the MPR* for the scene of the 1921 events. The *History*—especially the footnotes—and N. D. Shulunov, *Stanovlenie sovetskoi natsional 'noi gosudarstvennosti v Buryatii (1919–1923 gody),* provide much information about the people and events. See also Rupen, *Mongols of the Twentieth Century,* Volume 1, Chapter 5.

first he seemed to be as alert to military-strategic considerations as to ideological ones. The Civil War and the Allied intervention were obviously overriding concerns. His advice to Sukhe Bator in November 1921 included his assertions that Mongolia was strategically important to Russia, and that it was a society in which a socialist regime could be built.

BORIS ZAKHAROVICH SHUMYATSKY [ANDREI CHERVONNYI] (1886–1943), operating primarily as Comintern representative, mainly at Irkutsk, masterminded the Mongolian operation. He later went to Persia (1922–1925), then edited *Revolyutsionnyi Vostok,* and, in 1937, the *Sibirskaya Sovetskaya Entsiklopediya* (which was never completed). He was another victim of Stalin's purges.

EL'BEKDORJ RINCHINO (1885–1937), a Buryat, though far more radical than Jamtsarano, nonetheless was not classified with the true Red Communists, and was castigated for pan-Mongolism and bourgeois nationalism. He was exiled to Moscow in 1928, and executed in 1937.

SERGEI STEPANOVICH BORISOV [SORIKTU] played an important part in Tuva as well as in Mongolia. His Altai Oirat nationality made him unique among the significant actors. He was Shumyatsky's agent in Mongolia, and did not initiate policy independently. He was probably the least influential of the eight most important participants.

SUKHE BATOR (1893–1923), a Khalkha Mongol, remains an enigmatic and vague figure, uniformly praised but never really portrayed as a living personality. He appears more a propaganda invention: an artificiality pervades the accounts supplied about him. His death was long ascribed to poisoning by enemies, but for some time now it has been ascribed to natural causes.

KHORLOIN CHOIBALSAN (1895–1952), a Khalkha, was not always prominent in the leadership during the revolution, but his unique fluency in the Russian language unquestionably placed him in an important position. He functioned for many years on special commissions and investigatory bodies from which emanated the unsavory odor of secret police. He was undoubtedly not the forthright soldier that some accounts try to make him seem.

BARON ROMAN VON UNGERN-STERNBÈRG (1887–1921), the anti-Bolshevik leader, was certainly mad, but many of the Mongols initially welcomed him as a savior. He was executed in Novonikolaevsk (Novosibirsk) on September 15, 1921.

CHANG TSO-LIN (1875–1928) was a Manchurian warlord, a Japanese puppet, and perhaps a Chinese nationalist. He was certainly the enemy of the USSR most of the time, although he was rarely involved in any direct confrontation. His was almost the only military force that was conceivably capable of controlling Outer Mongolia for China.

IMPORTANT, BUT SECONDARY, FIGURES

STALIN, according to Amur-Sanan, showed little interest in or knowledge of Mongolia; he simply followed Lenin's lead in his policy toward Mongolia. Later, he was far more concerned about Mongolia in relation to the Japanese threat than as a Marxist-Leninist society. He probably had a "bird-in-the-hand" philosophy: he preferred to hang on to the Mongolia he had in his control rather than gamble with it to gain favor with the Chinese. Partly through his insistence on dominating Mongolia he lost his chance to win China.

GEORGYI V. CHICHERIN (1872–1936) was a close ally and patron of Maisky's and probably had privileged access to Maisky's information, but there is nothing from the record to show that he had a special interest in Mongolia; he always regarded China as far more important. A famous and widely reproduced photograph shows Chicherin in full Mongolian regalia.

ANTON MUDRENOVICH AMUR-SANAN (1888–1940), the Kalmyk revolutionary leader, wrote an interesting autobiographical account. Like so many who were leaders during the Revolution and the 1920s, he fell in Stalin's purges. He was never closely involved with the MPR, except for the October 1920 Politburo meeting and the arrangement made with Rinchino at that time for Kalmyk military instructors.

AGVAN DORJEEV (1850–1938), a Buryat, also died in the purges, but he spent many of his later years living in the Tibetan-style temple whose construction in Leningrad he had originally inspired. It was at least a fitting house-arrest.

VITALY IVANOVICH YUDIN represented the Narkomindel (NKID) at Irkutsk, and participated in the Fifth Army's military-council meeting that planned the entry into Urga. He continued to represent the NKID with the Russian troops in Urga for several years.

VASILY KONSTANTINOVICH BLYUKHER [GALEN] (1889–1938) came to Chita in June 1921 and served as the minister of war and the commander in chief for the Far Eastern Republic. The FER was founded at Verkhneudinsk on April 6, 1920; moved to Chita on October 28, 1920; and was liquidated by incorporation into the RSFSR on November 16, 1922. Blyukher of course served many years in China, then became commander of the Special Far Eastern Army, only to be executed in Stalin's purges.

O. IVANOVICH [S. YA.] MAKSTENEK was NKID (Narkomindel) border representative at Kyakhta-Troitskosavsk, and as such he met and dealt with most of the revolutionary-minded Khalkhas. Sukhe Bator and Choibalsan stayed with him, and his house was the scene of the First Party Congress.

KONSTANTIN AVGUSTOVICH NEIMAN, commander of the 35th Division, Fifth Red Army, led the combined Soviet-Mongolian forces to Urga in July 1921.

KONSTANTIN KONSTANTINOVICH ROKOSSOVSKY (1896–1968) commanded the 35th Cavalry Regiment in the expeditionary forces to Urga; his troops captured von Ungern-Sternberg's deputy, Rezukhin. Rokossovsky served in the Far East for many years in the 1930s; after World War II he became defense minister for Poland, from 1949 through 1956.

KANUKOV and V. A. KHOMUTNIKOV were the leading Kalmyks in the Mongolian army. Kanukov was named first commandant of the City of Urga in July 1921. Khomutnikov commanded a cavalry division in World War II and died in street fighting in Budapest. He was buried in Novodevichy Cemetery in Moscow.

MATVEI INNOKENTOVICH AMAGAEV [AMUGA] (1897–1938), a Buryat, filled important economic jobs and served as Comintern agent in the MPR, but like many others he suffered a two-stage de-escalatory purge: he served at KUTV (the Communist University of the Toilers of the East) and the Institute of Oriental Studies from 1929 until his arrest and disappearance in late 1937.

FEOFAN ROMANOVICH KONYAEV (b. 1900), a Buryat, actively participated in the founding of the Mongolian Revsomols in 1921; in 1927–1928 he was in the MPR as director of the Party School. He was reportedly working in Irkutsk in 1958.

IVAN VASIL'EVICH CHENKIROV (b. 1898), a Buryat and Comintern representative, was a founder of the Tuva Revolutionary Party in 1921; in the early 1930s he led Buryats into the MPR to enforce the radical Comintern-inspired program.

SIREN ARABDYNOVICH NATSOV [SHOIZHELOV] (1899–1938), a Buryat, played an active part in western Mongolia and then served in Tuva for many years. He was a bitter enemy of Jamtsarano, and attacked him mercilessly and unceasingly. Certainly he was partially responsible for bringing down Jamtsarano, but he himself was later purged and met the same fate as his "enemy." Natsov was politically one of the most important Buryats in the 1920s.

PETR EFIMOVICH SHCHETINKIN [TOMOR BATOR] (1885–1927) led Bolshevik partisans in Tuva and western Mongolia, and his guerrillas constituted part of the expeditionary force that advanced into Urga in July 1921. Shchetinkin died in Ulan Bator, where he was serving as an inspector of the Secret Police.

In addition to Sukhe Bator and Choibalsan, the "Khalkha Seven"—the Mongols who formed the first group to enter the USSR seeking assistance in July-August 1920—included Bodo, Chakdorjav, Danzan, Doksom, and Losol.

DOGSOMYN BODO (1885–1922) served as prime minister of the new MPR government in 1921, but was relieved from his official position January 1922 and executed in August. Pershin claimed that Bodo actually formed the revolutionary circle that has been accredited to Choibalsan's initiative, and that Bodo was in fact Choibalsan's brother! For Bodo's contacts with the American Sokobin, see *History of the MPR,* pp. 790 n. 198 and 796 n. 45.

CHAKDORJAV (d. 1922) was executed with Bodo. He had been an original member of a revolutionary circle in Urga in 1920, attended the Kyakhta First Party Congress in March 1921, was a leader of the provisional government formed in March 1921, and was later active in western Mongolia.

DANZAN (1873–1924) was characterized by Genkin in 1928 as having been "clever in a way, very energetic, and a great hater of theocratic rule." The Soviet diplomatic representative in Urga in August 1924, Vasil'ev, is reported to have said about Danzan's execution: "Such incidents occur not only in Mongolia, but in Russia also. . . . [W]hat you have done is correct. . . ." (Xenia J. Eudin and Robert C. North, *Soviet Russia and the East,* pp. 201, 256).

DAMSRANBELEGIIN DOKSOM [DEMBREL] (1884–1939) and DAR'ZAVYN LOSOL (1890–1939), like so many others, lost their lives in the purges. Doksom served in the Moscow embassy in 1927, and was the MPR's representative in Tuva from 1933 through 1934. Both Doksom and Losol were rehabilitated in 1962.

JA LAMA (1860-1922), the Kalmyk adventurer, was one of the most remarkable in a group of very unusual personalities. The crosscurrents of cultural change were certainly the cause of some of his bizarre behavior.

IVAN MAISKY (1884-1975) was only a secondary actor in Mongolian events. His book is an excellent piece of work, and there is no doubt of his formidable ability.

TSYBEN JAMTSARANO (1880-1940) had probably the most impressive intellect of all the Buryats. He served mainly in the Scientific Committee rather than directly in politics after the revolution. His moderation and his integrity soon became unacceptable to the new regime.

ATAMAN SEMENOV (1891-1946), who was descended from Buryat Cossacks, continued his fight against the Bolsheviks for decades. He was captured and executed when the Red Army marched across Manchuria in August 1945.

Five figures died or left the scene before the actual revolution of July 1921, but they still exerted considerable influence on that event.

MIKHAIL IVANOVICH KUCHERENKO (1889-1921) worked in the Russian printing plant in Urga before the revolution, and was one of Choibalsan's Bolshevik contacts. He was from Irkutsk. Von Ungern-Sternberg killed him when he entered Urga in February 1921.

YAKOB VASIL'EVICH GEMBARZHEVSKY (d. 1921) was, with Kucherenko, the main Bolshevik contact of Choibalsan in Urga; von Ungern-Sternberg killed him in February 1921 also.

SANJIMITAB BUDAJAPOVICH TSYBYKTAROV (d. 1921), the first Buryat medical doctor, had worked as a physician in the Russian consulate in Urga since 1910. He was a Bolshevik and became one of von Ungern-Sternberg's first victims in February 1921.

CH'EN YI seems to have been both reasonable and capable, but he was thrust into an impossible situation. He had no stable government to back him up, and no armed force paid any attention to him.

HSÜ SHU-CH'ENG (d. 1925), or "Little Hsü," forcibly abolished Mongolian autonomy on November 16, 1919, and by his aggressive and arrogant behavior antagonized the Mongols. He was a representative of the Anfu Clique in Peking, and the clique's fall from power brought Hsü down with it.

FIFTY-TWO OTHER PARTICIPANTS

The chronology in June 1921 is important in assessing the role played particularly by the less conspicuous actors in the revolution. Although the chronology that appears in the official *History of the MPR* is often quite detailed, it becomes very thin in that important month. The re-creation offered here by no means resolves all the ambiguity and confusion (cf. *History of the MPR*, p. 782 n. 105), but it does give some assistance in sorting out people and events.

June/July 1921

June   7. Boris Shumyatsky in Moscow for Narkomnats Commissariat of Nationalities) meeting (at least ostensibly).

        8. Soviet Army reported pursuing Ungernists toward Urga.

   14. Sergei Kamenev's order to Fifth Red Army to move to Urga.

   15. Chicherin's note warning Peking that Red Army would cross border.

   16. Politburo directive to advance to Urga and occupy it.

June 22– July 12. Third Comintern Congress in Moscow (Jamtsarano was the Mongolian delegate).

June 24. Blyukher's move to Chita and assumption of post as minister of war, Far Eastern Republic. FER Military Council formed.

   26. Move of Yudin, Mulin, Kosich, and Lyubimov from Irkutsk to Kyakhta-Maimaicheng.

   27. Meeting of FER Military Council (chairman: Blyukher; members: Gubel'man, Borov, and Seryshev).
Neiman and two columns crossed Mongolian border.

   28. Meeting of Yudin, Mulin, Kosich, and Lyubimov assigning Neiman responsibility for leading joint Soviet-Mongolian forces to Urga and eliminating von Ungern-Sternberg.
Meeting of the Mongolian Party's Central Committee, and provisional government. The Mongolian order to liberate Urga was issued at this time.

Military Personnel and Officials

SERGEI S. KAMENEV was a former tsarist officer who became commander in chief of the Red Army in July 1918. He was fully aware of Mongolian developments, and had received the delegation that came to Moscow and saw Lenin in October 1920.

I. P. UBOREVICH (1896–1937) was commander of the Fifth Red Army in 1921; he succeeded Blyukher as Far East commander in 1922. He was purged at the same time as Tukhachevsky.

V. M. MULIN was head of the political administration of the army in Siberia. He accompanied the Mongolian army to Urga as military adviser.

D. I. KOSICH, a member of the Revolutionary Military Council of the Fifth Red Army, led the Soviet military instructors in Ulan Bator in 1923 and served at that time as chief of staff of the Mongolian army.

P. N. LYUBIMOV, chief of staff of the Fifth Red Army, helped to plan the July military operation in the MPR. In 1927 he was a member of the Buryat Oblast's Executive Committee.

LITVINTSEV, who commanded a border battalion of the Red Army—the Sretensky Cavalry Brigade—became Sukhe Bator's chief of staff and fought Ungernist remnant forces with Sukhe Bator around Urga in August 1921.

IVANOV-RIMSKY, commander of Soviet border troops, served with Litvintsev, as Sukhe Bator's deputy chief of staff. Thus the "Mongolian" army staff included Russians as chief of staff and deputy chief of staff, a Russian military adviser (Mulin), and a Soviet citizen (Borisov) as head of the political administration of the Mongolian army.

V. I. BOROV and S. M. SERYSHEV, along with M. I. GUBEL'MAN [YAROSLAVSKY], formed the Far Eastern Republic's Military Council, which was headed by Blyukher. Gubel'man had founded Marxist groups in Transbaikalia as early as 1899.

GRIGORY MIKHAILOVICH CHEREMISINOV was Neiman's chief of staff.

Political Personnel

Although the line separating military from political personnel in mid-1921 was tenuous indeed, the group above included those who were most closely connected to military units and events, and the following are more "political" figures: those identified with the Comintern and the Russian Communist Party (Bolshevik) rather than the Red Army.

NIKOLAI IVANOVICH BUKHARIN (1888–1938) participated in Lenin's October 1920 meeting with the Mongols, but he had few other direct contacts with them that were ever reported. His own involvement with Trotsky against Stalin, which led to his removal from the Party in 1929 and then his trial and execution in 1938, set a pattern that was typical for many of the leading Buryat Mongols. A large number of them lost their Comintern or other jobs in the MPR in 1928–1932, and then were arrested and killed in 1937–1938.

INNOKENTY ASENKRITOVICH SOROKOVIKOV was "assigned to gain a clear understanding of the desires and aspirations of the Khuree [Urga] group." In April 1920 he met five Mongols, including Sukhe Bator, through Kucherenko and Gembarzhevsky. In May he reported back to Irkutsk, to Borisov and Shumyatsky (see *History of the MPR*, p.71).

ARISTARKH TIKHONOVICH YAKIMOV (1895–1976) became head of the political section of the military-political administration, Far Eastern Republic Army, in April 1921. He had been editor of the journal of the central organization of Siberian Communists, *Tsentrosibir'*. Later (from 1940 through 1952) he served in the Soviet army. He was one of the signers of the attack on Rinchen in 1959.

I. N. SMIRNOV (1881–1936) was a member of the Military Council and of the Fifth Army from 1918 through 1919; he systematically informed Lenin about the situation in Siberia. (See Serdobov, *Istoriya formirovaniya tuvinskoi natsii;* Kyzyl, 1971.)

YAKOV DAVIDOVICH YANSON [HAYAMA] (b. 1886), a Latvian, was assigned as NKID representative in Siberia in March 1920. Rinchino contacted him at that time, and "Yanson agreed to set up special machinery to promote revolutionary work among the Mongols" (Eudin and North, *Soviet Foreign Policy*). He was chairman of the Irkutsk Guberniya Revolutionary Committee at that time. He served as minister of foreign affairs for the Far Eastern Republic from 1921 through 1922, and in 1925–1928 was

Soviet trade representative in Japan (and reportedly also Comintern agent there). He served as chairman of ARCOS in London, 1930-1932, and was one of the Soviet members of the USSR Council for the Institute of Pacific Relations (IPR).

YAROSLAV HASHEK, the famous Czech writer, was in Eastern Siberia for only a few months in 1920, but he did have direct contact with Mongols there at that time. He was officially a deputy head of the political administration, Fifth Red Army.

VLADIMIR YAKUBEVICH ZAZUBRIN [ZUBTSOV] (1895-1938) edited the newspaper of the Fifth Red Army in Irkutsk. Later, from 1923 through 1928, he edited *Sibirskie ogni,* and he went with Burdukov to Tuva in 1926. (See Burdukov, *V staroi i novoi Mongolii,* p. 389 n. 95.)

S. E. CHUTSKAEV was deputy chairman of the Siberian Revolutionary Committee, directly under Boris Shumyatsky.

Buryat-Mongols

MIKHAIL NIKOLAEVICH ERBANOV (1889-1937) was chairman of the Buryat Revolutionary Committee (Amagaev was deputy chairman). In 1925 Erbanov served concurrently as NKID representative at Verkhneudinsk for Buryat Mongolia, Irkutsk, and Transbaikalia.

VASILY IL'ICH TRUBACHEEV (1895-1937) served in *Tsentrosibir',* Irkutsk, in 1918, and in the Far Eastern Republic in May 1920. In May 1923 he was a member of the Buryat Revolutionary Committee, and became first secretary of the Buryat Mongolian Party. In 1928 he went to the MPR, where he served a year as secretary to the Russian diplomatic representative in Ulan Bator. He worked at the University of the Toilers of the East 1931-1932.

IL'YA STEPANOVICH ARKHINCHEEV (1891-1938) was a Buryat delegate to Moscow on June 7, 1921, and wrote for the Comintern.

EVDOKHIN IVANOVICH LOSOV (b. 1898) was active on special courts for the Buryat Revolutionary Committee; he was secretary of the Aga District Communist Party Committee from 1923 through 1929, and worked in the MPR for several years during the 1930s as head of "Mongol'stroi" and a member of the Economic Council.

MARIYA MIKHAILOVNA SAKH'YANOVA [POSEIDON] (b. 1896) served as secretary of the Far Eastern Committee, Communist Party (Bolshevik), from early 1919 to March 1920; from the fall of 1920 to April 1921 she was in China, probably in Manchuria. From April to June, 1921, she was in the Mongol-Tibetan section of the Far Eastern Secretariat of the Comintern.

GEORGY GEORGIEVICH DANCHINOV (1894-1954) served for several years as chairman of the Buryat section, Russian Communist Party (Bolshevik). He accompanied the Fifth Red Army to Urga in July 1921, and became secretary of the Mongolian Section of the ECCI.

TSERENGIIN BALMASO (1892-1934) was secretary at the First Party Congress at Kyakhta, March 1921, and was an active Comintern agent.

TSOGTO GARMAEV BADMAJAPOV was a wealthy and influential Buryat in Urga active in business dealings and relations with Westerners—an entrepreneur. (See Marguerite Harrison, *Red Bear or Yellow Dragon,* p. 203; London, 1924.)

Participants from the Far Eastern Republic

ALEKSANDR MIKHAILOVICH KRASNOSHCHEKOV (b. 1880) worked with Boris Shumyatsky in Tsentrosibir' in 1917–1918 and became prime minister of the Far Eastern Republic in April 1920. Differences reportedly arose between Krasnoshchekov and B. Shumyatsky; in any case Krasnoshchekov was recalled to Moscow in mid-1921. Later he became a director of the Industrial Bank, and was imprisoned for embezzlement in 1924.

BOBROV represented the ministry of foreign affairs of the Far Eastern Republic at the border-town of Troitskosavsk; he was thus the opposite number of Makstenek. (He played no notable role in the events of 1921, however, whereas Makstenek did.)

Western Mongolian Participants

K. K. NEKUNDE-BAIKALOV led Red Army forces in the Russian and Mongolian Altai. He was at Biisk in May 1920, at Kosh Agach in June 1921, and fought with Khas Bator in the siege of Tolbo Nur, October 17–December 1, 1921.

SERGEI YUL'EVICH SHIROKIKH-POLYANSKY (1898–1922) was on Nekunde-Baikalov's political staff. In January of 1921 he was put in charge of agitation and propaganda for the Pribaikal section of the Russian Communist Party (Bolshevik), and from April to December 1921 he served as representative of the Far Eastern Secretariat of the Comintern in western Mongolia. In 1922 he went to Yakutia, and was killed there.

KHAS BATOR (1883–1921) was minister of war and commander in chief of the army, West Mongolian government, in mid-1921. Nekunde-Baikalov, Damba Dorji, and Khas Bator fought together, and Khas Bator was killed at Tolbo Nur in late 1921. He was born in Inner Mongolia, and had joined Khalkha in 1911.

F. G. FAL'SKY [F. GORELIK]. The authorities in Irkutsk sent Fal'sky to contact the Jalkhandza Khutukhtu, who communicated with Boris Shumyatsky via Fal'sky on June 20, 1921.

ALEKSEI VASIL'EVICH BURDUKOV [CHUETS] (1883–1943) was the merchant who worked for decades in western Mongolia and who hosted Maisky while he wrote his book in 1919–1920.

ANATOLY DMITRIEVICH KALINNIKOV [ANTOV; ERDENI] (1899–1937) was Maisky's assistant in 1919–1920. The *History of the MPR* (p. 33) assessed his numerous writings. He served as an official Russian representative in the MPR, 1925–1930.

Manchurian Participants

IGNATIUS A. YURIN (b. 1880) was minister of foreign affairs for the Far Eastern Republic, and was at Mukden with Chang Tso-lin in July 1921.

P. F. ALEKSANDROVSKY, the NKID border representative at Manchuli, was in contact with staff of Chang Tso-lin throughout early 1921.

Anti-Bolsheviks

KAZAGRANDI (d. 1921), an Altai Oirat, was near Lake Khubsugul, headed for Irkutsk with a special cavalry brigade, attempting to divert attention from von Ungern-Sternberg's main force to the Soviet Fifth Army. Von Ungern-Sternberg suspected Kazagrandi of treachery, and ordered the Ataman Sukharev to shoot him; he was executed on August 17, 1921.

A. P. KAIGORODOV headed a detachment that was stationed in Altai area, then around Kobdo; it later headed for the Yenesei River. Kaigorodov and Bakich surrounded Khas Bator and Nekunde-Baikalov at Tolbo Nur, 100 km. north of Kobdo, in Oct.–Dec. 1921.

BAKICH (d. 1922). In May 1921, Bakich was in Sinkiang, but after the Soviets negotiated the "Ili Protocol," on May 27, 1921, he moved into western Mongolia, then fled into Tuva, and finally was again forced back into Mongolia. His last stand was at Ulankom. He was captured by Maksorjav at end of December 1921 or early January 1922 and shot.

KAZANTSEV killed a Mongolian official at Ulyasutai in June 1921. He later moved from Tuva to Kobdo, and in September 1921 he joined Kaigorodov at Tolbo Nur.

REZUKHIN (d. 1921) was von Ungern-Sternberg's deputy and longtime friend. He had been a Cossack officer at Kobdo in 1913. On July 1, 1921, he was with twenty-six hundred men in the Selenga Valley, and he was killed in August 1921.

MERKULOV led the Japanese-supported coup at Vladivostok, May 26, 1921. A document of June 9, 1921, found among Merkulov's papers, purported to prove a coordinated anti-Bolshevik offensive supported by the Japanese. (See E. H. Carr, *The Bolshevik Revolution, 1917–1923*, p. 360 and 360 n. 1.)

Pre-1921 Personnel

Ten figures either died or left the scene of the action before July 1921, but they or their actions nonetheless affected the course of the 1921 Mongolian Revolution.

NAUM BURTMAN (1900–1920). Sukhe Bator had undertaken political studies with Burtman at Irkutsk in 1920. Burtman had left Harbin and come through Urga in March 1920; he met Mongols and Russian revolutionaries there. At Irkutsk he was Chairman of *Sekvostnarod*—the section for Asian Peoples of the Russian Communist Party (Bolshevik). He was killed at Irkutsk in 1920.

SERGEI GEORG'EVICH LAZO (1894–1920). Lazo and Boris Shumyatsky received the first Khalkha Mongolian delegation to Russia in June 1918 (led by the Sain Noyan Khan). Lazo was arrested by the Japanese in April 1920 and shot; his body was then burned in a locomotive at the station on the Trans-Siberian Railroad that now bears the name Lazo.

F. I. GAPON was chief of the Far Eastern section of the Russian Communist Party (Bolshevik). Sukhe Bator was sent to him by Boris Shumyatsky from Verkhneudinsk in August 1920, but soon Shumyatsky began to handle all Mongolian matters himself.

NIKOLAI TARASEVICH DANCHINOV (1886–1916) was the Buryat Bolshevik who taught at Jamtsarano's school in Urga beginning in 1912. He became Choibalsan's mentor.

Tserempil Tserempilovich Ranzhurov (1882–1918) was a Cossack and the first Buryat Bolshevik.

Pantaleimon Parnyakov (d. 1921) was an outstanding revolutionary in Eastern Siberia. His father, an Orthodox priest in Urga, was among those killed by von Ungern-Sternberg in 1921.

Dmitry Petrovich Pershin [Daursky], an anti-Bolshevik, was an assistant to the Irkutsk governor-general, then director of the Russo-Asiatic Bank in Urga. He emigrated in 1920.

Li Yuan came to Urga in 1917 and was left in charge when Hsü returned to Peking on July 26, 1919. In October he managed to form an army sufficiently effective to stave off von Ungern-Sternberg's attack at that time. When Ch'en Yi came to Urga in December 1920, Li Yuan served as his assistant. On March 3, 1921, after having been forced out of Urga by von Ungern-Sternberg, Li Yuan endorsed Ch'en Yi's request for Soviet assistance against the baron, but Peking disavowed both those requests.

Charles C. Eberhardt. In April 1920, Eberhardt, a U.S. foreign service officer, visited Urga. At that time he met the Jalkhandza Khutukhtu and others, who requested American help for relief from Hsu's oppression. Nothing could be done, however, save to record the request. (See *History of the MPR*, p. 759 n. 110.)

2. Central Committee, Mongolian People's Revolutionary Party, Elected at the Seventeenth Congress in June 1976

POLITBURO MEMBERS

*YUMJAGIIN TSEDENBAL (b. 1916). First secretary of the MPRP since November 23, 1958. Former prime minister (from May 1952–June 1974). Went to Peking for the signing of the border treaty in December 1962. Former chairman, Gosplan, and director, Economics Institute.

JAMBYN BATMUNKH (b. 1926). Prime minister (Chairman, Council of Ministers) since June 1974. Wrote a dissertation on economic planning at the Academy of Social Sciences, Central Committee, CPSU, Moscow 1961. Former director of the Economics Institute at Ulan Bator.

*NYAMYN JAGVARAL. Politburo member since July 4, 1960; secretary of the Central Committee since December 22, 1963. Wrote a dissertation on state farms, Moscow, 1945. Former minister of agriculture.

*SAMPILYN JALAN-AJAV. Vice-president since June 1977. Politburo member since 1972; secretary of the Central Committee. Former state prosecutor.

*NAMSRAIN LUVSANRAVDAN. Chairman of the Committee on Party Control. Elected vice-president in 1969; re-elected in June 1977. Politburo member since July 4, 1960. Former first secretary of the Ulan Bator City Party Committee.

*DAMDINJAVYN MAIDAR (b. 1916). First deputy prime minister. Politburo member since February 7, 1963. Wrote a dissertation on veterinary service, Moscow, 1958. Former chairman of Gosplan. Chairman of the Mongolian side of the Mongolian-Soviet Intergovernmental Commission 1975–1977. Chairman of the Society for Protection of Nature and the Environment since December 5, 1975. Chairman of the State Committee for Science and Technology.

*DEMCHIGIIN MOLOMJAMTS. Politburo member since December 17, 1959; secretary of the Central Committee since December 22, 1964. Former chairman of Gosplan, former first deputy prime minister, and long-time MPR representative to CMEA.

---

*Central Committee members or candidate-members elected in December 1963. The 1963 list of seventy-eight members and forty-six candidate-members appears in Rupen, *Mongols of the Twentieth Century*, 1:393–402.

*TUMENBAYARYN RAGCHA (b. 1917). First deputy prime minister since November 1976. Politburo member since June 1976. Former chairman of Gosplan.

POLITBURO CANDIDATE-MEMBERS

*BAT-OCHIRYN ALTANGEREL. First secretary of the Ulan Bator City Party Committee since May 1963.

*DAMDINY GOMBOJAV. Politburo candidate-member and secretary of the Central Committee since June 1976. Former deputy prime minister (dropped in July 1977). Chairman of the Mongolian-Soviet Friendship Association since January 1977. Former counsellor at the MPR embassy in Moscow; former minister of foreign trade. Published a book on economic cooperation in the development of the MPR (Moscow, 1969).

SECRETARY, CENTRAL COMMITTEE

SANDAGIIN SOSORBORAM. Minister of culture. Former first deputy minister of foreign affairs. Went to Peking in December 1962 for signing of border treaty.

Other secretaries of the Central Committee include: Tsedenbal, Molomjamts, Jagvaral, Jalan-Ajav, and Gombojav.

CHIEFS OF DEPARTMENTS OF THE CENTRAL COMMITTEE OF THE MONGOLIAN PEOPLE'S REVOLUTIONARY PARTY

Tsereviin Davagsuren	. Chief, International Relations Department.
Gelegiin Ad'yaa	Chief, Party Organization Department.
Tserenpiliin Balkhajav	Chief, Ideology Department.
Yadamyn Tsegmid	Acting Chief, Agriculture Department.
Tserengiin Gurbadam	Chief, Industrial Department.
Lkhamyn Tserendondog	Chief, Construction Department.
Sanjiin Bata	Chief, Administrative Organization Department (Military Affairs).
Chuvandorjiin Molom	Chief, Trade and Transport Department.
Chimediin Sereiter	Chief, Science and Education Department.
Tserendashiin Namsrai	Chief, Main Department.
Banzragchiin Lamjav	Chief, Cadre Department.
Puntsagiin Jasray	Chief, Economics, Planning and Finance Department. (Replaced in May 1978)

CENTRAL COMMITTEE MEMBERS

GELEGIIN AD'YAA. Head of Central Committee's Department for Party Organizations.

TSENDIIN AD'YA. First secretary, Selenga Aimak.

*DARIIN AR'YA. Not further identified.

JARANTAIN AVKHIA. (b. 1923). Lieutenant General. Minister of Defense. Former First Deputy Minister of Defense (April–September 1978); State Prosecutor; Deputy Chairman, Mongolian Parliamentary Group. Writer on law.

*BALDANGIIN BADARCH (b. 1916). General representative of Council of Ministers. Deputy chairman, Gosplan. Deputy chairman, Mongol-Soviet Friendship Association.

LUVSANNYAMYN BALDANDASH. Head of Central Committee's Agriculture Department (reported inactive in 1977). Former deputy minister of rural economy.

TSERENPILIIN BALKHAJAV. Head of Central Committee's Ideology Department. Chairman of the Great Khural Committee for Youth Questions since December 4, 1975.

JAM'YANGIIN BANZRAGCH. First secretary, Erdenet City Committee.

*KHAYANGIIN BANZRAGCH. Ambassador to the USSR since August 31, 1973. Former chairman, Goskhoz Commission.

*SANJIIN BATA. Head of the Central Committee's Administrative Organization Department (a euphemism for the Department of Military Affairs). Member of the Presidium of the Great Khural. Former ambassador to USSR (1956–1959). Former deputy minister of defense. Went to Peking in December 1962 for signing of border treaty.

BALDANDORJIIN BEGESUREN. First secretary, Dzabkhan Aimak.

VANCHINSURENGIIN BUNCHIN. Deputy Chief, Party Organization Department, Central Committee, MPRP. Former first secretary, Ubur Khangai Aimak.

*GOMBO-OCHIRYN CHIMID. Chief editor, *Namyn Amdral*. Secretary, Union of Journalists. Former director, Central Committee's Culture and Propaganda Department. Signatory of August 1959 attack on Rinchen. Published article on the MPRP in *Kommunist,* no. 9 (June 1968), pp. 64–71.

*MAGSARYN CHIMIDDORJ. Deputy chairman, Mongolian side of Mongolian-Soviet Intergovernmental Commission (assimilated rank of a minister in the government). Former minister of transport and communications. Attended July 1974 "Erdenet meeting" in Ulan Bator.

PUNTSAGIIN CHOGDON. No information available.

LUVSANGIIN CHOIJILSUREN. Chairman, Council for Prose, Union of Mongolian Writers.

*PAVANGIIN DAMDIN. Minister of light and food industry.

LEGDENGIIN DAMDINJAV. Chairman, People's Control Committee. Former chairman, Committee on Transport, Council of Ministers.

*TUVSHINTSERIIN DANGA. Secretary, United Party Organizations of Production Units of Leather and Wool-Working Enterprises. Former director, Ulan Bator Industrial Kombinat.

GOMBYN DARAMBAZAR. First secretary, Central Gobi Aimak.

TSEREVIIN DAVAGSUREN. Head of Central Committee's International Relations Department. Deputy chairman of the Great Khural Foreign Affairs Commission. Wrote a dissertation on the economy of the MPR, Academy of Social Sciences (AON), Central Committee, CPSU, Moscow, 1961. Central Committee member since 1966. Appointed Ambassador to East Germany, August 1978.

BUGYN DEJID LT.-GENERAL (b. 1927). Minister of security. Central Committee member since 1966.

BATYN DORJ, GENERAL (b. 1914). Chairman, Committee of Veterans of Revolutionary Struggle. Former minister of defense. Former minister of public security.

MANGALYN DUGERSUREN (b. 1922). Minister of foreign affairs since August 25, 1976. Head of the MPR's delegation to the Geneva disarmament talks. Former representative at the United Nations. Former minister of foreign affairs (1963–1968). Central Committee member since 1966.

BATMUNKHIIN ENEBISH. Minister of transport.

SUNDEVIIN GOMBOSUREN, MAJOR GENERAL. First deputy chief of the political administration of the army, and director of the Ideological Department, General Political Department of the army.

*DAKHYN GOTOV. Minister of communications since 1966. Member, Central Council, Mongolian Soviet Friendship Association.

TSEDENDAMBYN GOTOV. Secretary of the Presidium of the Great Khural since 1966. Was a member of the official delegation to Japan in February 1977. Wrote a dissertation on the Mongolian intelligentsia, Academy of Social Sciences (AON), Central Committee, CPSU, Moscow 1959. Published an article on "The People's State" in *World Marxist Review,* no. 11 (Oct.–Nov. 1968), pp. 18–21. Central Committee member since 1966.

*RAVDANGIIN GUNSEN, MAJ.-GENERAL (b. 1923). State prosecutor since April 1978. Former Chairman of the Supreme Court since November 1970. Former deputy minister of public security. Earned a doctorate in juridical science from the Institute of State and Law, USSR Academy of Sciences, in June 1974. Wrote a dissertation on guarding state property.

TSERENGIIN GURBADAM. Head of the Central Committee's Industry Department. Chairman of Great Khural Planning and Budget Commission. Former deputy minister of industry. Chief editor, Mongolian version of *Voprosy Ekonomiki.*

*JAMBYN JAM'YAN, LT.-GENERAL. Director of the Foreign Affairs Department, ministry of defense. Chairman of the Society for Promotion of Defense. Chairman, Mongolian-Vietnamese Friendship Association. Former chairman of the Commission on State Control. Former Chairman of Civil Defense.

PUNTSAGIIN JASRAY. First Deputy Chairman, Gosplan. Assimilated rank of Government minister May 1, 1978. Former Chairman, State Committee for Prices and Standards (1975–1977), and Chief of Economics, Planning and Finance Department, Central Committee, MPRP.

SHAGDARYN KHASBAZAR. First secretary, Selenga Aimak.

LUVSANJAVYN KHURLE. First secretary, Bayan-Ulegei Aimak. Former first secretary, Gobi Altai Aimak.

*BAITAZAGIIN KHURMETBEG. A Kazakh. Director of the Higher Party School. Former deputy director, Culture and Propaganda Department, Central Committee.

*BANZRAGCHIIN LAMJAV. Head of the Central Committee's Cadre Department.

*BADAMYN LKHAMSUREN. Representative of the MPR on the editorial board of *Problems of Peace and Socialism.* Former Politburo member (approximately 1954–1957; 1962–1973). Wrote a dissertation on Mongolian foreign policy, Moscow 1958; doctorate at Institute of Marxism-Leninism, Central Committee, CPSU, Moscow, 1975.

MYATAVYN LKHAMSUREN. Former chairman of the State Committee for Labor and Wages. Central Committee member since 1966.

GOMBYN LODOIKHU. May be the "Labor Hero Lodoikhu" mentioned in *History of the MPR* on p. 612.

*SONOMYN LUVSAN (b. 1912). Former Politburo member (Dec. 1963–June 1976). Former first deputy chairman of the Great Khural, and former chairman of the Mongolian-Soviet Friendship Association. Former ambassador to Peking (1957–1959) and ambassador to Moscow (1960–1964). Former first deputy prime minister.

*NYAMYN LUVSANCHULTEM (b. 1916). Chairman of the Great Khural. Chairman of the Executive Committee, Federation of Organizations for Peace and Friendship. Former ambassador to the USSR (Feb. 1964–1973). Studied at Ulan Ude and Irkutsk in the 1930s. Counsellor of the MPR embassy at Peking, 1954–1955. *Aspirant* at Institute of Oriental Studies, Moscow, 1957–1960.

SONOMYN LUVSANGOMBO. Deputy prime minister. Chairman of the Construction and Architecture Commission, Council of Ministers. Deputy chairman, Society for the Protection of Nature and the Environment. Candidate-member of Central Committee 1966–1976.

JARGALYN LUVSANJAMTS (b. 1928). First secretary, Khentei Aimak.

CHUVANDORJIIN MOLOM. Head of the Central Committee's Trade and Transport Department.

TSENDIIN MOLOM. Minister of finance. Member of the Central Revision Commission of the MPRP. Former minister of the fishing industry. Candidate-member of the Central Committee 1966–1976.

†TSENDIIN NAMSRAI (b. 1926). Chairman of the Journalists Union. Deputy chairman of the Parliamentary Group. Chief editor of *Unen.* Former head of the Propaganda and Culture Department of the Central Committee. Attended the Higher Party School, Central Committee, MPRP, and Higher Party School, Academy of Social Sciences, Central Committee, CPSU.

---

†Two Central Committee members and two candidate-members are all named Namsrai, and it is all too easy to confuse their names and positions. References to them are often difficult to sort out.

TSERENDASHIIN NAMSRAI. Head of the Central Committee's Main Department.

YONDONGIIN OCHIR. Minister of foreign trade. Former first deputy minister of foreign trade (1966).

*GOMBOJAVYN OCHIRBAT. Member of the Presidium of the Great Khural. Chairman of the Trade Unions. Former chairman, Union of Journalists. Former deputy chief editor of *Unen*. Former head of a Central Committee department. Wrote a dissertation on harmonizing "national" and "international" factors in building socialism, Academy of Social Sciences, Central Committee, CPSU, Moscow, 1972.

PUNSALMAGIIN OCHIRBAT. Minister of fuel and power.

JIGMEDIIN OTGONTSAGAN. May be the "outstanding miner" mentioned in *History of the MPR,* p. 571.

*MYATAVYN PELJE. Deputy prime minister. MPR Representative to CMEA. Former minister of geology and mining (1966–1976). Wrote a dissertation on foreign trade, Moscow, 1960.

UL'ZIIN PULJIN. No information available.

*TSEVEGJAVYN PUNTSUKNOROV. Permanent representative of the MPR United Nations delegation to New York. Former deputy prime minister. Attended Moscow University.

CHOIDONGIIN PUREVDORJ, MAJ.-GENERAL. First deputy minister of defense and chief of staff of the army since 1974. Former director, Bureau of Chinese Workers' Affairs, State Committee on Labor (1963).

*BYAMBYN RINCHENPELJE. Chairman, State Committee for Materials and Technical Supply. First deputy chairman of Gosplan.

*LODONGIIN RINCHIN (b. 1929). Minister of agriculture. Former minister of foreign affairs (1970–1977). Former first secretary, Selenga Aimak. Received his higher education in the USSR.

DANGASURENGIIN SALDAN. Chairman, State Committee on Foreign Economic Relations (assimilated rank of government minister). Adviser for economic questions at the MPR embassy in Moscow. Deputy chairman of the Mongolian side of Mongolian-Soviet Intergovernmental Commission. Former deputy chairman for Industry and Construction of Gosplan. Candidate-member of the Central Committee 1966–1976.

CHIMEDIIN SEREITER. Head of the Central Committee's Science and Education Department. Former scientific secretary, Mongolian Academy of Sciences. Wrote a dissertation on socialist property in industry, Moscow State Economics Institute, 1957. Candidate-member of the Central Committee 1966–1976.

*PUNTSAGIIN SHAGDARSUREN (b. 1918). Ambassador to East Germany until relieved August, 1978. Former minister of foreign affairs (1959–1963). Former director, International Relations Department of the Central Committee. Went to Peking in December 1962 for signing of border treaty.

*BAZARYN SHIRENDYB (b. 1912). President of the Mongolian Academy of Sciences since 1960. Deputy chairman of the Great Khural. Deputy chairman, Society for

Protection of Nature and the Environment. Former Politburo member and first deputy prime minister. Wrote a dissertation on the Mongolian Revolution at the Institute of Oriental Studies, Moscow, 1954, and a dissertation on the history of the revolution, 1960. Currently chairman of the Mongolian Alumni of Soviet Educational Institutions.

DUMAGIIN SODNOM. Deputy prime minister since June 1975. Chairman of Gosplan. Former minister of finance. Central Committee member since 1966.

TSERENNAMJILYN SODNOMJAMTS. First secretary, Bulgan Aimak.

CHOINORYN SUREN (b. 1932). Deputy prime minister since 1974. Former economic adviser, Moscow embassy. Former deputy chairman, Darkhan City Khural (1967–1972). Received his engineering training in the USSR.

ORONYN TLEIKHAN. Minister of construction and construction-industry materials since 1964. Central Committee member since 1966.

PUNTSAGIIN TOGTOKH (b. 1889). Veteran of 1921 revolution.

YADAMSURENGIIN TOIVGO. First secretary, Eastern Aimak.

NURJAVYN TSEDENPIL. Reference to him is ambiguous; may be deputy chairman of the Great Khural.

OCHIRYN TSENDE. Chairman, Ulan Bator City Khural. Recalled from North Korea (he was ambassador) on May 21, 1976. Former chairman of the State Statistical Administration (1966). Wrote a dissertation on Mongolian finances, Moscow University, 1964. Central Committee candidate-member 1966–1976.

LKHAMYN TSERENDONDOG. Head of the Central Committee's Construction Department. Deputy minister of construction and construction-materials since May 1963.

SHURKHUGIIN TSEREVSAMBA. Deputy chairman, Party Control Committee. Former secretary, Ulan Bator City Party Committee. Former Member of the Presidium of the Mongolian-Chinese Friendship Association (1964).

*DONDOGIIN TSEVEGMID (b. 1915). Deputy prime minister. Chairman, Committee for Higher, Secondary Specialized, and Vocational and Technical Institutions. Chairman, Atomic Energy Committee. Former chairman, Scientific Committee. Former ambassador to Peking. Former delegate to the United Nations. Currently chairman of the Parliamentary Group. Directed the attack on Rinchen in 1959.

*BUTAGIIN TSOG, COL.-GENERAL. First deputy minister of defense. Chairman, Society for Promotion of Defense. Was at Nomonkhan with Choibalsan in 1939.

SONOMTSEVENIIN TSOGTGEREL. No information available.

LODONGIIN TUDEV. First secretary of the Revsomols since June 20, 1975. Former chairman of Mongolian Writers (July 1974–October 1975). Former head of the Great Khural Youth Commission.

JAMBYN TUMENJARGAL. First secretary, Kobdo Aimak.

*SONOMYN UDVAL. Chairperson of the Mongolian Women's Committee since 1964. Former Chairperson of the Mongolian Writers' Union.

DARAMYN YONDON. First deputy minister of foreign affairs.

DONDOVYN YONDONDUICHIR, LT.-GENERAL. Head of the political administration of the army. Former State prosecutor.

CANDIDATE-MEMBERS, CENTRAL COMMITTEE

DASHIIN ADILBISH (b. 1917). Ambassador to Yugoslavia. Former ambassador to Moscow (1954–1955). Former minister of foreign affairs (1956).

SHARAVYN AGVAN. Chairman, Commission for Socialist Legality and Social Order.

MYAGMARYN ALTANGEREL. No information available.

TSEVEGIIN AMGALAN. No information available.

SHAVIIN ARVAI, MAJ.-GENERAL. Deputy minister of public security. Chairman, Directorate of Frontier and Internal Troops.

*DAMBYN BABUU, MAJ.-GENERAL. Deputy minister of defense. Chief of the Main Army Construction Troops Administration. Former chief of the Darkhan Military Construction Project (1964).

SANDAGSURENGIIN BADAMKHATAN. Second secretary, Revsomols.

UNURIIN BANDI. No information available.

JAMBALYN BANZAR (b. 1920). Deputy minister of foreign affairs. Former ambassador to West Germany. Former first secretary, Moscow embassy (1950–1954). Former ambassador to Poland. Candidate-member of the Central Committee since 1966.

BILEGTIIN BANZRAGCH. Secretary of the Erdenet City Party Committee.

BABUDORJIIN BARS. Minister of irrigation.

DAGDALYN BARS. Ambassador to Turkey and Bulgaria.

*NYAMJAVYN BASANJAV. Secretary, Ulan Bator City Party Committee.

BEGZIIN BATCHULUN. No information available.

GENDENGIIN BIZ'YA. First secretary, Ubsa Nur Aimak.

SODNOMBALJIRYN BUDRAGCHA, MAJ.-GENERAL. First deputy minister of public security. Chief of militia.

DELGERIIN BYAMBA, MAJ.-GENERAL. Commanded Ulan Bator parade on June 13, 1975. Former first deputy chief of the Darkhan Military Construction Project (1964). Full member of the Central Committee 1966–1976.

SHIRENGIIN DAGVA. Deputy head of a Central Committee department.

TSERENBALYN DALAI. Chairman of the Khural, Sukhe Bator Aimak.

CHLUNY DAMCHAJAMTS. No information available.

*KHORLOGIIN DAMDIN. Ambassador to Cuba and Mexico. Former ambassador to East Germany.

NYAMBYN DAMDIN. No information available.

SANJIDYN DAR'SUREN. No information available.

DUGERIIN DAVATSEREN. No information available.

*MANGALJAVYN DASH. Deputy Chairman, State Committee for Science and Technology. Former Ambassador to West Germany. Former minister of agriculture, chairman, SKhO Council; head of a Central Committee department. Wrote a dissertation on Gobi sheep, Moscow (1954).

NYAMJILJAVYN DASHNYAM. Head of a department in the ministry of foreign affairs.

PUNTSAGIIN DECHIN. First deputy minister of public security.

*DUNJMAGIIN DORJGOTOV. Minister of trade and procurement. Former deputy minister of industry and minister of trade resources since July 1960.

*BAMDARYN DUGERSUREN. Former Ambassador to Rumania and Hungary. Former deputy prime minister (July 1963–December 1974). Participated in the July 1974 "Erdenet meeting" in Ulan Bator.

*TSAGANLAMYN DUGERSUREN. Vice-president (deputy chairman of the Presidium of the Great Khural). Former member of the Politburo (1954–1974). Former Party secretary. Former chairman of Gosplan. Former deputy prime minister.

JAMSRANGIIN DULMA. Deputy minister of food industry since 1964.

DUGERIIN GOMBOJAV. Former deputy minister of defense and chief of staff of the army (appointed August 1962).

CHOIJILYN GUNSEN. First secretary, Party Committee, Ulan Bator Railroad. Wrote a dissertation on the economic effectiveness of railroad transport at the Railroad Institute in Moscow, 1975.

DENZHEGIIN ISHTSEREN (d. March 25, 1978). Former minister of education (December 1965–March 1978). Former Chairman of the National Committee for UNESCO. Candidate-member of the Central Committee (1966–1978).

BURALYN JADAMBA. Chief of a department, Council of Ministers.

SHARAVDORJIIN JADAMBA. Deputy chief of a Central Committee department.

BUYANDELGERIIN JAMSRAN. First secretary, East Gobi Aimak.

SHADAMYN KHOKHIISUREN. No information available.

TUVSHINGIIN KHORKHOI. First secretary, South Gobi Aimak.

CHOIJINGIIN KHURTS. Minister of geology and mining.

DONDOVOGIIN LKHAGVASUREN. First secretary, Ulan Bator Revsomols. Former first deputy general director of Mongolian-Soviet Enterprises at Erdenet.

*JAMYANGIIN LKHAGVASUREN, COL.-GENERAL (Retired). Deputy Chairman of the Great Khural. Former minister of defense. Former minister of justice.

URJINGIIN MAGSARJAV. No information available.

NARANGERELIIN MYATAV. First deputy chairman, State Committee on Information, Radio, and Television.

DORJDEREMIIN NAMSRAI. Deputy chairman, Committee on People's Control.

TSOGTYN NAMSRAI. Secretary, Khural Foreign Affairs Commission.

JADAMBYN NARAN. Secretary, Trade Unions Council.

DAR'SURENGIIN NYAM-OSOR. Minister of health. Former director, State Enterprise for Production and Supply of Medical Goods in the ministry of health (1964).

JUMDANY ROZON. Head of a Central Committee department. Former deputy head of the Ideological Department of the Central Committee. Led MPRP delegation to Moscow, September 4–15, 1972.

ASGANBAIN SARAI. Chairman, Bulgan Aimak.

NAMSRAIN SODNOM. Rector of Mongolian State University since 1964. Chairman, Mongolian Committee for the Defense of Peace. Deputy chairman, Atomic Energy Commission.

YADAMYN TSEGMID. Acting Head, Agricultural Department of the Central Committee. Wrote a dissertation on harmonizing collective and private economies in the SKhO Academy of Social Sciences, Central Committee CPSU (Moscow, 1974).

DORLINGIIN TSEREN. First secretary, Sukhe Bator Aimak.

NAVAN-JAMBYN TSERENNOROV. First deputy chairman of the Ulan Bator Railroad since 1966. Attended a railway meeting in Peking in August 1977.

CHOIDOVYN TUMENDELGER. Deputy chief of the Ideology Department, Central Committee. Former chairman, Mongolian Red Cross (1964).

Notes

1. Introduction

1. Cf. the following views:

"The Mongols of the small Mongolian party were . . . used ruthlessly . . . to bring about the extension of Soviet power. . . . The Mongols who had joined [the People's Party] are simply native puppets, acting as a screen for the desire of the Soviet Union to move into this part of Central Asia." George Murphy, *Soviet Mongolia*, p. 3.

"It would oversimplify matters to assert that everything which happened in Mongolia after 1921 was directed by Soviet interests and Soviet intervention. . . . Still, Soviet influence in Mongolia was continuous and paramount after 1921. . . . Mongolia's whole contemporary ethos is something new and originating from abroad. Ideologically, at the official level, she is a Soviet creation." Charles R. Bawden, *The Modern History of Mongolia*, pp. 239, 241.

"Neither the assertion on the one hand that Soviet imperialism achieved a disguised annexation of Mongolia, nor the vigorous denial that Soviet Russia was prompted by anything but feelings of brotherly Socialist help toward Outer Mongolia on the other, is likely to lead to an understanding of the situation." Gerard M. Friters, *Outer Mongolia and Its International Position*, p. 147.

"In Outer Mongolia Soviet policy has indisputably used the power thus accruing to it in the interests of the Mongol people as a whole. . . . [T]he Khalkha Mongols now have, under the MPR, the most popular and representative government they have ever had. . . ." Owen Lattimore, *Inner Asian Frontiers of China*, p. 199.

"[I]t would be a mistake to assume that Mongolia is no more than an outlying province of the Soviet Empire. . . . [T]he MPR gives in many ways a greater impression of independence than do some Communist countries in Eastern Europe. . . . [T]hough in foreign policy the Mongolian Government regularly follows the Soviet line, there is little or no indication of Russification or of active Soviet interference in Mongolian internal affairs." Sir Fitzroy Maclean, *To the Back of Beyond*, pp. 137, 139.

"Why has Mongolia succeeded so well, while other nations are left burdened with the same kinds of problems (e.g., poverty and lack of development) which once plagued Mongolia?" Daniel Rosenberg, *"Negdel* Development," p. 62.

M. I. Gol'man devoted a whole book to attacking most of the U.S. and Western judgments about the MPR: *Problemy noveishei istorii MNR v burzhuaznoi istoriografii SShA*. See S. D. Miliband, *Biobibliograficheskii slovar' sovetskikh vostokovedov*, pp. 145–146, for information about Gol'man and citations of other writings of his.

2. What the Mongolian regime says of itself is conveniently available in English translation: *History of the Mongolian People's Republic*, translated and annotated by William A. Brown and Urgunge Onon.

2. Roots: 1900–1920

1. Charles R. Bawden, in *The Modern History of Mongolia,* supplies an excellent overview of the prerevolutionary period. George A. Cheney provides a useful survey of "The Pre-Revolutionary Culture of Outer Mongolia." Robert B. Valliant gives information about "Japanese Involvement in Mongol Independence Movements, 1912–1919." A. V. Burdukov's memoirs and letters in *V staroi i novoi Mongolii,* especially the extensive footnotes in that book, compiled by Elena Darevskaya, illuminate many persons and events.

2. William Gardener, "China and Russia: The Beginnings of Contact"; idem, "Peking to Moscow." A map of 1763 reproduced on p. 211 of the latter shows the Baikal Corridor clearly.

3. Gerard M. Friters, *Outer Mongolia and Its International Position* p. 55. I. Ya. Korostovets wrote an indispensable book about Mongolia before 1921: *Von Chinggis Khan zur Sowjetrepublik.* His diary for the Russo-Japanese negotiations is also available: *Stranitsa iz istorii russkoi diplomatii: Russko-Yaponskie peregovory v Portsmut'e v 1905 (Peking 1923).* (The English translation is *Pre-War Diplomacy, The Russo-Japanese Problem. Diary of J. J. Korostovetz* [London, 1920].) His dispatch from Peking of November 16, 1910, is one of the most important single documents for Mongolia: in B. von Siebert, ed., *Graf Benckendorffs Diplomatischer Schriftwechsel,* no. 302 (Berlin and Leipzig, 1928), pp. 378–383.

The 1977 Simulations Publications, Inc., war game, "Red Sun Rising," (New York) includes discussion in its "Rules of Play" of "The Trans-Siberian Railroad: Critical Bottleneck or Source of Superiority?" See also Denis and Peggy Warner, *The Tide at Sunrise: A History of the Russo-Japanese War, 1904–1905,* especially pp. 76 and 552; see also Christopher Martin, *The Russo-Japanese War.*

4. Friters, *Outer Mongolia,* pp. 57, 60, and 162, indicated that Russian agents played an active role in fomenting the Mongolian revolt; he referred in particular to Captain Makushek and his "rebellion" memorandum. Bawden stated in *Modern History,* p. 194, that "the Russian attitude was very cautious," and that the Mongols "broke away from China in spite of Russian warnings to be moderate." Bawden was probably closer to the mark, since tsarist officials leashed the Barga leader Togtokho and did not send him to Urga until independence had already been declared. Togtokho was at Chita after having fled with his troops from Manchuria and eastern Outer Mongolia; he would have been an ideal tool for subversive employment. Urgunge Onon translated Navannamjil's account of Togtokho's career in *Mongolian Heroes of the Twentieth Century* (see especially pp. 63–66).

5. The text of the 1911 letter, and the quotations from Murav'ev (1861) and Badmaev (1893) can be found in Robert A. Rupen, *Mongols of the Twentieth Century,* 1:60–61, 54, 158. A. M. Pozdneyev indicated in *Mongolia and the Mongols,* p. 137, that in 1890 "The Khalkhas [were] firmly convinced that the Russians are going to come to these parts and take possession of them and all the Khalkhas." The translators' note in *History of the MPR,* p. 750 n. 58, reported the Jebtsun Damba's 1895 request. Bawden referred to earlier Mongol-Russian contacts in *Modern History,* pp. 52, 62, 70–74, 76–77.

Harrison Salisbury paid considerable attention to Badmaev in *Black Night, White Snow,* pp. 73, 208, 280, 296, 296n, 304, 608, 620 (Semennikov), 641 n. 8 (especially), 658 n. 21.

6. The Buryat Cossacks constituted a unique group, more denationalized and Russified than other Mongols. The first Buryat Communist, Ranzhurov, was a

Cossack; and so was the anti-Bolshevik and pro-Japanese leader Ataman Semenov. See Rupen, *Mongols,* 1:10–11, 131, and 152 n. 44.

7. Albert von Le Coq, *Buried Treasures of Chinese Turkestan,* p. 50.

8. Agvan Dorjeev deliberately cultivated contacts with Kalmyks, and Kozin and Vladimirtsov worked with them for many years. A conference at Elista (Kalmyk Republic) in 1972 paid tribute to Kotvich's role in Kalmyk studies. *Narody Azii i Afriki,* no. 1 (1973): 225–230 (translation in *Mongolia Society Bulletin* 12, nos. 1–2 [1973]: 94–109). See also Walter Kolarz, *Russia and Her Colonies,* pp. 81–86, and numerous indexed references to Kalmyks in both volumes of Rupen, *Mongols.* A recent book is *Ocherki istorii Kalmytskoi ASSR.* Burdukov worked with the Kalmyks from 1932 through 1939 (Burdukov *V staroi,* p. 21).

9. Burdukov (April 25, 1912), *V staroi,* p. 267. Cf. Rupen, "The Absorption of Tuva," and V. L. Popov, *Uryankhai'skii pogranichnyi vopros. Doklad.*

10. Muslim-Buddhist rivalry was deep-seated and built into the beliefs of both sides: the future Utopian Buddhist kingdom was supposed to put an end to the spread of Mohammedanism; the "ancient iconoclasm" of the Muslims led to such phenomena as Dungan vandalism of the Buddhist sacred relics at Ejen Khoro in Inner Mongolia in the 1870s and the destruction in 1925 in Sinkiang of nearly seventy Buddhist monasteries. "The Dungan armies . . . used machine guns. Many Tanguts [Mongols] perished. . . . The Dungans [or "Hui"—ethnic Chinese who were Muslims] occupy a strange position. They are frankly disliked by Moslem, Chinese, and Kalmyks. The word 'Dungan' itself is pronounced with a certain contempt. . . ." Nicholas Roerich, *Altai-Himalaya: A Travel Diary,* pp. 213, 247, 295. See also Sir Charles Bell, *Tibet Past and Present,* p. 63; Rinchen, *Zum Kult Tschinggis-Khans bei den Mongolen;* and M. Sushanlo, *Dungane—istoriko-demograficheskii ocherk.*

11. In 1910 Gabrik had completed studies in the Chinese-Mongolian section of the Institute of Oriental Studies at Vladivostok (Burdukov, *V staroi,* pp. 156, 391 n. 105, 106, and 393 n. 111; photograph in Rupen, *Mongols,* 1:124).

12. J. R. V. Prescott, *Map of Mainland Asia by Treaty,* p. 275. The Simla Conference took place from October 1913 through June 1914. See Alastair Lamb, *The McMahon Line,* vol. 2, and Friters, *Outer Mongolia,* pp. 252–253, 259.

13. V. P. Leont'ev, *Inostrannaya ekspansiya v Tibete, 1888–1919* (Moscow, 1956), p. 161.

14. For Maksorjav, see Onon's translation of Choibalsan's account in *Mongolian Heroes,* pp. 105–142. For an account of Maksorjav's acquisition of Russian weapons, see Burdukov, *V staroi,* p. 17. The Russian treaties with Japan were of critical importance to the outcome of the Kyakhta Conference. Ernest B. Price, *The Russian-Japanese Treaties of 1907–1916 Concerning Manchuria and Mongolia;* see also Friters, *Outer Mongolia,* pp. 217–221.

The adviser to the Chinese delegation at Kyakhta was Ch'en Yi, who emerged as deputy commissioner for Outer Mongolia in June 1915 and formally succeeded Ch'en Lu (a Chinese negotiator at Kyakhta) as commissioner on August 7, 1917. Ch'en Yi was relieved by Hsü Shu-ch'eng, and after Hsü's recall in July 1920, Ch'en Yi succeeded him as China's principal representative in Urga. Ch'en Yi published a memoir on the 1915 Kyakhta Conference: see *History of the MPR,* 746 n. 25. Ch'en Lu served as Chinese minister to France, 1920–1927, and was assassinated in Shanghai on February 20, 1939. Other Chinese negotiators at Kyakhta were Chen I-fan (Ivan Chen), who had been Peking's representative in Tibet in June 1913, and General Pi Kuei-fang, who had dominated Heilungkiang province in 1913.

15. For Babojab, see Gavan McCormack, *Chang Tso-lin in Northeast China, 1911–1928,* pp. 28–30; Valliant, "Japanese Involvement," pp. 9, 11, 26 n. 41 (especially), and 29 n. 64; Friters, *Outer Mongolia,* pp. 223–224; and the Japanese source cited in *History of the MPR,* p. 762 n. 1. Ch'en Lu left a detailed account of Sino-Mongolian negotiations about Babojab in *Chih-shih-pi-chi* (Shanghai, 1917).

16. For some aspects of developments concerning Tibet, Great Britain, and Russia at that time, see Salisbury, *Black Night,* pp. 73–74, 641 n. 8, and 642 n. 13; Burdukov, *V staroi,* p. 378 n. 42; Kyuner in S. D. Miliband, *Biobibliografscheskii slovar' sovetskikh vostokovedov,* pp. 298–299 and the citation concerning the Tibetan-Uighur connection in Miliband, p. 688. See also E. F. Knight, *Where Three Empires Meet,* pp. 289–290, 504. Many aspects of Manchurian developments and the Japanese influence are illuminated by Andrew Malozemoff in *Russian Far Eastern Policy, 1881–1904, With Special Emphasis on the Causes of the Russo-Japanese War;* note also Burdukov, *V staroi,* pp. 381 n. 54 and 403 n. 163, and Sapozhnikov in Miliband, p. 496.

Concerning the formation of a Mongolian army, which Sazonov considered "a necessary factor of our influence," see Rupen, *Mongols,* 1:78–79; Friters, *Outer Mongolia,* pp. 82–83 and 92–93; and Burdukov, *V staroi,* pp. 79, 382 n. 55, 383 n. 61, and 383 n. 64.

17. Discussions of Mongolian feudalism include those by B. Ya. Vladimirtsov in *Obshchestvennyi stroi mongolov—Mongol'skii kochevoi feodalizm* (Leningrad, 1934—translated by Michael Carsow as *Le regime social des mongols* [Paris, 1948]; of N. N. Koz'min in *K voprosu o turetsko-mongol'skom feodalizme;* of Owen Lattimore in *Inner Asian Frontiers of China;* of George Cheney in "Pre-Revolutionary Culture"; and of Sh. Natsokdorj in "The Economic Basis of Feudalism in Mongolia." For biographical and bibliographical information on Vladimirtsov, see Miliband, *Biobibliografscheskii,* pp. 115–116, and I. Ya. Zlatkin, "Ak. B. Ya. Vladimirtsov—istorik-vostokoved." For information on Zlatkin, see Miliband, *Biobibliografscheskii,* pp. 216–217.

18. A. M. Pozdneyev, *Mongolia,* pp. 377–378. See also Charles R. Bawden, "An Event in the Life of the Eighth Jebtsun Damba Khutukhtu."

19. Pozdneyev, *Mongolia,* pp. 281–282.

20. Sir Charles Bell, *Portrait of the Dalai Lama;* see Rupen, *Mongols,* 1:107–110 and for the Dalai Lama's itinerary, p. 113 n. 34. The Younghusband Expedition occupied Lhasa from August 4 through September 23, 1904.

21. P. L. Mehra, "Tibet and Russian Intrigue."

22. Buddhist, Sanskrit, and Indian studies in Russia comprised part of Russian-Mongolian and Russian-Tibetan relations. Individuals important in these academic specialties before and after 1917 included: Vladimirtsov (d. 1931); Tsybikov (d. 1932); Ol'denburg and Rozenberg (d. 1934); Kozlov and Obermiller (d. 1935); Shcherbatskoi (d. 1942); Vorob'ev-Desyatskii (d. 1956); and Monzeler (d. 1959). Nicholas Roerich (d. 1947) pursued Buddhist studies from America and India, and his son George (d. 1960) published an article titled "Indology in Russia" in 1945 and two articles on Mongolian-Tibetan relations in 1958 and 1959, just after his return to the USSR in 1957; his book on the Tibetan language was published in 1961. See the bibliography for examples of the work of these Russian scholars. Also see Rinchen, "Sanskrit in Mongolia."

23. In 1931 George Roerich wrote in *Trails to Inmost Asia* (p. 157):

The doctrine of Shambhala is the hidden doctrine of Tibet and Mongolia. . . . Even in distant Buryatia is to be observed the same movement. . . . Shambhala is not only considered to be the abode of hidden Buddhist learning, it is the guiding principle of the coming . . . cosmic age. . . . A western observer is apt to belittle the importance of this name or to relegate the voluminous literature about Shambhala and the still vaster oral tradition into the class of folklore or mythology; but those who have studied both literary and popular Buddhism know the terrific force that this name possesses among the masses of Buddhists of higher Asia. . . . Let us not diminish the importance of this awakening force, that is treasured in the tents of the nomads and the numerous monasteries of Lamaist central Asia.

Compare his comments on the Geser saga, the great epic poem of Mongolia and Tibet (*Trails,* pp. 360–361):

In its present form the ballad is extremely popular in Mongolia. . . . In Tibet and Mongolia, the epic . . . is still constantly enriching itself with new songs and episodes. . . . In Mongolia . . . a new chapter on the future exploits of Geser is in process of creation. . . . These new additions have the character of prophetic songs. . . . It seems as if the nomad tribes of Mongolia and Tibet, agitated by some hidden unrest, seek inspiration in the ancient lore of their past.

(*Novye knigi,* no. 16 (Apr. 21, 1978) announced that the first complete Russian-language edition of the Buryat version of the epic will be published in 1978 as *Geser, Narodnyi epos* [Ulan Ude] in 25,000 copies.)

Sir Charles Bell noted that the Buryat confidant of the Dalai Lama, Agvan Dorjeev, spread the story that Shambhala was Russia and that the tsar would restore the Buddhist kingdom (*Tibet Past and Present,* p. 63). Also see Rupen, *Mongols,* 1:106–107.

In 1926–1927, when they were in Ulan Bator, Nicholas and George Roerich found the Mongolian cavalry singing "The War of Northern Shambhala," which was allegedly composed by Sukhe Bator himself. "Even in new Mongolia they know the reality of Shambhala. In Ulan Bator, the site for the future [temple] of Shambhala is already fenced around" (George Roerich, *Trails to Inmost Asia,* pp. 156–157; Nicholas Roerich, *Altai-Himalaya,* pp. 143, 168, 257, 352–354). Nicholas Roerich presented a painting entitled "The Ruler of Shambhala" to the Mongolian government, and it then asked him to design a temple shrine for the painting and for other venerated objects. Nicholas Roerich published a book in 1930 entitled *Shambhala— The Resplendent,* which dealt with the hope of Asia for a new spiritual renaissance. See also P. Belikov and V. Knyazeva, *Rerikh,* pp. 183–184.

24. The temple is a fine building, still standing today. It has, however, had its political ups and downs—most recently a "down" described by Alexander Piatigorsky in "The Departure of Dandaron," pp. 173 and 173 n. 5. Information on and bibliography for Radlov appear in Miliband, *Biobibliograficheskii,* pp. 460–461.

25. Ongons are discussed by Piers Vitebsky in "Some Medieval Views of Mongolian Shamanism"; he referred on p. 40 n. 20 to a bibliography of Russian sources by C. Humphrey, *Magical Drawings in the Religion of the Buryat.*

26. Sh. Bira, *Mongolian Historical Literature of the XVII–XIX Centuries Written in Tibetan,* p. 54, referred to an 1819 source dealing with the conflict between lamaism and shamanism. *Ateisticheskie chtenie* presented a color photograph of a Tuvan shaman on the cover, along with an article on the subject, "Shamany i shamanstvo," pp. 32–43, and a poem, "The Last Shaman," by Semen Gudzenko.

E. F. Knight, writing of Ladakh and Tibet in 1891, recorded a situation similar to that in Mongolia (*Three Empires,* pp. 131–132):

[T]hese inhabitants of the Himalayan highlands have corrupted almost beyond recognition his [Buddha's] pure and wise doctrines, and have buried with absurdities all that was eternally true in them. A visit to Tibet is apt to destroy many illusions. It is better to read of Buddhism . . . than to contemplate it from too near. As it exists in these regions, Buddhism is fantastic, and most interesting to study; but it is as degraded a system of idolatry as has ever been practiced by a people outside savagery. The priests themselves have long since forgotten the signification of the many complicated ceremonies, forms, and symbols of their religion, and all that remains is an unmeaning superstition.

Writing on the basis of decades of detailed study and the immediate experience of travel in Tibet in 1927–1928, Nicholas Roerich was less negative (*Altai-Himalaya,* p. 390):

[W]e distinguish two Tibets: One is the Tibet of officialdom—of those officials . . . who reflect so much prejudice and violence and falsehood, who desecrate art and petrify learning. . . . [W]e also discern another Tibet, even though it is smaller in numbers. This is the Tibet of the few educated lamas and of an even smaller number of enlightened laymen. This is the Tibet which guards the essence of the teaching and aspires towards enlightenment. It is the Tibet of its spiritual leaders.

27. Ivan Maisky, in *Sovremennaya Mongoliya,* pp. 96–97, cataloged Russian influence.

28. Bawden, *Modern History,* pp. 28–35. "[T]he lamas took care to identify themselves with the Mongolian ruling class" (p. 33).

29. The first autonomous government included: as premier, the Sain Noyan Khan; as minister of foreign affairs, Dalai Wang; as minister of finance, the Tushetu Khan; as minister of war, Khanda Dorji Wang; and as director of the Urga monasteries and the Jebtsun Damba's lamas, Da Lama Tseren Chimet. See the 1913 photograph of these officials in Hermann Consten, *Die Weideplaetze der Mongolen,* vol. 2, opposite p. 16.

30. For a discussion of the outrageously excessive expenditures and the economic consequences, see Pozdneyev, *Mongolia,* pp. 249–250, 274, 276–277; Bawden, *Modern History,* pp. 146–147; G. E. Grumm-Grzhimailo, *Zapadnaya Mongoliya i Uryankhaiskii Krai,* vol 3, pt. 2, pp. 478–479 (quoted in Rupen, *Mongols,* 1:59). See George Murphy, *Soviet Mongolia,* pp. 43–49. Murphy believed that "[T]he picture of heavy Mongol indebtedness to the Chinese . . . definitely seems overdrawn" (p. 46). Grumm-Grzhimailo played an important part in economic forecasting and analysis on Mongolia. See Rupen, *Mongols,* 1:90 n. 13.

31. Kozlov published a great deal about Mongolia and Tibet (see Rupen, *Mongols,* vol. 2 [Bibliography], Items 1063–1071, pp. 57–58). Friters, *Outer Mongolia,* p. 110, quoted Rockhill.

32. V. L. Kotvich, *Kratkii obzor istorii i sovremennogo politicheskogo polozheniya Mongolii,* presented clearly the administrative organization of the country at that time. Grumm-Grzhimailo described the hoshun-princes as in complete control: "customarily a hoshun responded with all its property to the demands of its master" (*Zapadnaya,* vol. 3, pt. 1, pp. 411–412).

33. Beatrix Bulstrode, *A Tour in Mongolia,* pp. 150–153; Rupen, "The City of Urga in the Manchu Period," pp. 157–169.

34. Julius Price, *From the Arctic Ocean to the Yellow Sea,* p. 256. See also Le Coq's description (in *Buried Treasures,* p. 112) of the Russian official at Kashgar:

The Russian Representative in Kashgar, the well-known Consul-general Pietrowsky. . . . Pietrowsky was an extraordinarily gifted man, and was in his time the real ruler of Eastern Turkestan. No man was better acquainted than he with the history, religion, and character both of the Chinese and the Turks, no one knew more than he did of the economic, military, and other resources of the country. . . .

35. Burdukov, *V staroi*, p. 392 n. 108.

36. For Lyuba, see Burdukov, *V staroi*, p. 383 n. 65. For Miller and related matters, see Korostovets, *Cinggis Khan*, p. 148; *Die internationalen Beziehungen im Zeitalter des Imperialismus*, Document no. 57 vol. 1(i).

37. M. I. Bogolepov and M. N. Sobolev, *Ocherki russko-mongol'skoi torgovli;* Burdukov, *V staroi*, p. 393 n. 110; Friters, *Outer Mongolia*, p. 53; *Moskovskaya torgovaya ekspeditsiya v Mongoliyu* (MTE); and A. P. Boloban, *Mongoliya v ee sovremennom torgovo-ekonomicheskom otnoshenii.*

38. For references to several versions of the quotation and information concerning Kuropatkin, see Rupen, *Mongols,* 1:22 n. 15.

39. Price, *Russian-Japanese Treaties.*

3. Revolution. Buryats, Comintern, and Revsomols: 1920–1928

1. Altai Oirats live in what is now called the Gorno-Altai autonomous oblast, which was from June 1922 to 1948 the Oirat autonomous oblast. The total population of this autonomous oblast was 168,000 in 1970, including 47,000 Altais (Oirats), 110,000 Russians, and 7,000 Kazakhs. A description of the area as it was in 1895–1899 and information on the Chuisk Road at the turn of the century appear in V. V. Sapozhnikov, *Po russkomu i mongol'skomu Altayu* especially p. 499 n. 4.

Kolchak elements led by Kaigorodov were defeated and fled across the border to Mongolia in April 1920 (V. A. Demidov, "Sovety v bor'be s natsionalisticheskoi kontrrevolyutsiei v Gornom Altae," pp. 25–53 [bibliography, pp. 25–29]; L. P. Mamet, *Oirotiya).* When Nicholas Roerich travelled in the area in 1926, he wrote: "Everything bears the traces of the civil war. Here on the highway a Red regiment was destroyed by ambush. Here in the Katun [River] they drowned the Whites. On the mountain ridge are lying the Red commissars. . . . [There are] many graves on the roads . . ." (*Altai-Himalaya,* p. 340).

2. Hashek was at Irkutsk from June through October 1920. In September he introduced Choibalsan and other Mongols to the political administration of the Fifth Red Army. He initiated, briefly edited, and wrote for a Buryat-language newspaper, which may have served as a model for the Khalkhas' *Unen.* See Yu. Shcherbakov, *Pisatel', Agitator, Boets,* pp. 100–103; B. S. Sanzhiev, *Yaroslav Gashek v Vostochnoi Sibiri;* Emanuel Frynta, *Hasek the Creator of Schweik; Novosti Mongolii,* September 10, 1974; and Afrikan Bal'burov, *Dvenadtsat' moikh dragotsennostei,* p. 27.

3. "To the Bolsheviks . . . Ungern's campaign was rather advantageous, as they themselves thus avoided an armed clash with the Chinese. Such a clash they wanted to avoid by all means, so as not to interrupt their peaceful relations with China" (D. P. Pershin, *Baron Ungern, Urga and Altan-Bulak,* p. 23; see also pp. 70–71).

For information about Pershin, A. V. Burdukov, *V staroi i novoi Mongolii,* p. 388 n. 88. For von Ungern-Sternberg as simply an excuse for the Red Army's invasion see Thomas T. Hammond, "The Communist Takeover of Outer Mongolia," p. 118;

George G. Murphy, *Soviet Mongolia*, pp. 6–10, 26; and Rupen, *Mongols*, 1:155 n. 67. The order signed by Blyukher and Gubel'man (the chairman and a member of the FER Military Council) instructed the Red Army units to avoid confrontation with Chinese and to treat any they encountered as allies in the fight against the Whites (John Erickson, *The Soviet High Command*, p. 223).

Sergei Lazo had signed an agreement with local Chinese in 1918 concerning "hot-pursuit" operations (James W. Morley, *The Japanese Thrust into Siberia, 1918*, Appendix M, pp. 361–362). In Sinkiang, where the Chinese remained in control of the province, the Red Army incursions lasted only as long as it took to suppress Russian anti-Bolshevik forces.

4. Zlatkin indicated that between February 4 and 8, 1921, von Ungern-Sternberg killed 40 Jews and 80 Russians and Mongols (*Ocherki novoi i noveishei istorii Mongolii*, p. 167). *The History of the MPR* stated: "the Ungernists burned old men, children, and old women alive, hanged them to death from trees, and confiscated their property. Hating revolutionary-minded Russians, the Ungernists resorted to such brutalities as shooting, hanging, hacking, and torturing them to death. They hacked and tortured to death such people as Kucherenko, Gembarzhevskiy, and the doctor Tsybyktarov, who were a leading element of the revolutionary Russians . . ." (p. 92). Pershin says that von Ungern-Sternberg was responsible for killing 50 Jews and 150 Russians, including the Russian veterinarian Gei and Father Parnyakov, who was sabered to death (pp. 75, 103). See "The Mad Baron," Chapter 14 in Sir Fitzroy Maclean, *To the Back of Beyond*, pp. 121–133, and B. D. Tsibikov, *Razgrom ungernovshchiny*, pp. 82–88. There is a brief biography of von Ungern-Sternberg in Xenia J. Eudin and Robert C. North, *Soviet Russia and the East, 1920–1927*, p. 463. See also Enders and Anthony, *Nowhere Else in the World* (1935), pp. 184–189.

5. The role of Ivan Maisky in 1919–1921 is somewhat obscure. He was in Urga from May to October 1919, then in western Mongolia with Burdukov preparing his famous book (*Sovremennaya Mongoliya*); he returned to Irkutsk around July 1920 (where he received ten pounds of butter and seventy pounds of flour for the manuscript). His official position was that of representative of *Tsentrosoyuz*, a Siberian trading organization. George Murphy stated: "We do not know definitely whether Maisky's mission was confined to examining the possibility of trade in Mongolia for Tsentrosoyuz, or had the wider purpose of arranging entry of Soviet forces into Outer Mongolia" (*Soviet Mongolia*, pp. 8–9). Murphy based his suspicions mainly on the testimony of D. P. Pershin, the tsarist official who emigrated and prepared a 1933 report (*Baron Ungern, Urga and Altan-Bulak*) filed at the Hoover Institution. Pershin, who was in Urga at the time, stated, for example: "Maisky acquainted himself with Urga and its inhabitants, found personnel suitable to the Bolsheviks, and inoculated them with Bolshevism" (p. 20).

It seems unlikely that Maisky was directly involved in "arranging entry of Soviet forces into Outer Mongolia," or in organizing the Mongolian revolutionary movement. He was isolated in western Mongolia when Hsü Shu-ch'eng's oppression led to anti-Chinese organization of Mongols. Shumyatsky and *Tsentrosibir'* returned to Irkutsk-Verkhneudinsk in February 1920 (when the defeated Kolchak was executed), and the Comintern connection with Urga was activated then. Maisky reappeared in Irkutsk (via Lake Khubsugul, rather than Urga) in June or July, but a letter of his written in early December was from Novonikolaevsk (Novosibirsk). Von Ungern-Sternberg's takeover of Urga occurred in February 1921. Khomutov, one of Burdukov's co-workers, sought out Maisky some time after von Ungern-Sternberg took over and before the Soviet Army's move in July; at that time Maisky was in

Novonikolaevsk serving as chairman of Siberian Gosplan, with no apparent connection to Mongolia. Shumyatsky, not Maisky, was the moving spirit in the Mongolian affair.

Maisky was a Menshevik who became a member of the Communist Party (Bolshevik) only in February 1921; he was still an active Menshevik in 1919. Except for the famous book published at Irkutsk in 1921, and one six-page article published in 1921, Maisky's prolific writing, including many book reviews, dealt entirely with European subjects: books on Germany in 1916 and 1917 when he was still in exile; a long pamphlet on the Hague Conference in 1922, and another book on Germany in 1924. His involvement with Mongolia was an aberration in his career, and it probably occurred because when he returned from exile to his family home at Omsk, the anti-Bolshevik success of the Czechs and of Kolchak forced him to leave Siberia.

A small Russian Bolshevik community already existed in Urga in 1919; Maisky was probably in contact with it, and perhaps met Choibalsan there. Sukhe Bator and most of the "revolutionary" Mongols were activated more by the oppression of Hsü Shu-ch'eng between October 1919 and July 1920 than by their "inoculation" by Maisky in mid-1919.

When Maisky was in Mongolia, he was thirty-five to thirty-six years old, and Burdukov was about the same age. Assisting Maisky were a twenty-year-old Irkutsk student, A. D. Kalinnikov, and an interpreter from the Mongolian school in Urga, Erdeni Batukhan, a Buryat Mongol who was then between twenty-five and thirty years old. Kalinnikov served as Russian diplomatic representative in Ulan Bator from 1925 through 1930 and wrote extensively about Mongolia; Batukhan became minister of education for the MPR. The Stalinist purges took both their lives in 1937, along with Burdukov's in 1943. Maisky was Soviet ambassador to England from 1932 through 1943, but he was arrested in February 1953 and was not freed and rehabilitated until 1956. He died in September 1975 at the age of ninety-one. A biography of Maisky and a bibliography appear in *Mezhdunarodnye otnosheniya*, pp. 3–22. See Burdukov, *V staroi*, pp. 389 n. 92, 394 n. 120, 395 n. 129, and 396 n. 130; S. D. Miliband, *Biobibliograficheskii slovar' sovetskikh vostokovedon*, pp. 663–664 (on Maisky) and p. 237 (on Kalinnikov).

6. Robert B. Valliant, "Japanese Involvement in Mongol Independence Movements, 1912–1919"; Gavan McCormack, *Chang Tso-lin in Northeast China, 1911–1928*.

7. B. D. Tsibikov, *Razgrom ungernovshchiny*, pp. 53–54; quoted in Rupen, *Mongols* 1:135. A. T. Yakimov, in "Bratstvo po oruzhiyu (Vospominaniya politrabotnika)" praised Rinchino for his services to the Bolsheviks during the Civil War, but N. D. Shulunov stated in "Obrazovanie buryatskoi ASSR" that Rinchino was a Japanese agent and a counterrevolutionary. Shulunov's book (*Stanovlenie sovetskoi natsional'noi gosudarstvennosti v Buryatii* [*1919–1923 gody*]) mercilessly attacked Rinchino as a bourgeois nationalist and a pan-Mongolist (pp. 88, 102, 262), as a sympathizer with Semenov (p. 105), and as an opponent of the Communist Konyaev in the summer of 1920 (p. 112 n. 2).

8. General William S. Graves, commander of the American Expeditionary Forces in Siberia, concluded: "No one could have been associated with Japanese military representatives as I was in Siberia, and escape the conviction that they always hoped to occupy Eastern Siberia" (*America's Siberian Adventure, 1918–1920*, p. 62). Evidence that the Japanese supplied arms to Semenov can be found in Morley, *Japanese Thrust*, Appendix J, pp. 354–355.

9. Pershin stated, for example, that Hsü Shu-ch'eng left behind in Urga "a

demoralized band of soldiers commanded by quarreling officers" (*Baron Ungern,* p. 17).

10. Ken S. Weigh argued that Chang procrastinated because of collusion with von Ungern-Sternberg (*Russo-Chinese Diplomacy, 1689–1924,* pp. 200–202). McCormack doubted that view (*Chang Tso-lin,* p. 275 n. 39), and found Chang Tso-lin less a Japanese puppet and more a Chinese nationalist than many believe. Japan generally supported Chang as a ruler in Manchuria, but not as a unifier of all China. Chang's plan for entering Mongolia from Mukden and Manchuli and moving on Urga along the Kerulen River from the east was supposed to culminate in a triumphal automobile caravan from Urga to Peking (p. 55).

Ignatius L. Yurin was named to negotiate with the Chinese in May 1920, and he was at Kyakhta in June and July waiting for China's acknowledgement and acquiescence. He finally arrived in Peking on August 26. He was recalled to Chita in May 1921, almost certainly in relation to events in Mongolia. As the official minister of foreign affairs for the Far Eastern Republic, Yurin left for Peking on July 16, and stopped at Mukden for discussions with Chang Tso-lin on July 23–24. Reportedly he offered Chang the withdrawal of Soviet forces from Urga in return for full Soviet participation in the management of the Chinese Eastern Railway, but Chang refused. See Sow-theng Leong, *Sino-Soviet Diplomatic Relations, 1917–1926,* pp. 154–156, 189–190. Also note Leong's quotations from Vilensky, Trotsky, and Lenin on pp. 136–137.

11. See *History of the MPR,* pp. 778 n. 31, 780 n. 75, and 782 n. 105.

12. Murphy, *Soviet Mongolia,* p. 2 n. 5.

13. Henry K. Norton, *The Far Eastern Republic of Siberia,* pp. 227–228. The Far Eastern Republic was founded April 6, 1920, at Verkhneudinsk (now Ulan Ude) as a buffer separating the regular Russian forces and the Japanese interventionists in Siberia. It was centered in Chita from October 28, 1920, until its incorporation into the RSFSR on November 16, 1922. The Far East Buro of the Russian Communist Party (Bolshevik)—CP(b)—became the Dal'buro Russian CP(b) in August 1920 and insured Russian control of the FER "to secure absolute and unconditional influence of the Central Committee Russian CP(b) and the Government of the RSFSR on the resolution of all important questions of internal and especially foreign policy" (I. Molokov, "Voennaya i ekonomicheskaya pomoshch' RSFSR DVR-e (1920–1922 gg.)," p. 75 n. 4).

Blyukher attended the FER-Japan conference at Dal'ny (Dairen) from August 1921 through April 1922, which arranged details of the evacuation of the Japanese from the Soviet Far East and Northern Sakhalin. A. I. Kartunova, *V. K. Blyukher v Kitae 1924–1927 gg.,* p. 32 n. 39. N. I. Lukashuk provided information about the army of the FER, and B. M. Shereshevskii described the FER's party organization and its economic situation (*Voprosy istorii Sovetskoi Sibiri,* no. 1 and no. 5 (1957 and 1962)).

14. See Allen S. Whiting, *Soviet Policies in China, 1917–1924,* pp. 81–82.

15. Ibid., pp. 73–74, concerning the anti-British thrust; see also Conrad Brandt, *Stalin's Failure in China, 1924–1927,* p. 15. For information on Tibet, see Amur-Sanan, "The Importance of Buddhist Mongolia to the World Revolution"; idem, *Mudreshkin syn;* and L. Berlin [B–n], "Khambo-Agvan Dorzhiev (k bor'be Tibeta za nezavisimost')." Stalin noted in 1923: "All we have to do is make one small mistake in relation to the small territory of the Kalmyks, who have ties with Tibet and China, and that will affect our work in a far worse way than mistakes in regard to the Ukraine" (Aleksandr Nekrich, *The Punished Peoples: The Deportation and Fate of Soviet Minorities at the End of the Second World War,* p. 99).

16. Pershin, *Baron Ungern*, p. 30. The *History of the MPR*, Brown and Onon (trans.) indicated that there was a lack of unity: "there was a strong, sharp struggle between Sukhe Bator's adherents and certain members of the bourgeois nationalist-minded group who were attempting to limit their goals to the restoration of Autonomy" (p. 77).

17. Murphy, *Soviet Mongolia*, pp. 6–7, 10; and Hammond, "Communist Take-over," pp. 118, 120, 122, 125, considered the von Ungern-Sternberg factor only an excuse. See note 3, chapter 3.

18. Moves in the fall of 1920 toward starting the Mongolian youth movement were described by Ts. Erdenebilig in "U istokov Revsomola," *Novosti Mongolii*, June 24, 1977. F. R. Konyaev played an important role. See also Rupen, *Mongols*, 1:195, and 215 n. 68.

19. Rupen, *Mongols*, 1:194 (Lenin, point 3); for the early oath and platform, and other documents, see pp. 136–141 in that book.

20. References in *History of the MPR* for Shumyatsky are pp. 74 and 758 n. 104; for Borisov, pp. 72 and 758 n. 103: and for Rinchino, pp. 74, 758 n. 106, and 771 n. 103.

21. A. T. Yakimov listed the following as having been Russian Bolsheviks active in Urga: Gembarzhevsky, Kucherenko, Sorokovikov, Cherepanov, Maslakov, Agafonov, Anchugov, Zaporin, Kopyton, and Byzov ("MNRP–organizator i vdokhnovitel' pobed mongol'skago naroda," p. 57). The *History of the MPR* noted: "The fact that Choibalsan interpreted when members of the groups met with Gembarzhevsky and Kucherenko greatly helped him to gain an even more profound understanding of the ideology of the October Revolution" (p. 69).

22. There was at least one active female Buryat Bolshevik: Mariya Sakh'yanova (see Rupen, *Mongols*, 1:150 n. 26). Her daughter, Larissa, became prima ballerina of the Buryat Mongolian company; see Afrikan Bal'burov, *Dvenadtsot' moikh dragotsennostei*, p. 80, and a photograph of Larissa just before p. 129.

23. The first military commandant of the city of Urga, named on July 8, 1921, was the Kalmyk K. B. Kanukov. Fifty Kalmyk veterans from Astrakhan arrived in Urga in August 1921: "We were proud in the knowledge of the high honor of being sent to assist the fraternal Mongolian people" (S. G. Baltykov, "V ryadakh mongol'skoi narodnoi armii. Vospominaniya." *Kniga bratstva*, p. 108). For information on Khomutnikov, see *Novosti Mongolii*, June 21, 1974.

24. The twelve Soviet military instructors who began to work in the MPR in September 1923 were: D. I. Kosich (leader); N. S. Sorkin; V. I. Dmitrenko; L. Ya. Vainer; Beloglazov; A. O. Petrov; N. M. Glavatsky; Boiko; A. S. Orlov; Petrovsky; Shamin; and Yakimovich. N. S. Sorkin, *V nachale puti (zapiski instruktora mongol'skoi armii)*.

25. See Charles R. Bawden, *The Modern History of Mongolia*, pp. 277–282.

26. Barbara Tuchman, *Stilwell and the American Experience in China, 1911–1945*, p. 89.

27. For the sad state of the Mongolian army, see Marguerite Harrison, *Red Bear or Yellow Dragon*, p. 202 (quoted in Rupen, *Mongols*, p. 208). Ma Ho-tien's view was not as negative (*Chinese Agent in Mongolia*, pp. 104–106). The Russian chief of staff, whom Ma referred to as K'ang-ko-la-li, was Kangelari, who succeeded Kosich.

28. Rupen, *Mongols*, 1:198–199, 217 n. 83. For information on American officials who visited Urga and reported on conditions there, see *History of the MPR*, pp. 753 n. 74, 759 n. 110, and 788 n. 190.

29. K. A. Neiman led the Red Army into Mongolia on June 27, 1921; see Murphy, *Soviet Mongolia*, p. 1, and *Novosti Mongolii*, August 20, 1974. The fact that K. K. Rokossovsky took an active part (Rokossovsky, "My vsegda vmeste," *Narody brat'ya*, pp. 5–11 and Burdukov, *V staroi*, p. 398 n. 140) adds force to Thomas T. Hammond's suggestion that Mongolia served as a model for the Communist takeover in Eastern Europe ("Communist Takeover," pp. 127–128), where Hammond compared the roles of Choibalsan in Mongolia and Rokossovsky in Eastern Europe after World War II. See also Shulunov, *Stanovlenie*, pp. 302–303.

30. The siege of Tolbo Nur of 1921 wherein the Red Army saved the encircled Mongols from the Whites is described by Damba Dorji [Ulan Otorchi] in "Ozero Tolbo." A monument was erected at Tolbo Nur on February 19, 1958.

31. See Rupen, *Mongols*, 1:214 n. 56 and *History of the MPR*, p. 799 n. 64.

32. Burdukov, *V staroi*, p. 117.

33. *History of the MPR*, p. 273. Nicholas Roerich noted that "All through the Central Gobi, the legend of Ja Lama will persist for a long time" (*Altai-Himalaya*, pp. 355–357). George Roerich reported that "The deeds and cruel massacres of Ja Lama were still on the lips of local nomads. . . . Even at present, some six years after the death of the man, Mongols feel an unholy dread of him" (*Trails to Inmost Asia*, pp. 190, 223; also pp. 209–213 and 223–234).

34. Soviet military aid to Feng Yu-hsiang is thoroughly documented: Brandt, *Stalin's Failure*, p. 204 n. 23; Rupen, *Mongols*, 1:107–108 211 n. 19 (Feng's career). See James E. Sheridan, *Chinese Warlord*.

35. Rupen, *Mongols*, 1:211 n. 17.

36. *History of the MPR*, p. 273.

In January 1928, in Tibet not far from Lhasa, George Roerich heard a version of the Russian Revolution that included an account of the fate of the tsar ("Tsagan-bator khan," the White tsar) and of the attempted assassination of Lenin (*Trails to Inmost Asia*, p. 389):

> The khan-po [Tibetan official] told us that formerly the religion of Russia had been somewhat similar to the religion of Tibet, but since the victory of the Reds, there was no religion in Russia. Present-day Russia was ruled by a man who killed the Tsagan-bator Khan with a revolver. Pictures of this man were to be seen everywhere and his name was Nenin. This man on committing the deed, climbed a high tree and proclaimed from the top of it that Tsagan-bator Khan was no more, and that the religion of Yisu (Jesus) and Buddha had been destroyed. But, unfortunately for him, a woman possessing the knowledge of Red and White customs, who was formerly the wife of a big official under the Tsagan-bator Khan, was still alive, and resolved to revenge the death of the great Khan. She approached the man ruling Russia and shot him dead, after which she committed suicide! That is the story of the Russian Revolution according to Lhasa.

37. O. Edmund Clubb, *China and Russia*, p. 237.

38. Tsedenbal, *Izbrannye stat'i i rechi, 1962–1973*, p. 552.

39. Sheridan, *Chinese Warlord*, pp. 151–152.

40. McCormack, *Chang Tso-lin*, p. 175.

41. Ibid., pp. 118–119, 175, 256, 288 n. 30; Leong, *Sino-Soviet Relations*, pp. 282–283, 288. McCormack noted (p. 305 n. 126): "Evidently Chang Hsueh-liang . . . made a special trip to see General Shirakawa, Kwantung Army commander, at the critical

time in December 1925, and it is worth noting that Chang Tso-lin made a special, and most unusual, visit to Shirakawa in the summer of 1926 to express thanks for the aid given him." Leong recorded that "The Japanese military attache in Peking . . . argues quite plausibly that Japan's military occupation of north Manchuria was one reason for Soviet military intervention in Outer Mongolia" (p. 320 n. 7).

42. Ma Ho-tien, *Chinese Agent,* pp. 115, 162.

43. Sheridan, *Chinese Warlord,* pp. 197–202. Feng went on to Moscow from Ulan Bator, and left there to return to China in September 1926. Mao I-heng, Feng's aide, accompanied his patron to Moscow and wrote about his experiences in *O-meng Hui-i-lu* [Reminiscences of Russia and Mongolia]. See Yueh Sheng, *Sun Yat-sen University in Moscow and the Chinese Revolution,* p. 98 and 105 n. 4.

44. M. F. Perkins's report of August 1928, in U.S. Department of State, *Foreign Relations of the United States,* vol. 2, pp. 166–167:

> During the middle of the month a series of raids took place in the Barga district of Inner Mongolia, organized by "young Mongols" with communistic leanings. A small body of Outer Mongolian troops officered by Russians crossed the Barga frontier and clashed with Chinese troops near Arshan, and Mongol cavalry cut the western line of the Chinese Eastern Railway as far south as Barim. It is possible that there was here involved a movement instigated by Soviet agents for reasons not clear at this time, forcibly to bring about the unification of the various Mongol tribes under the aegis of the red Mongolian Republic whose capital is Urga. . . . The movement had apparently been temporarily suppressed and . . . railway traffic had been resumed.

A press report of September 8, 1928, quoted in Perkins, indicated: "According to a Reuter message from Mukden, the Mongolian Soviet Republic, probably with the foreknowledge and approval of Soviet Russia, is plotting to detach this district [Barga] and incorporate it with Outer Mongolia, thus extending the territory of the latter across the Western branch of the Chinese Eastern Railroad." In fact, Manchurian troops quickly drove out the Mongols. In November 1929 a Comintern journal attacked Merse as a renegade and traitor to the Mongolian Revolution; in the interim (October 3–December 10, 1928) the Seventh Congress of the MPRP had deposed Damba Dorji and condemned rightist deviation, and in December 1928 the young marshal subordinated himself and Manchuria to Chiang Kai-shek and the Kuomintang. Chang Tso-lin had been killed in early June 1928. See V. A. Kormazov, "Kochevaya Barga." J. B. Powell based his articles in *The China Weekly Review* ("The Soviet Atrocities in Barga" and "The Sino-Russian-Mongolian Struggle in Barga") on Kormazov. See also Gerard M. Friters, *Outer Mongolia and Its International Position,* p. 133; Merse [Kuo Tao-fu] *Meng-ku wen-t'i chiang-yen lu* [Discussion of the Mongolian Question]; and *History of the MPR,* p. 811 n. 66.

45. Alonzo W. Pond, *Andrews,* p. 149. For Andrews's connection with U.S. Naval Intelligence, see pp. 83, 147. Andrews's agent in Urga was Larsen (p. 123); the U.S. consul at Kalgan, Sokobin, dealt with Larsen and went to Urga several times, and the U.S. military attaché in Peking, *the* Joseph Stilwell, went to Urga in June 1923. Note also the novel by M. S. Kolesnikov, "A Soviet Historical Novel About Mongolia," which deals extensively with Roy Chapman Andrews and Mongolian suspicions about him. Compare my review "A Soviet Historical Novel About Mongolia" [Kolesnikov]. For Sokobin, see *History of the MPR,* pp. 753 n. 74, 796 n. 45, and 801 n. 80.

George Roerich's "defection" to the USSR in 1957 after four decades of life in America and India (including higher education in London, at Harvard in the United States, and at the Sorbonne in Paris), as well as Nicholas Roerich's pro-Soviet stance in the 1930s and 1940s, suggest the possibility of espionage activity. Ambiguity and scarcity of relevant evidence for the years 1924–1927, and the apparent suppression of facts about the Roerichs' visit to Moscow in the summer of 1926 in George's book *Trails to Inmost Asia* raise questions that are difficult to answer. Chronological coincidence—or was it more than coincidence?—had the Roerichs in Moscow at the same time Feng Yu-hsiang was there (Roerichs—June 13 to early August 1926; Feng—May 9 to August 17), and the Roerichs were in Urga from September 26, 1926, to April 15, 1927, while Ma Ho-tien, a Kuomintang representative, was there from December 22, 1926, to February 12, 1927. Roy Chapman Andrews complained that official harassment made it impossible for foreigners to work in Mongolia in 1926, and the Austrian artist, Roland Strasser, was jailed when he arrived in Urga without permission. The Roerichs' "American Expedition" had no trouble at all, however; it enjoyed full official Soviet and Mongolian cooperation and encouragement.

There appear to be three competing scenarios: (1) what actually happened; (2) selective and misleading reporting by the Roerichs; and (3) the version appearing in recent Soviet publications that adds considerable misleading embellishment to selective factual review and some deliberate misstatement of fact.

The facts seem to be that the Roerichs (Nicholas, his wife, and his son George) went from New York to northern India and that Nicholas arranged passports and American political and financial support for the "Roerich American Artistic-Cultural Expedition" in New York and Washington in September 1924. Nicholas then went to Berlin and contacted a Soviet representative there to try to arrange approval for the part of the journey planned in Soviet and Soviet-controlled territory (Altai, Baikal, and MPR). The Soviet commissar for foreign affairs, G. V. Chicherin, knew about Nicholas Roerich and was sympathetic to his plan, but nothing was finally arranged in 1924. The Roerichs were in contact with Soviet officials in Kashgar and Urumchi (Sinkiang), and they intended all along to go into the USSR as part of the trip. They crossed into the Soviet Union on May 17, 1926, went to Moscow—where they met Chicherin and A. V. Lunacharsky, Russian commissar for education, and where two colleagues from New York, M. M. Lichtman and Mrs. Lichtman, joined them. The Lichtmans and the Roerichs went on a tour of the Altai region of Western Siberia (Barnaul, Biisk, and so on) in August, and then the Roerichs proceeded to Baikal and arrived in Urga on September 26. Mr. and Mrs. Lichtman later came from New York with supplies and equipment, joining the Roerichs in Urga in March 1927. The Roerichs left Urga for Lhasa on April 15, 1927. They were never permitted to go to Lhasa, however, and only after severe hardship on the northern border of Tibet were they permitted to cross Tibetan territory to Northern India, which they finally reached in May 1928.

The accounts published by the Roerichs make no mention of the 1924 Berlin contact, the Moscow portion of the sojourn in the USSR, or any Russian background and connections. Both Nicholas and George Roerich generously acknowledge the assistance of Americans and of British officials in Sinkiang and northern India (particularly Colonel F. M. Bailey, British political officer in Tibet, Sikkim, and Bhutan, and Major Gillian, British consul-general at Kashgar), but do not mention Chicherin or any Russian or Soviet assistance. They said that the USSR portion of the expedition's route stemmed from their unhappy experiences with Chinese authorities in Sinkiang and warnings at Kashgar and Urumchi that Chinese would continue to hinder their work—that because of inevitable Chinese obstructionism and the unsettled political and military conditions then prevailing in Kansu province, they would be better advised to go via Siberia. In their published accounts the Roerichs said that they relied on the precedent of Soviet approval six months earlier of transit via Siberia for Alan Priest (a friend of George Roerich and later curator of Oriental art at the Metropolitan Museum in New York City).

Recent books published in the USSR indicate that in Berlin in December 1924 Nicholas Roerich assured the Soviet representative there that he was a close friend of Indian and Asian leaders who believed in the future of Russia and its mission of liberation from British imperialism. Soviet consuls at Kashgar and Urumchi supplied the Roerichs with Soviet newspapers and information, while the British were spreading unfounded rumors that the Roerichs were "Red spies." At Kashgar in February 1926 Nicholas Roerich purportedly underlined the anticolonial significance of his work and in Urumchi he was in almost daily direct contact with the Soviet consul. The Moscow visit was known only to a few people. Nicholas Roerich extended to Chicherin a greeting from Mahatma Gandhi to the Soviet people, expressed his enthusiasm for the October Revolution, and clearly indicated his undying patriotic feelings for Russia. Chicherin and Lunacharsky encouraged the Roerichs to continue to work for the close connection of the Soviet Union with Asian countries and peoples. Charges published in the USSR in the 1930s that Nicholas Roerich had "rejected the Bolsheviks" and had in fact "served world capitalism" were said by Soviet authors in the 1970s to have been absurd.

The account above is based principally on George Roerich, *Trails to Inmost Asia;* Nicholas Roerich, *Altai-Himalaya;* P. Belikov and V. Knyazeva, *Rerikh;* and E. I. Polyakova, *Nikolai Rerikh.*

46. See note 19, Chapter 3.

47. Charles R. Bawden, "An Event in the Life of the Eighth Jebtsun Damba Khutukhtu." Near the Russian border north of Ulan Bator, George Roerich noted stories circulating in 1926 about the finding of a ninth Jebtsun Damba Khutukhtu (*Trails to Inmost Asia,* p. 132):

> Here on the banks of the Iro, a boy was recently born who manifested strange faculties. Mysterious signs accompanied his birth. His mother, a shaman woman, heard mysterious voices, and the boy himself uttered amazing prophecies about the future glory of Buddhist Mongolia. The news of the appearance of the strange child spread like lightning all over Mongolia. The lamas everywhere whispered about the coming of a new incarnation of Jebtsun Damba Khutukhtu. The Government of the Republic was obliged to send out a commission of inquiry and to post proclamations in Urga [Ulan Bator] to calm the population. It is sometimes difficult to discount rumors by printed words and the news about the new Bogdo Gegen [Jebtsun Damba Khutukhtu] continues to agitate the minds of the deeply religious Mongols. This boy is not the only candidate to the vacant throne of the Mongolian Pontiff. There is another—a boy known to have appeared in Inner Mongolia, who is now studying in some of the lamaseries within the Chinese border.

See also N. Roerich, *Altai-Himalaya,* p. 343.

48. Natsov in *Kommunisticheskii Internatsional',* no. 33–34 (August 31, 1928), p. 71. Belikov and Knyazeva, in *Rerikh,* ascribed authorship of the pamphlets to E. I. Roerich, Nicholas's wife (pp. 80–81). She had allegedly written a book published in Urga and known in Buryat Mongolia that "bases socialism on principles of ancient Buddhism," and that book was included unchanged as part of another anonymous one. George Roerich observed of Jamtsarano, whom he met when he was in Urga, that "in his deep knowledge he possesses a singular gift of unfolding the ancient sacred lore of Mongolia and Tibet"; Jamtsarano accompanied the Roerich caravan

for some distance when it left Urga in April 1927. (George Roerich, *Trails to Inmost Asia*, pp. 151, 178.) Chicherin called Nicholas Roerich "half Communist-half Buddhist" (Belikov and Knyazeva, *Rerikh*, p. 183), and Batorov stated that the "chief ideologue" of the modernization of Buddhism was Agvan Dorjeev (p. 333). Belikov and Knyazeva indicated that Nicholas Roerich knew Agvan Dorjeev in Russia before 1917 (pp. 127–128). See also Rupen, *Mongols*, 1:36.

49. Sorkin, *V nachale puti. Narody Azii i Afriki*, no. 4 (1976), pp. 213–14, reported publication of a new book, *Materialy po izucheniyu istochnikov indo-tibetskoi meditsiny*. Tibetan medicine was a particular subject of inquiry at the Roerich Institute's laboratory in northern India in the 1930s and 1940s.

50. Walter Kolarz, *The Peoples of the Soviet Far East*, p. 117. Sir Charles Bell, *Portrait of the Dalai Lama*, pp. 366–367, reported that there were Mongols in Lhasa in 1927: "They were clearly agents of the Soviet." See also Rupen, *Mongols*, 1:209–210. The Roerichs reported that a representative of the Lhasa government was in Urga, Buryat pilgrims were going to Tibet, and trading caravans were going in both directions in 1927–1928 (Nicholas Roerich, *Altai-Himalaya*, pp. 290 and 351; George Roerich, *Trails to Inmost Asia*, p. 301; and Belikov and Knyazeva, *Rerikh*, p. 184).

51. Xenia J. Eudin and Robert M. Slusser, *Soviet Foreign Policy, 1928–1934*, vol. 1, p. 21.

52. Ma Ho-tien, *Chinese Agent*, pp. 37, 45–46, 68, 79, 91, 95, 102. Other especially useful sources describing Mongolia and Urga from firsthand experience in the mid-1920s include George Roerich, *Trails to Inmost Asia*, pp. 133–164; Fritz Weiske, "Die wirtschaftlichen Verhältnisse in der Äusseren Mongolei" (Weiske was a mining engineer who worked for a year and a half as an adviser to the Mongolian government); and Roland Strasser, *The Mongolian Horde* (New York, 1930; Strasser was an Austrian artist who came without authorization via Tibet and spent some time in prison in Urga).

53. See photographs Nos. 34 and 37 in Rupen, *Mongols*, vol. 1. It cost more than ten times as much to send a Mongolian student to Germany or France and maintain him there as it did in Moscow. Cf. Rupen, *Mongols*, 1:222 n. 137. See Serge Wolff, "Mongolian Educational Venture in Western Europe (1926–1929)." Between 1922 and 1972, 15,104 Mongols received higher education in the USSR, including 2,209 at Moscow, 704 at Irkutsk, 648 at Leningrad, 400 at Ulan Ude, 220 at Kiev, and 154 at Sverdlovsk (B. Shirendyb, *Izbrannye proizvodeniya*, p. 332). For the Communist University of the Toilers of the East (KUTV), see Rupen, *Mongols*, 1:222 n.136, and N. N. Timofeeva, "KUTV (1921–1925)." Between 1921 and 1936, 229 Mongols attended KUTV (*Ocherki istorii kul'tury MNR*, p. 310).

Sun Yat-sen University opened in Moscow in 1925, became KUTK (Communist University for Workers of China) in 1928, and closed in 1930. Ulanfu, who became the leader of Inner Mongolia in the Communist regime after World War II, attended Sun Yat-sen University, but most of the students were ethnic Chinese. Teng Hsiao-p'ing is also a graduate. (Yueh Sheng, *Sun Yat-sen University in Moscow and the Chinese Revolution*.)

54. Ma Ho-tien, *Chinese Agent*, pp. 18–20, 74–75. Fritz Weiske judged that "Development of Mongolia without the Chinese is impossible" ("Die wirtschaftlichen Verhältnisse in der Äusseren Mongolei," p. 165).

55. In addition to Amagaev, the editorial board of *Khozyaistvo Mongolii* consisted of L. G. Gavrilov, D. D. Mikhel'man, and B. I. Onishchenko; all three were board members of the Mongolian Bank. See "Soderzhanie zhurnala 'Khozyaistvo Mongolii' (Ulan Bator 1926–1931 gg.)."

56. *History of the MPR,* p. 221.

57. Violet Conolly concluded in 1933: "The large increase in all Soviet manufactured goods exported to Mongolia is certainly not a question of superior quality and better assortment, but is mainly due to the fact that the Soviets have succeeded in excluding their foreign competitors . . . from the market as a result of the Mongolian foreign-trade monopoly." (*Soviet Economic Policy in the East,* p. 10; see also p. 108).

Choibalsan blamed "enemies of the Revolution" for the loss in 1924 of 5.7 million head of livestock, at least one third of the total. There was no collectivization policy to explain such massive destruction. The most likely source of trouble for the regime was the Buddhist Church. The death of the Jebtsun Damba Khutukhtu in May and plans for the confiscation and redistribution of church property (which included as much as 4 million head of livestock) are a possible explanation. The *History of the MPR,* pp. 191–192, noted "the powerful spread of counter-revolutionary rumors among the population that the People's Government intended to attack religion." Nonetheless, the loss of almost 6 million head, in the conditions of 1924, is very difficult to explain by political reasons alone. Very bad weather combined with political unrest might have caused heavy losses. Any set of data related to the early 1920s is suspect because of the very poor statistical base; to treat Maisky's data (the 1918 census) as though they were reliable would be, in my opinion, a serious mistake. He admitted to adding large round figures, such as "25 percent," because the census count must have been too low (it did not even pretend to cover western Mongolia). My assumption had always been that Choibalsan would never have wanted the losses to look worse than they actually were, so I have accepted his 5.7 million figure, but I am unable to explain it in any convincing manner.

58. *History of the MPR,* p. 236.

59. Shoizhelov [Natsov], "Sotsial'no-ekonomicheskie korni pravyi opasnosti v MNRP," pp. 38–47.

60. A. L. Strong, *China's Millions. Book 2: Across China's Northwest and Gobi Desert to Moscow with Borodin and Marshal Feng.* For an account of Borodin's ignominious return to Moscow, see Yueh Sheng, *Sun Yat-sen University,* pp. 129–130.

Comintern representatives in Mongolia included the Buryats Rinchen, and Amagaev; the Altai Oirat Borisov; the Kazakh Ryskulov; the Czech Shmeral; and the Bulgarian Kolarov.

61. *History of the MPR,* p. 238. Reports on the Seventh MPRP Congress can be found in: *Revolyutsionnyi Vostok,* no. 17 (1929), and *Khozyaistvo Mongolii,* no. 1(14; Jan.–Feb. 1929).

62. While both the Russians and the Mongols wanted to exclude the Chinese from any effective political role in Outer Mongolia, the Russians also wanted to influence the revolutionary movement in China. That dilemma was never satisfactorily resolved. It was dramatized in 1921 when the Mongol-Soviet Conference met in Moscow on October 26, just two days after Alexander K. Paikes had left Moscow for Peking. Russia and Mongolia concluded a treaty on November 5; the Paikes mission arrived in Peking on December 12, 1921. As Whiting put it, "There was no reason to assume that this treaty [Russia-Mongolia] aimed at anything other than the establishment of an independent Mongolian government" (*Soviet Policies in China 1917–1924,* pp. 173–174). Paikes's position in China was rendered awkward, if not impossible.

63. The negotiators included Sukhe Bator, Danzan, Tseren Dorji, Shirnin (representing the Jebtsun Damba Khutukhtu), Dava (the secretary), Batukhan (the interpreter), and the Russians, L. Berlin (the NKID representative), S. I. Dukhovsky (of the Far Eastern section, NKID), B. F. Gets (of the Economic and Legal section,

Narkomindel), Ochirov (a Buryat, an interpreter), Chicherin (the commissar for Foreign Affairs), and B. Shumyatsky. (L. E. Berlin, "U istokov Sovetsko-mongol'skoi druzhby.") Note also G. S. Matveeva, "V. I. Lenin i mongol'skie revolyutsionary" and I. M. Shastitko, "Novye materialy o vzglyadakh V. I. Lenina u natsional'no-kolonial'nomu voprosu."

N. Tsultem, who is now a candidate-member of the Central Committee of the MPRP and has been chairman of the Union of Mongolian Artists for more than twenty years, gained fame and fortune for his painting of Sukhe Bator meeting Lenin (reproduced opposite p. 128 in *Ocherki istorii kul'tury MNR*). On pages 413–415 the painting is described and analyzed. Tsultem studied with Russians at the Moscow Artists' Institute.

64. *History of the MPR*, p. 789 n. 193.

65. See Ma Ho-tien, *Chinese Agent*, p. 115:

[M]ost of the leaders in the Mongol People's Party are Rightists who advocate union with China. Damba Dorji, the present chairman of the Central Executive Committee, is an example. Although educated in Russia, he is antagonistic to that country and is strongly in favor of joining with the Chinese Kuomintang in order to reduce the power of the Russians. He is especially disliked by the Revolutionary Youth League. The Chinese Kuomintang should find a way to work with him so as to strengthen his hand. Otherwise it is to be feared that the Revolutionary Youth League, under the manipulation and guidance of Soviet Russia, will make it impossible to entertain any hopes for the future of Outer Mongolia.

66. Conrad Brandt, *Stalin's Failure*, p. 47.

67. Ibid., p. 127.

68. For information about the Communist Youth International and Comintern, see E. H. Carr, *The Bolshevik Revolution, 1917–1923*, vol. 3, pp. 401–404. See also Carr, *Socialism in One Country, 1924–1926*, vol. 2, pp. 88–107, where he concluded: "The 14th Party Congress [1926] marked the end of an illusion. . . . Henceforth the Komsomol was a junior branch of the Party, echoing its doctrines and practices, and following its fortunes in every detail" (page 107).

69. A Revsomol representative at the Third Mongolian Party Congress of 1924 indicated that relations between the party and the Revsomols in Mongolia would be decided by the Comintern in Moscow. See Rupen, *Mongols*, 1:197.

70. Most important in Tuva, but also often of great importance in the MPR were the Russians Shchetinkin and Starkov, and the Buryats Chenkirov and Natsov.

71. V. A. Kuchumov was a Mongolian specialist in the Comintern who in the 1920s led the Chinese students of Sun Yat-sen University on tours of the MPR; he later became vice-rector of that school (Yueh Sheng, *Sun Yat-sen University*, p. 38). The bibliography lists two articles on Mongolia that he published in 1931.

O. S. Tarkhanov [S. P. Razumov; Yang Chu-lai—1901–1944] worked in China 1925–1926 and in Mongolia 1934–1937. His writings dealt with China and Japan (see Miliband, *Biobibliograficheskii*, pp. 543–544).

M. I. Tubyanskii (1893–1943) taught Bengali in Leningrad 1920–1927, then worked as an adviser to the Soviet representative in the MPR 1927–1936, and also as scientific secretary of the Mongolian Scientific Committee 1930–1936. In 1937 he returned to teaching and writing about Bengali language and literature (Miliband, *Bio-bibliograficheskii*, p. 557).

4. Stalin and Japan: 1929–1939

1. Stalin to Chiang Ching-kuo, July 1945, as paraphrased in O. Edmund Clubb, *China and Russia*, p. 344.

2. An especially fine overall survey is provided by O. Edmund Clubb in "Armed Conflict in the Chinese Borderlands, 1917–1950."

3. Clubb, *China and Russia*, p. 318. See also George Lensen, "Yalta and the Far East," p. 130. *History of the MPR* suggested that: "There is basis for believing that the failure of the Japanese militarists to attack the Soviet nation simultaneously with Hitler's Germany in 1941, and their awaiting the weakening of Soviet forces, was connected with the historical lesson of Khalkin-gol [Nomonkhan]" (p. 356). In *Unconquered* (pp. 317–18), James Bertram stated his belief that the turning point came more than a year before Nomonkhan:

> Up to the spring of 1938 . . . an extension of the Far East hostilities to include the Soviet Union seemed by no means unlikely. . . . the preponderant Japanese strength accumulated at this time in Manchuria. But the events of that spring completely altered the picture.
> [T]he battle of Taierchwan . . . ushered in an entirely new phase of the war. . . .
> More troops, and good troops, were badly needed in Central China; and they could only come from the North.
> [F]or the first time Japan was drawing upon the reserves hitherto kept for action against the USSR. Any attack on Russia must now be abandoned, probably for the duration of the China war.
> I traveled across Manchuria in April [1938]. Several divisions had already left for the south.

See Gerard M. Friters, *Outer Mongolia and Its International Position*, pp. 147–148 and 238–241; Clubb, "Armed Conflict," pp. 30–40; N. N. Kuznetsov, *Podvigi geroev Khalkin-gola;* S. Shishkin, *Khalkin-gol;* Larry Moses, "Soviet-Japanese Confrontation in Outer Mongolia." See also several articles in *Voenno-istoricheskii zhurnal:* no. 7 (July 1964), pp. 126–128; no. 8 (Aug. 1969), pp. 31–41; no. 9 (Sept. 1969), pp. 74–76; no. 6 (June 1971), pp. 38–47; no. 11 (Nov. 1971), pp. 38–47; and no. 8 (Aug. 1975), pp. 72–77 (by Fedyuninsky). More extensive bibliographies can be found in G. S. Gorodova, "Sovetskaya memuarnaya literatura o Mongolii," p. 169 n. 7; *History of the MPR*, pp. 822 n. 79 and 823 n. 85; and Rupen, *Mongols*, 1:247 n. 11.

4. A. I. Gekker was commander of the Eleventh Red Army in 1920. He served as military attaché in Peking in 1925, and probably worked with Blyukher in China. He became a trouble-shooting inspector in the army and was Head of Red Army Foreign Liaison; he disappeared in April 1937 and was reportedly shot on July 1, 1937. See Rupen, *Mongols*, 1:223 n. 143.

5. See Clubb, "Armed Conflict," p. 27. In the latter part of 1934 there were rumors of Inner Mongolian-Outer Mongolian (that is, Chinese-Russian) agreement to cooperate on roads and communications, but the Japanese advance aborted it. See Rupen, *Mongols*, 1:246 n. 2. Robert M. Slusser and Jan F. Triska, in *A Calendar of Soviet Treaties, 1917–1957*, cited an exchange of notes between the USSR and Japan (i.e., Manchukuo) concerning sale of the CER (June 3, 1933), and a protocol fixing payment by Manchukuo to the USSR (Mar. 23, 1935).

The Manchuli (Manchukuo-MPR) Conference, held from June through November 1935, was a politically sensitive affair, with the Japanese later executing several of the Hsingan-Mongol participants (F. C. Jones, *Manchuria Since 1931*, pp. 60–68). The charges made in the MPR in 1937 against Demid and Gendun included the allegation that they sent "pro-Japanese spies" to Manchuli in 1935 (Rupen, *Mongols,* 1:250 n. 47).

Nicholas and George Roerich were in Manchuria and at Kalgan in 1934–1935, at least nominally for scientific purposes. Henry Wallace, who was then U.S. secretary of agriculture, was influential in obtaining permission from the Japanese government for them to work in Manchuria; he also interceded with the Chinese government at Peking to try to gain permission for the Roerichs to tour North China and Inner Mongolia extensively. The Roerichs were actually in Manchuria, in Barga and other areas bordering on the USSR and the MPR, as well as at Harbin and Kalgan. Officially it was an "expedition for U.S. Department of Agriculture through China and Mongolia in search of drought resisting grasses for America" (*Who Was Who in America,* vol. 2 [Chicago, 1950], p. 456).

Nicholas Roerich himself, as well as societies and organizations sponsored by him or bearing his name and indeed most activities in any way connected with him, had by this time taken on a strong "peace" orientation, and increasingly a role as a public defender of the USSR. Since he spent much of his five months in Harbin in 1934–1935 delivering "patriotic" lectures vigorously defending the peaceful intentions and the Russian-nationalist legitimacy of the Soviet regime, the anti-Communist Russian emigrés in Harbin, Paris, and elsewhere, attacked him as a dupe and/or a spy. He became extremely controversial, but gave no ground to his detractors and opponents. Emigré Russian communities everywhere, as well as many non-Russians all over the world, faced a choice between supporting the defense of Russia against German and Japanese Fascism, or condemning Stalin and Communism. Nicholas Roerich seemed to find no dilemma; he did not appear to be torn by any doubt. President Roosevelt's favorable mention of the Roerich "Peace Pact" in a radio speech in April 1935 was a proud "victory" for Roerich's cause, but of course it only intensified the controversy. The reference by FDR was in a brief statement on Pan-American Day, April 15, 1935, congratulating the Latin Americans on signing a "Treaty on the Protection of Artistic and Scientific Institutions and Historic Monuments." The text of that treaty did indeed come directly from Nicholas Roerich's "Peace Pact." See Belikov and Knyazeva, *Rerikh,* pp. 220–224; Polyakova, *Nikolai Rerikh,* pp. 274–275.

6. G. K. Plotnikov, *Mongol'skaya narodnaya armiya.*

7. Aleksander Solzhenitsyn, *Gulag Archipelago Two,* pp. 377–378.

8. Walter Kolarz, *Russia and Her Colonies,* p. 173.

9. See Robert Conquest, *The Great Terror,* p. 247, for Stalin's rage at Vareikis and the sensitivity regarding Blyukher and the Far East Army at that time. For more information concerning Vareikis in 1925, see E. H. Carr, *Socialism in One Country, 1924–1926* vol. 2, p. 96 n. 5.

See also Z. Sh. Yanguzov, *OKDVA na strazhe mira i bezopasnosti SSSR (1929–1938 gg.),* pp. 226–231, wherein the name list indicates that twenty-one of twenty-eight leading officers of the Special Far Eastern Army died between 1937 and 1943: eight in 1937, four in 1938, two in 1939, three in 1940, two in 1941, one in 1942, and one in 1943. Four of the twenty-eight were still alive in 1970.

10. Alvin D. Coox, *"L'Affaire* Lyushkov." Lyushkov was captured by the Red Army in Manchuria in 1945, and was undoubtedly executed.

11. Rupen, *Mongols,* 1:246 n. 7, concerning Blyukher's posthumous rehabilitation.

12. *History of the MPR,* p. 345. A biographical sketch of Demid appeared in *Sovremennaya Mongoliya,* no. 4–5 (17–18), 1936. Demid published a *History of the*

Development of the Red Army (in Mongolian) in Ulan Bator in 1931. Choibalsan, Demid, and Losol jointly published a *History of the Mongolian Revolution* in 1935. In 1937 Demid died and Losol was purged, and in 1939 the book was published in Choibalsan's name alone.

13. *History of the MPR*, p. 345; Urgunge Onon, *Mongolian Heroes of the Twentieth Century*, pp. 213–214. For many indications of the rehabilitation of Choibalsan, see, for example, Orlov and Plotnikov, "Slavnyi syn mongol'skogo naroda (k 80-letiyu so dnya rozhdeniya marshala MNR Kh. Choibalsana)" and *Spravochnik propagandista-mezhdunarodnika*, pp. 253–254. *Novosti Mongolii*, Feb. 8, 1975, published an article entitled "Plamennyi revolyutsioner, vydayushchiisya partiinoi i gosudarstvennyi deyatel'," and the issue of February 11 reported a special Politburo meeting in Ulan Bator to honor Choibalsan. See Tsedenbal's speech of August 1969 in the 1974 volume of his speeches entitled *Izbrannye stat'i i rechi*, pp. 296–306.

14. Owen Lattimore, "The Unknown Frontiers of Manchuria," *Foreign Affairs* II (Jan. 1933), p. 326.

15. See Clubb, *China and Russia*, p. 296; Friters, *Outer Mongolia*, p. 239; Kolarz, *The Peoples of the Soviet Far East*, p. 137.

A Japanese propaganda publication ("Meng Chiang [Autonomous Government of Inner Mongolia]," *The Peking Chronicle* [Peking 1939]) argued in 1939:

> Out of the Sino-Japanese conflict has arisen a new opportunity. The Japanese Army, in its operations against the Kuomintang forces, passed through the Mongol Borderland regions, and with an understanding of the native mind they assisted the Mongols to create an autonomous state . . . The goal of the entire program in the Mongol borderland area is to create a strong buffer state against the extension of Communist influence into East Asia. And with an eye to the ultimate union of Outer Mongols with the anti-Communist bloc, Japan is aiding in the regeneration of the Mongol nation.

16. Kolarz, *Peoples of the Soviet Far East*, p. 120; G. D. R. Phillips, *Dawn in Siberia*, p. 168. For Unkrig's description of Shambhala, see Rupen, *Mongols*, 1:106–107.

17. Charles R. Bawden, *The Modern History of Mongolia*, p.359.

18. *History of the MPR*, p. 345.

19. In Ma Ho-tien, *Chinese Agent in Mongolia*, pp. 202–203.

20. See F. C. Jones, *Manchuria Since 1931*, pp. 60–68, and Teh Wang's statement quoted in Rupen, *Mongols*, 1:227.

21. Clubb, *China and Russia*, p. 290.

22. Kolarz, *Peoples of the Soviet Far East*, p. 37. Note Miliband, *Bio-bibliograficheskii slovar' sovetskikh vostokovedov*, p. 415, who cited B. D. Pak on the Korean question in Russia, 1910–1914.

23. U.S. Department of State, *Foreign Relations of the United States. 1943*, p. 254. By January 1934 the USSR had already transferred seven thousand of these Chinese refugees to Sinkiang to strengthen Sheng Shih-tsai's forces (Jack Chen, *The Sinkiang Story*, pp. 180–181).

24. See Rupen, *Mongols*, 1:253 n. 53 and 255 n. 83.

25. A more extensive quotation appears in Rupen, *Mongols*, 1:248 n. 28.

26. *History of the MPR*, pp. 343–344.

27. Kolarz, *Russia and Her Colonies*, p. 37.

Latinization of the written Mongolian language was proposed as early as 1910 by Agvan Dorjeev; at that time Rinchino was involved in the same project. Nevertheless, traditional vertical script continued to be the standard throughout all the Mongolian areas for many years after 1910. A conference at Baku in 1926 approved Latinization of alphabets of Oriental peoples of the USSR, including Mongols and Central Asians (a unified Turkic Latin alphabet for all Soviet Central Asia). The new writing was adopted by the Kalmyks in 1927, the Altai Oirats in 1928, the Tuvans in 1930, and the Buryat Mongols in 1931, and there was discussion at that time of a single Mongolian language and alphabet for them all. Latinization was officially adopted in the MPR in April 1930, and a few postage stamps, some currency, and a dictionary and textbook were issued in the new form. It was not seriously introduced in the MPR, however, and was abandoned completely in mid-1932. Thus a policy enforced for the Mongols of the USSR was not effectively implemented in the MPR.

At the same time the Latin alphabet was replacing traditional scripts of minority nationalities all over the USSR, many Chinese who were in the Soviet Union for study at Sun Yat-sen University-KUTK wanted to adopt a Latin alphabet to replace the ideographs of the traditional Chinese language. Seventy-three Chinese and fourteen Russians met to discuss the Latinization of Chinese at Vladivostok in September 1931, and a so-called "Far Eastern Committee for a New Alphabet" (DVKNA) functioned at Vladivostok until its liquidation in September 1937. A journal entitled "Yngxu Sin Wenz" ("For a New Alphabet") was published at Khabarovsk, as were several books in Latinized Chinese, between 1933 and 1936.

Traditional language and script meant continuing access to and knowledge of the history and religion of the past, and also encouraged contact with nonrevolutionary traditional peoples and cultures bordering the USSR. Latinization tended to break the connections with the past, and encouraged "progressive" global connections—that is, Latinization and Comintern expansionism seemed to go together. Language reform and a change in alphabet were projects favored by the Comintern and the intellectuals of the 1920s and early 1930s. The impulse came to the MPR from the USSR, and in 1930 it was a weak impulse that was not vigorously fortified by any active pressure.

See Rupen, *Mongols,* 1:43 n. 43; Charles R. Bawden, *The Modern History of Mongolia,* pp. 250, 344; Paul Henze, "Politics and Alphabets in Central Asia"; Yueh Sheng, *Sun Yat-sen University in Moscow and the Chinese Revolution,* pp. 4, 55, 71; A. G. Shprintsin, "Iz istorii novago kitaiskogo alfavita (1928–1931 gg.)," pp. 126–135. A list of books published in Latinized Chinese at Khabarovsk from 1933 through 1936 is in Shprintsin, "O literature na kitaiskom yazke," p. 266. See also works cited in the bibliography for V. M. Alekseev, V. S. Kolokolov, A. A. and E. N. Dragunov, Shprintsin, and E. D. Polivanov.

28. Bawden, in *Modern History,* pp. 370–373, carefully examined this question. Suggestive remarks about practical aspects of acculturation appeared in E. Nelson Fell, *Russian and Nomad,* referring to Kazakhs in 1916; his comments were especially apt since copper mining is becoming a large industry in Mongolia (see Rupen, *Mongols,* 1:364 n. 17). The effects of collectivization were explored in a fascinating study of the Uzbeks and Kirgiz in 1931–1932, A. R. Luria's *Cognitive Development.*

29. Ma Ho-tien, *Chinese Agent,* p. 56. There were 7,500 pupils in secular schools in 1931, and 18,000 in religious schools in 1932; in 1935 there were 3,725 in secular schools and 18,000 in religious ones; in 1939 there were 9,707 in secular schools and none in religious schools; and in 1940 there were 21,700 in secular schools (no other schools existed). Note also Choibalsan's ideas about the use of the Tibetan language (Rupen, *Mongols,* 1:229–230).

30. Xenia J. Eudin and Robert C. North, *Soviet Russia and the East, 1920–1927*, pp. 177–179.

31. Xenia J. Eudin and Robert M. Slusser, *Soviet Foreign Policy, 1928–1934*, vol. 1, p. 202.

32. Chenkirov, "Vospominaniya o mongolii," pp. 225–227. Other Buryats important in the MPR in the late 1920s and the 1930s included N. M. Baldaev (GVO, 1929–1930); V. I. Trubacheev (secretary to the Russian diplomatic representative in Mongolia, 1928); E. I. Losov (head of "Mongol'stroi" 1930–1934 and then a member of the Economic Council); and A. O. Nazarov (adviser for health, 1936–1940).

33. *History of the MPR*, p. 269.

34. Eudin and North, *Soviet Russia*, p. 288. Pavel Mif (1901–1939) began teaching at KUTV in 1921, was rector of KUTK 1927–1929 (he replaced Karl Radek), and worked in the Far Eastern section of the Comintern 1928–1937 (Miliband, *Bio-bibliograficheskii solvar' sovetskikh vostokovedov*, pp. 362–363). Yueh Sheng commented on Pavel Mif: "Mif was young, inexperienced, and generally unpopular. . . . he compared to Karl Radek as a drop of water to an ocean. . . . With the backing of Stalin and the Comintern, he played an important role in trying to shape the Chinese revolution and CCP affairs. . . ." (*Sun Yat-sen University*, pp. 38–40).

35. McClosky, H., and Turner, J. E., *The Soviet Dictatorship* (New York, 1960), p. 131.

36. Rupen, *Mongols*, 1:256 n.91 and 1:233.

37. *History of the MPR*, pp. 280, 703.

38. *Ibid.*, p. 283. Sudets, in *Novosti Mongolii*, Nov. 1 and 5, 1974. V. N. Markelov, *Ugolovnoe pravo MNR*, pp. 148–165, referred to several specific acts of sabotage in the 1930s.

39. Rupen, *Mongols*, 1:241–242. George S. Murphy, *Soviet Mongolia*, p. 129; Bawden, *Modern History*, pp. 323–324.

40. Details of the abortive plan were published: I. L. Baevskii, "O pyatiletnem plane razvitiya narodnogo khozyaistva i kul'tury MNR." *Khozyaistvo Mongolii*, no. 5(18). (Sept.–Oct. 1929), pp. 26–35; Baevskii, "Pyatiletnii plan razvitiya zdravookhraneniya MNR," *Khozyaistvo Mongolii*, no. 2(20), (March–April 1930), pp. 87–113; Erdeni Ochir, "Pyatiletka sotsialisticheskogo razvitiya Mongolii," *Zhizn' Buryatii*, no. 4 (1930), pp. 105–111; I. O. Shleifer, "Osnovnye problemy pyatiletnego plana khozyaistvennogo i kul'turnogo stroitel'stva MNR," *Khozyaistvo Mongolii*, no. 3(21), (May–June 1930), pp. 5–25; A. P. Tsirnyuk, "K predstoyashchemu sostavleniyu pyatiletnego perspektivnogo plana razvitiya Mongol'skoi narodnoi kooperatsii," *Khozyaistvo Mongolii*, no. 2(20), (March–April 1930).

41. Rupen, *Mongols*, 1:233.

42. *History of the MPR*, p. 362.

43. Bawden, *Modern History*, p. 379, suggested caution: "If the statistics are to be believed, all earlier losses of livestock had been made good, and the national stocks stood at nearly 27,500,000 head. This figure has subsequently been scaled down by a million or so, and as it represents a total never achieved, by several million either before or after 1940–41, it may well have been a euphoric exaggeration."

44. See the detailed argument in Murphy, *Soviet Mongolia*.

45. Rupen, *Mongols*, 1:234.

46. *History of the MPR*, p. 261.

47. Rupen, *Mongols*, 1:232.

48. Shmeral (1880–1941) worked for the Comintern until he returned to Prague in 1938. He fled when the Germans invaded Czechoslovakia and died in Moscow. Vasil Kolarov (1877–1950) was a member of the Bulgarian Politburo in exile from 1936 through 1945.

49. *History of the MPR*, pp. 197–198.

50. Little Khural membership lists can be found in Rupen, *Mongols*, 1:432–435.

51. Ibid., p. 234; Bawden, *Modern History*, pp. 333–334.

52. See a discussion of the reputations of Sukhe Bator and Choibalsan in Owen Lattimore, *Nationalism and Revolution in Mongolia*, pp. 67–81.

53. The Russian officer Litvintsev served as first chief of Staff of the Mongolian People's Army. *History of the MPR*, p. 786 n. 154.

54. Murphy, *Soviet Mongolia*, p. 128 n. 53.

55. *Novosti Mongolii*, Nov. 1 and 5, 1974; for information on Sudets, see *Voenno-istoricheskii zhurnal*, no. 10 (Oct. 1974), pp. 120–124.

56. Bawden, *Modern History*, p. 349. See also Rupen, *Mongols*, 1:35 and 1:49 n. 11 on Aga. Blyukher was apparently the agent of the destruction of Aga (Rupen, *Mongols*, .1:35). See L. N. Gumil'ev, *Staroburyatskaya zhivopis'*, which catalogs the surviving Aga collection; and Dandaron, "Aga Monastery."

Two years of destruction in Buryat Mongolia left but 40 of 299 Buddhist religious structures (temples, monasteries, and other buildings) standing in 1937. The vigorous activity of the Buryat League of Militant Godless was commended to the Kalmyk Komsomols as a model for emulation (B. N. Batorov, "K istorii i bor'by buryatskoi partiinoi organizatsii za preodolenie lamaizma v gody sotsialisticheskogo stroi-tel'stva," pp. 334, 336).

57. In 1934–1935, 48 percent of eighteen-year-old boys went into the church to avoid the army (*History of the MPR*, p. 329).

58. *History of the MPR*, pp. 299, 378; Rupen, *Mongols*, 1:231.

59. Bawden, *Modern History*, p. 331.

60. *History of the MPR*, pp. 338, 345, Many plots, especially those of the 1930s, were reported in V. N. Markelov, *Ugolovnoe pravo MNR* and in Misshima and Goto, *A Japanese View of Outer Mongolia*.

61. Rupen, *Mongols*, 1:252 n. 51. A Soviet *kandidat*-dissertation was reported in 1973: A. B. Dubinin, *Problemy politiki Kominterna v natsional'no-kolonial'nom voprose (na primere Mongolii 1919–1928 gg)*.

62. See the chapter entitled "The Russian Elder Brother" in Walter Kolarz, *Communism and Colonialism*, pp. 24–30. *Novosti Mongolii*, Nov. 26, 1974, showed Sukhe Bator in the orthodox younger-brother position in relation to Lenin. See also General Kuropatkin in 1916: "To the Russians must belong the foremost role in all corners of Russia since they contributed more than all others in toil and sacrifice for the creation of Russia. . . . In this numerous family [of peoples] the Russians must be the elder brothers of all the rest . . ." (Richard A. Pierce, *Russian Central Asia, 1867–1912*, p. 284).

63. See note 5 in Chapter 4.

64. Markelov, *Ugolovnoe pravo*, presented the plot version, while ten years later, Sorkin told a totally different story in *V nachale puti*. See Bawden, *Modern History*, pp. 336–342.

65. See Chapter 11, "The Great Trial," in Conquest, *The Great Terror*.

66. Solzhenitsyn, *Gulag Archipelago Two*, p. 379.

67. Left: 1928–June 1932; Right: June 1932–March 1936; Left: March 1936–1940.

5. *World War II and the Death of Choibalsan: 1940–1952*

1. *History of the MPR*, pp. 405, 455–456, and 826 ns. 1 and 2. In 1942 Maurice Hindus considered a war between Russia and Japan inevitable. Chapter 13 of his *Russia and Japan* was entitled "Japan Must Strike." He believed that the 1941 Neutrality Pact was the exact Asian equivalent of the Hitler-Stalin pact, concluded for the same delaying purpose and bound to have the same end result. His assessment of the strategic role of the MPR appears on pp. 128–130. See also Iolk in Miliband, *Biobibliograficheskii slovar' sovetskikh vostokovedov*, p. 228.

The Mongols assisted the Soviet war effort by financing a tank unit, "Revolutionary Mongolia" and an air squadron, "Mongolian Arat," and by sending half a million horses. See *History of the MPR*, p. 822 n.19. Gusakovsky, commander of the tank unit, visited Ulan Bator several times after the war.

2. *History of the MPR*, pp. 469–470; see Grechko in *Pravda*, Sept. 3, 1975. The MPR declared war on Japan on August 10, 1945.

3. In the 1960s and 1970s *Voenno-istoricheskii zhurnal* published more than twenty articles dealing with general as well as specific tactical aspects of the 1945 Far Eastern campaign. See also A. M. Dubinskii, *Osvoboditel'naya missiya Sovetskogo Soyuza na Dal'nem Vostoke*. Memoirs that had been originally published in small editions were reissued around the time of the Damansky Island incident in much larger ones: L. N. Vnotchenko, *Pobeda na Dal'nem Vostoke*, was published in an edition of 19,000 in 1966 and 40,000 in 1971; idem, *Final: Istoriko-memuarnyi ocherk o razgrome imperialisticheskoi yaponii v 1945 g.*, had an edition of 35,500 in 1966 and 50,000 in 1969 (it went to press November 28, 1968—before the Damansky Island incident). Pliev's memoirs, published in 1965 as *Cherez Gobi i Khingan*, appeared in 1969 as *Konets Kvantunskoi armii*, in an edition of 40,000.

John Erickson noted in *Soviet Military Power* (pp. 27, 73):

> The Soviet Far Eastern campaign of 1945 [was] a high-speed conventional operation which could well serve as a model for any punitive demonstrative Soviet intervention [against China]: the 1945 Far East campaign, planned as a *blitzkrieg* operation, approximates most closely to the type of rapid advance with armored and motorized forces presently contemplated in Soviet ideas about the Ground Forces, with flexible logistics support and airborne troops dropped ahead of the strike forces. . . . As an example of the Soviet *blitzkrieg* (for all the lack of a major encounter battle) the Far East campaign is a much more realistic "model" than the majority of the operations in the European theater during the period 1941–1945.

See also Harrison Salisbury, *War Between Russia and China*, pp. 158, 161.

4. Tsog, now first deputy minister of defense, was a colonel and commander of a division at age twenty-five, presumably at least partly as a result of the extensive purges of 1937–1938. The chief of the propaganda branch in the army's political administration in 1945, L. Toiv, attended the Soviet diplomats' school in Moscow, headed the Mongolian delegation to the UN in New York for a time, and became minister of foreign affairs (he died in July 1970). In 1945 he published *Khuv'sgalt Tsergiin 25 Jil* [25 Years of the Revolutionary Army] (see *History of the MPR*, p. 26). S.

Ravdan, who also died recently, became head of the army's political administration after serving with Pliev in 1945. He also served as minister of foreign affairs from 1955 through 1956. In 1974 D. O. Riizen completed a *kandidat*-dissertation entitled *Partiino-politicheskaya rabota v MNR voiskakh v gody vtoroi mirnoi voiny (1939–1945 gg.)* at the Military-Political Academy in Moscow.

5. In Pliev's KMG were 42,000 men; 23,000 horses; and 403 tanks (Khetagrov, "General armii P. A. Pliev," *Voenno-istoricheskii zhurnal,* no. 11 [November 1973], p. 124). When Pliev later became commander of the North Caucasus Military District, he directed the slaughter at Novocherkassk on June 2, 1962, to suppress a strike there (Solzhenitsyn, *Gulag Archipelago Three,* p. 509 n. 2).

6. For example, *Novosti Mongolii* (March 16 and 19, 1976) reported the visit of a Soviet military delegation to celebrate Mongolian Army Day, March 18.

7. *Velikoderzhavnaya politika Maoistov v natsional'nykh raionakh KNR,* pp. 30–31. See also Ivor Montagu, *Land of Blue Sky,* pp. 158–159; and Rupen, *Mongols,* 1:259.

8. It was also thought that the USSR might well take over Manchuria: see O. Edmund Clubb in U.S. Department of State, *Foreign Relations of the United States, 1947* vol. 7, p. 705; and Clubb, "Manchuria in the Balance, 1945–1946." The 1947 *Foreign Relations* volume included a Joint Chiefs of Staff "Study of the Military Aspects of U.S. Policy Toward China," dated June 9, that stated: "There is evidence that current Soviet intentions are to remove Manchuria from the Chinese economy and integrate it into the economy of Eastern Siberia." Dean Acheson believed that the Soviet Union was "attempting to spread its influence even to the extent of detaching Outer Mongolia, Inner Mongolia, Sinkiang, and Manchuria" (*Present at the Creation,*) p. 356, referring to his well-known speech of January 12, 1950, "Crisis in China").

A description of the Russian return to Port Arthur appeared in *Final,* pp. 333–339. Stalin had said, "For forty years we the people of the older generation have waited for this day" (quoted in George Lensen, "Yalta and the Far East," p. 163).

9. See James Burke, "China's Losing Game in Mongolia"; Doak Barnett, *China on the Eve of Communist Takeover,* pp. 195–214; Howard Boorman, "The Borderlands and the Sino-Soviet Alliance," pp. 156–173; Rupen, *Mongols,* 1:259–261; *History of the MPR,* p. 827 n. 21; and June Dreyer, *China's Forty Millions,* pp. 79–83.

10. Teh Wang had often expressed himself clearly and forcefully against the MPR and the Soviets, but members of his family had been removed to Ulan Bator by the retreating Communist forces in 1946. The Mongolian government later extradited Teh Wang to Peking, where he was tried as a war criminal and imprisoned. He was pardoned and released on April 9, 1963, and reportedly died in China in 1965 (see *History of the MPR,* p. 827 n. 21).

James Burke discussed Fu Tso-yi's overbearing attitude toward and treatment of Teh Wang and the Mongols (in "China's Losing Game"; also cited in Rupen, *Mongols,* 1:261), and the Ulan Bator newspaper bitterly attacked Peking's rehabilitation of Fu Tso-yi (*Novosti Mongolii,* April 25, 1975).

11. Sheng Shih-tsai was responsible for the deaths of four sons, four daughters, and the only brother of Osman Bator.

12. U.S. Department of State, *Foreign Relations, 1944,* vol. 6, pp. 42, 767, 799–800. See the first-class reporting by Doak Barnett in *China on the Eve* in his dispatch from Sinkiang of September 1948 on pp. 236–281, especially pp. 266 and 275–276. He underlined the strategic importance of Peitashan, which "dominates the entire

Sinkiang-Outer Mongolia border, from a strategic point of view. . . . It flanks the Sinkiang supply line from Kansu; in non-Chinese hands, it could be a stronghold capable of severing Sinkiang from the rest of China."

George Roerich, at Urumchi in 1926, noted:

Disquieting reports were received from the Mongol border. Clashes with considerable loss of life had occurred between Mongolian frontier troops and Kirghiz tribesmen in the vicinity of the massive Baitik Bogdo, and large bands of Torguts and Kirghiz were fleeing into Jungaria, apprehending a Mongol raid. The atmosphere was charged with anxiety and war clouds gathered on the frontiers (*Trails to Inmost Asia*, p. 111).

Butterworth's dispatch of February 25, 1949 (in U.S. Department of State, *Foreign Relations, 1949*, vol. 9, pp. 1046–1047) is especially interesting:

The reported haste of the Soviets in pressing for an agreement [a Soviet agreement with Kuomintang China about Sinkiang trade] would seem to indicate that they are anxious to legalize and fortify their status in Sinkiang while there is still a Nationalist Government with which to deal, and, conversely, that they may wish to secure these special interests from a Nationalist Government which is fast dwindling in power and prestige rather than to risk waiting to deal with a Chinese Communist regime which is just beginning to flex its international muscles and in whose complete subservience the Kremlin may not have full confidence. It may also be that Russia is being motivated in her actions by her traditional apprehension of a strong, united China to her south and is therefore not averse to bolstering the Nationalist Government (while at the same time securing additional concessions for herself) just at the time when the Communists appear to have the military capability of destroying the Nationalist Government on the Chinese mainland. Even if the Chinese Communists have been fully apprised of Soviet intentions in Sinkiang and have been cajoled or forced into acquiescing to the present negotiations, the action of the Soviets in negotiating at this time a long-term agreement with the Nationalist Government involving special rights to the USSR would seem to indicate something less than comradely trust between the Chinese Communists and Moscow.

See also Allen S. Whiting, *Sinkiang: Pawn or Pivot?* p. 118; Clubb, *China and Russia*, p. 370.

For discussions and negotiations concerning the proposed Iran-USSR-Sinkiang route for United States aid to China, see U.S. Department of State, *Foreign Relations, 1942*, "China," pp. 591–623; and *1943*, "China," pp. 590–613. Herold J. Wiens, in "The Historical and Geographical Role of Urumchi, Capital of Chinese Central Asia," referred to Kashgar as controlling the pass into the Fergana Valley, which he judged unsuitable as a major trade route for modern transportation since the passes were too high and difficult.

For other sources of information, see Kutuklov in Miliband, *Biobibliograficheskii*, pp. 295–296, and Usmanov in Miliband, pp. 567–568.

13. U.S. Department of State, *Foreign Relations, 1944*, vol. 6, p. 240.

14. George Moseley, *A Sino-Soviet Cultural Frontier*, p. 113; and Rupen, "The Absorption of Tuva." See N. A. Serdobov, *Istoriya formirovaniya tuvinskoi natsii*. Note Potapov in Miliband, *Biobibliograficheskii*, pp. 452–453.

15. Gerard M. Friters, *Outer Mongolia and Its International Position*, pp. 5, 287, and 292, with footnotes citing UN documents.

16. Milton J. Clark, "How the Kazakhs Fled to Freedom" (including a fine photograph of Qali Bek). See Paxton's dispatch from Urumchi (Nov. 18, 1947) in U.S. Department of State, *Foreign Relations, 1947,* vol. 7, p. 580; Godfrey Lias, *Kazakh Exodus.*

17. Dagvadorj, *Novosti Mongolii,* Dec. 10, 1974. For sources on feudalism, see note 17, Chapter 2. The text of the 1924 Mongolian constitution can be found in *China Yearbook 1926* (Peking and Tientsin, Tientsin Press), pp. 795–800; the 1940 constitution in Friters, *Outer Mongolia,* pp. 325–344; the 1960 constitution, in Rupen, *Mongols,* 1:413–426.

18. I. M. Maisky, introduction to *MNR—strana novoi demokratii,* by I. Ya. Zlatkin, p. 8.

19. *Konstitutsiya i osnovnye zakonodatel'nye akty MNR* (1952), pp. 245–246, 248. See Paul Henze, "Politics and Alphabets in Central Asia," and "Alphabet Changes in Soviet Central Asia and Communist China"; and G. I. Mikhailov, "Yazykovedenie v MNR," *Voprosy yazykoznaniya,* no. 1 (1953), pp. 104–108. Choibalsan's speeches were published in Ulan Bator in 1951 in the old script.

Walter Kolarz referred to Irkutsk University's control over the Buryat language in 1952 (*Peoples of the Soviet Far East,* note on p. 123). For a discussion of Kazakh assistance to the western MPR, see *Druzhboi velikoi sil'ny,* pp. 298–299; 393–394. See also the chapter by Bakakov in a book listed in Miliband, *Biobibliograficheskii,* p. 684.

The policy of replacing the Latin alphabet with the Russian alphabet for the languages of minority nationalities in the USSR was adopted in 1937. The Kalmyks actually shifted from the Latin to the Russian alphabet in 1938; the Buryat Mongols and Altai Oirats in 1939; and the Tuvans in 1941. The Kazakhs shifted in 1938. The imposition of the Russian alphabet escalated the pressures of Russification and Russian nationalization, and reinforced isolation from foreign countries.

Paul Henze suggested that Sir Olaf Caroe first expressed the idea that Latinization in Turkey in 1928 led almost inevitably to the Soviet abandonment of Latinization and the adoption of the Russian alphabet for languages in Soviet Central Asia ("Politics and Alphabets in Central Asia," p. 49 n. 14). Even without the factor of Turkey's Latinization, however, the change to the Russian alphabet directed by Stalin in 1937 seems consistent with his character and his other actions at the time: he was girding for war and he feared disloyalty. It was simply a part of the larger strategic scene as Stalin saw it.

The MPR officially adopted Cyrillic in 1941, but during World War II that paper adoption was as little effective as the Latinization adopted by the MPR in 1930. Only after the war did any effective change from the traditional script to the Russian alphabet take place (see Bawden, *The Modern History of Mongolia,* pp. 17, 377; G. P. Serdyuchenko, *Russkaya transkriptsiya dlya yazykov zarubezhnego Vostoka;* and L. D. Shagdarov (on the Buryat language), I. K. Ilishkin (Kalmyk), D. A. Mongush (Tuvan), N. A. Kuchigasheva and E. N. Chunzhekova (Altai-Oirat), all in *Razvitie literatur'nykh yazykov narodov Sibiri v sovetskuyu epokhu.* Also see E. I. Ubryatova, *Nekotorye voprosy grafiki i orfografii pis'mennosti yazykov narodov SSSR, pol'zuyuschikhsya alfavitami na russkom osnove* and Chapter 4, note 27.

The Kalmyk case was unique because the Russian alphabet was employed from 1924 through 1931, the Latin alphabet from 1931 through 1938, and the Russian again since 1938 ("Kalmytskii yazyk," *Bol'shaya sovetskaya entsiklopediya,* vol. 11 [1973], p. 225).

20. A. G. Bannikov, "Pervye gody Mongol'skogo Universiteta," in *Narody Brat'ya* pp. 101–104. See also M. P. Khabaev, "Vospominaniya o Mongolii," *Trudy bur-*

yatskogo instituta, no. 23 (1974), pp. 222–223; and R. Zh. Zhalsonova and B. B. Shagdyrov, "Mongolrabfak."

V. V. Volkov, a Russian archaeologist, taught at the Ulan Bator University from 1956 through 1959, and E. A. Novgorodova, a biographer of Shirendyb (the president of the Mongolian Academy of Sciences), taught there from 1957 through 1961 (Miliband, *Biobibliograficheskii,* pp. 117, 391).

21. E. M. Murzaev, *Nepotorennymi put'yami,* pp. 267–384. The map opposite p. 272 in that book shows his travels in the MPR.

22. Harsh criticism was expressed and tightened control was enforced in a 1949 party resolution, "On the Teaching of MPR History and Literature in Schools." *History of the MPR,* pp. 497–498.

23. For Choimbol, see *Novosti Mongolii,* Dec. 6, 1977; and Gonchigsumla, *Novosti Mongolii,* Feb. 18, 1975, and Dec. 20, 1977.

24. Tsedenbal, *Izbrannye stat'i i rechi, 1941–1958.* Referring to the period 1940–1945, *History of the MPR* remarked on the "disorganized, disorderly, and backward practices and concepts of members of private household units" (p. 410). It also stated that: "Remnants of the old society such as shirking work and disliking work as an attitude toward manual labor were very powerful. . . . The carelessness of small owners caused serious losses . . . very many cases of instability in work and haphazardness. . . . The Party . . . aimed at getting rid of former habits such as dislike of labor, laziness, and procrastination" (pp. 412–413).

25. See George G. S. Murphy, *Soviet Mongolia,* and Rupen, *Mongols; History of the MPR,* p. 425, 510, 494, 511, 408–409.

26. *History of the MPR,* p. 437; Rupen, *Mongols,* 1:268 n. 25. M. V. Meshcheryakov, *Ocherk ekonomicheskogo sotrudnichestva sovetskogo soyuza i MNR.* See the annual volumes of *Vneshnyaya torgovlya SSSR,* which clearly show steadily increasing "subsidies" in the form of large Soviet exports to Mongolia and small Mongolian exports to the USSR.

27. Rupen, *Mongols,* 1:267 n.23.

28. *Mongol'skaya narodnaya respublika,* p. 169, indicated that it began on December 20, 1950.

29. Murzaev, *MNR,* p. 57. The first secretary of the railroad's Party committee, Ch. Gunsen, a candidate-member of the Central Committee, submitted a *kandidat-*dissertation in Moscow in 1975 entitled *Problemy povysheniya ekonomicheskii effektivnosti zhelezno-dorozhnogo transporta MNR.* The Russian director of the railroad from 1958 to 1967, Zaporozhtsev, wrote the book used as an instruction manual by Mongolian railroad workers (*Novosti Mongolii,* August 8, 1974). A radio broadcast in August 1977 listed V. A. Reimarov as director of the railroad, V. V. Kazimirov as chief engineer, V. Kapitsa as head of the section for labor and wages, and V. I. Krichigin as head of the signals and communications section.

30. Aleksander Solzhenitsyn, *Gulag Archipelago Two,* p. 241.

31. Prikhodov served as Soviet ambassador to Bulgaria from 1954 through 1960.

32. See Friters, *Outer Mongolia,* pp. 210–212.

6. China—Cooperation and Competition: 1952–1962

1. The official *History of the MPR* and Bawden use 1940 as the major dividing line. Bawden, in *The Modern History of Mongolia,* pp. 373–380, analyzes the significance of that year.

2. For the important potential of Sino-Soviet cooperation, with Mongolia as a bridge instead of a buffer or barrier, see two articles by Owen Lattimore, "Mongolia's Relations with Russia and China" and "Inner Asia: Sino-Soviet Bridge."

3. In 1964 Mao Tse-tung told visiting Japanese socialists that he had asked the Soviet leaders in 1954 "to restore Mongolian independence." That comment in effect confirmed C. L. Sulzberger's dispatch in early 1955 stating that there had been a shift affecting Mongolia that signified a return to Chinese domination. The text of Mao's statement and various commentaries on it appear in Dennis J. Doolin, *Territorial Claims in the Sino-Soviet Conflict.* Tsedenbal stated in 1975, "Talking to a Japanese Socialist Party delegation in July 1964 . . . Mao assailed the Soviet Union with slanderous accusations that it had 'suppressed' Mongolia and turned her into a 'colony' " ("Toward Socialism, Bypassing Capitalism," p. 25). Sulzberger, *New York Times,* dispatch of Feb. 14, 1955; quoted in Rupen, *Mongols,* 1:273.

4. June T. Dreyer, *China's Forty Millions,* p. 119. S. D. Dylykov, "Edzhen-Khoro"; Rinchen, *Zum Cult Tschinggis-Khans bei den Mongolen;* and George Cressey, "The Ordos Desert of Inner Mongolia." See also Rupen, *Mongols,* 1:311 n. 61 and Bawden, *The Modern History of Mongolia,* pp. 175 and 417. Rinchen recalled the sacking and destruction of the relics of Chinggis Khan at Ejen Khoro by the Muslims in the 1870s.

5. Chinese Buddhist Association, *Buddhists in New China;* see also China Islamic Association, *Chinese Muslims in Progress.* Two recent very favorable reports on Chinese policy toward religion are Han Suyin, *Lhasa, The Open City,* which includes much uncritical discussion about Buddhism in Tibet, and the similarly enthusiastic article by Jack Chen entitled "Islam in Sinkiang Today," *The Sinkiang Story,* appendix 2, pp. 327–337. Han Suyin was in Tibet October–November 1975, and Chen was in Sinkiang during the summer of 1957. Chen concluded that "the policies of the People's Government have enabled Islam to flourish in Sinkiang as never before" (p. 331).

6. The Kalmyk Republic was dissolved on December 27, 1943, and the native peoples were "reduced to the status of disenfranchised and persecuted beggars. The homes of the deportees were taken over by new settlers. Their property was plundered. Their personal belongings were appropriated by those who carried out the deportation. . . . Repatriation began at the end of 1956. . . . By the end of 1959 the resettlement was essentially completed" (Alexander M. Nekrich, *The Punished Peoples,* pp. 124, 142; see also the chapter "What Happened in the Kalmyk ASSR," pp. 66–85).

7. Alphabet and language played a part in Sino-Soviet cooperation from 1955 through 1958, as well as in the Sino-Soviet split in 1958 and after. The alphabets and languages of national minorities in China, including those of the Mongols, were involved, as well as the Chinese language and the question of adopting an alphabet for it. During the years of cooperation, the Russian alphabet and Russian language began to assume a significant place in China, but both alphabet and language were sent back to Russia with the Soviet experts when cooperation broke down. In August and October 1955, and in May 1956, Soviet and Chinese conferees in Peking and Kü-ke Khoto (an Inner Mongolian city) agreed that Chinese Inner Mongolia would employ the Russian alphabet in place of the traditional vertical Mongolian script, and serious discussion took place about future plans for the Chinese language itself.

Three of the Russians involved in negotiations with the Chinese on these matters were G. P. Serdyuchenko, adviser for linguistics to the Chinese Academy of Sciences and to the Central Institute of National Minorities of China; N. N. Korotkov, who had worked at the Bureau of Chinese Studies at the Far Eastern Institute at Vladivostok in 1931–1932 and was a participant in the 1956 conference for the reform of Chinese writing; and Bulgash Todaeva, a Kalmyk woman who was a linguistics expert from Astrakhan; she served from 1954 to 1957 as consultant for the Mongolian language at the Academy of National Minorities, and also taught at that time at Peking University.

The Chinese announced early in 1958 that only the Latin alphabet would be used for languages of national minorities in China, and that the former attitude of deference to Russia in such matters was completely abandoned. The Sino-Soviet border then marked a firm separation between the Russian alphabet and the Latin alphabet. In 1976, however, an American reporter found that the Soviet Union was publishing a newspaper with a circulation of eight thousand at Alma Ata in traditional script; it served refugees from Sinkiang (Christopher Wren, "Kazakhstan Beckons Refugees from China," *New York Times*, April 24, 1976).

See G. P. Serdyuchenko, "Iz istorii sozdaniya alfavitov na osnove russkoi grafiki," "O novom mongol'skom pis'me," and *Kitaiskaya pis'mennost' i ee reforma;* P. P. Nurmekund, "O reforme kitaiskoi pis'mennosti"; B. Kh. Todaeva, *Mongol'skie yazyki i dialekty Kitaya;* and Rupen, *Mongols,* 1:305 n. 14. See biographical and bibliographical information in S. D. Miliband, *Biobibliograficheskii slovar' sovetskikh vostokovedov,* for Serdyuchenko (pp. 507–508), Todaeva (p. 549), and Korotkov (pp. 274–275). Also see Rupen, *Mongols,* 1:243, 264, 275, and 305 n. 14; Charles R. Bawden, *The Modern History of Mongolia,* p. 344; as well as note 27, Chapter 4, and note 19, Chapter 5.

8. The following incomplete table shows arrivals and departures of Chinese laborers that were reported in the press:

Arrivals		Departures	
Early 1955	first agreement	April 1962	6,000 total remained
May 1955	first arrivals	May 1962	3,000 departed
By Aug. 1956	10,000 total	Sept. 22, 1963	309 departed
1958	2,400 more	Oct. 9, 1963	700 departed
July 1960	12,000 total	1966	4,000 total remained
Sept. 1960	signed new agreement	May 1973	formal termination, with Chinese turning over last unfinished projects to the MPR.
May 5, 1961	754 arrivals		

See *Vneshnyaya politika KNR,* pp. 63, 99; Harrison Salisbury, *War Between Russia and China,* p. 16, and the chapter entitled "The Blue Ants" in Salisbury, *To Moscow—and Beyond,* pp. 227–240.

9. Dreyer, *China's Forty Millions,* p. 148.

10. For information about Kao Kang's removal and his probable role as an agent of Stalin, see Schurmann and Schell, *Communist China,* pp. 5, 242, 243–244; for information on Edgar Snow, see p. 87 in the same book. See also Salisbury, *War Between Russia and China,* p. 96.

11. *Izvestiya,* May 17, 1957. The USSR made the following loans and gifts to the MPR: in 1954–1957, 900 million rubles in loans and gifts; in 1958–1960, a 200-

million-ruble loan and a 100-million-ruble gift; in 1961–1965, a 615-million-ruble loan and deferred payment of a 245-million-ruble debt. Chinese gifts and loans to the MPR included the following: in 1956–1959, a 160-million-ruble gift; in 1959–1961, a 100-million-ruble loan; in 1961–1965, a 200-million-ruble loan. See Rupen, *Mongols,* 1:290–291.

12. Rupen, *Mongols,* 1:308 n. 38.

13. Pasqualini (Bao Ruo-wang) and Chelminski, in *Prisoner of Mao,* pp. 197–202, discuss the settlement of Manchuria. See also Dreyer, *China's Forty Millions,* p. 164.

14. Why did George Roerich return to Russia in 1957? He left with his parents in 1916 when he was fourteen years old; was educated in England, the United States, and France; and spent several years in New York and a long time in India: it was from India that he returned to the USSR. He went back, voluntarily, after a life and a career spent mainly in the "free world."

Several factors probably motivated his "defection." Apparently, Nicholas Roerich, George's father, had been seriously contemplating returning to Russia at the time of his death in India in 1947. George's mother died at Calcutta in 1951.

The growing threat of Germany and Japan in the 1930s had caused Nicholas Roerich increasingly to praise the Soviet Union, and his stand had given rise to opposition and public attacks by Russian emigrés around the world. Nicholas served as honorary president of a so-called "American-Russian Cultural Association" (ARKA) in New York from 1942 through 1945 that maintained close connections with the Soviet embassy in Washington, D.C. Russians everywhere were reassessing their attitudes toward the Communist regime as the heroic defense against Hitler continued and then succeeded in turning the tide.

Stalin's death, Khrushchev's and Bulganin's trip to India in late 1955 (during which George Roerich spoke directly with Khrushchev), and Khrushchev's denunciation of the tyrant in 1956 led George Roerich and many others to hope for the reestablishment of scholarly, intellectual, and artistic continuity in Russian development. George's decision to return was evidently based on assurances that Nicholas and his art would be publicly honored and that he would get firm support for his own Buddhist studies and use of the Tibetan temple in Leningrad for that purpose. George arranged for about four hundred of his father's paintings to be shipped from India to the USSR, where they remain on exhibit in major museums.

The economic depression of 1929 and subsequent financial and legal difficulties in the United States in the mid-1930s (the twenty-nine-story building housing the Roerich Museum and its related activities was lost), the British government's obstructionist handling of Nicholas Roerich's request for a visa to return to the Institute in India in 1930, and the charges that the Roerichs were "Red spies" that were levelled with particular venom by Russian emigrés and "old friends" probably also affected George Roerich's decision.

In any case, George died in Moscow in May 1960 and his cremated remains were interred in Novodevichy Cemetery. Soviet reports say that a fatal heart attack struck him on May 21 without warning, but when I met him in Ulan Bator in September 1959, he certainly appeared healthy and vigorous, and his father, mother, and brother lived into their seventies.

George's surviving younger brother, Svyatoslav (b. 1904), went to Moscow for the funeral (a public exhibition of Svyatoslav's paintings was arranged at that time), and he went to the Soviet Union again in 1974–1975 for the centennial celebration of Nicholas Roerich's birth. The 1976 *American Art Directory* (p. 156) lists Svyatoslav as a board member of the Nicholas Roerich Museum at 319 W. 107th St., New York City,

"Established 1958 to show a permanent collection of paintings of Nicholas Roerich, internationally known artist, to promote his ideals as a great thinker, writer, humanitarian, scientist, explorer, to promote his Pact and The Banner of Peace. . . ."

Bol'shaya sovetskaya entsiklopediya, vol. 22 (1975), pp. 42–43, provides basic information about Nicholas, George, and Svyatoslav Roerich; and a biographical and bibliographical entry for George appears in Miliband, *Biobibliograficheskii,* pp. 471–472. *Narody Azii i Afriki,* no. 4 (1962), pp. 247–252, provided an obituary for George, including a list of his writings; and in *Narody Azii i Afriki* no. 3 (1975) pp. 239–241, S. I. Potabenko discussed Nicholas. The *New York Times* published Nicholas's obituary on December 16, 1947, and George's on May 23, 1960. Harrison Salisbury's *Black Night, White Snow* included references to Nicholas on pp. 188 and 665 n. 2. See also notes 45 and 48, Chapter 3, and note 5, Chapter 4.

The cause of George's death and details of the funeral arrangements are discussed in E. I. Polyakova, *Nicolai Rerikh,* p. 299. A. Piatigorsky supplied information about the bitter and ironic fate of the Buddhist temple in Leningrad, which never did become George Roerich's Institute of Buddhist Studies: it serves as a laboratory for animal experimentation! (Alexander Piatigorsky, "The Departure of Dandaron," p. 173 n. 5).

15. Rupen, *Mongols,* 1:306 n. 28; Dreyer, *China's Forty Millions,* p. 180. See note 7, Chapter 6, and A. G. Shprintsin, "Kitaiskii novyi alfavit (latinizatsiya), dialekty i obshch eliteraturnyi yazyk."

16. See the list of dissertation authors and titles in Rupen, *Mongols,* 1:442–445. In 1959 Tsedenbal complained that Soviet-trained specialists often did not work in their field of specialization—that much research was of no use, and especially that many dissertations were never finished but simply went on for years. He lamented "the sad fact" that of sixty-three degree-candidates, thirty-two were months or even years behind schedule, all at state expense. In a majority of cases, charged Tsedenbal, the research was not new, original, or creative, and the results had no practical application (Tsedenbal, *Izbrannye stat'i i rechi, 1959–1961,* p. 63).

17. S. K. Roshchin's description in *Sel'skoe khozyaistvo MNR na sotsialisticheskom puti,* pp. 193–207 of the operation of the MZhS in Mongolia is very similar to Fainsod's description (in *How Russia Is Ruled,* pp. 466–469) of the operation of the MTS in the USSR:

> The MTS constitute the most powerful instrument of State control in the countryside. . . . They are vested with extensive powers to plan and direct kolkhoz activities. . . . During the early years of the great collectivization drive, the MTS were used as a Party spearhead to penetrate the villages. . . . The MTS political departments . . . assumed leadership in the struggle to accelerate collectivization.

See also George Ginsburgs, "Local Government in the MPR, 1940–1960."

18. Dreyer, *China's Forty Millions,* p. 163. In China's Sinkiang Province 39 percent of the livestock in the Ili Kazakh Autonomous Chou were collectivized in 1957, and 100 percent were by 1958 (Jack Chen, "Ili—Autonomy Within Autonomy," in *The Sinkiang Story,* p. 308).

19. Dreyer, *China's Forty Millions,* p. 177. See note 13, Chapter 6.

20. Salisbury, *To Moscow—and Beyond,* pp. 230–231.

21. Rupen, *Mongols,* 1:338 n. 6.

22. See Doolin, *Territorial Claims,* p. 40, quoting a New China News Agency

(Peking) dispatch of April 28, 1964: "The authorities of the Soviet Union have . . . carried out large-scale subversive activities against Sinkiang, enticed and coerced tens of thousands of Chinese citizens into going to the Soviet Union." Jack Chen, in *The Sinkiang Story*, similarly charged that the USSR "inveigled 60,000 Kazakh nomads in April–May 1962 into the Soviet Union . . ." (p. 287).

23. J. R. V. Prescott, *Map of Mainland Asia by Treaty*. See also *History of the MPR*, p. 834 n. 4. The Mongolian delegation that went to Peking December 25–27, 1962, included Tsedenbal, N. Jagvaral, P. Shagdarsuren, S. Sosorbaram, S. Bata, and D. Chimiddorj. Tsedenbal, Jagvaral, Sosorbaram, and S. Bata maintained or bettered their political positions afterward, but Shagdarsuren and Chimiddorj, after rising to considerable prominence after the trip, fell far down the political ladder (Shagdarsuren in 1972 and Chimiddorj in 1976).

24. Dreyer, *China's Forty Millions*, pp. 187, 193, 199.

25. Kiselev led an expedition that thoroughly investigated Kara Korum in 1948–1949, and in 1952 a novel by M. S. Kolesnikov appeared that attacked the scientific committee and archaeological work in thinly veiled language. The novel showed Choibalsan complaining about "a plan to the Government suggesting the restoration of the ancient Mongolian capital of Kara Korum, the monastery of Erdeni Dzu, and other monuments of the former greatness of Mongolia." In the novel, Choibalsan termed this proposal a great waste of funds that could be better spent on practical things (M. S. Kolesnikov, "Shchastlivyi Oazis," pp. 7–8). See also Walter Kolarz, *The Peoples of the Soviet Far East*, p. 140, and my review "A Soviet Historical Novel about Mongolia [Kolesnikov]."

V. V. Volkov led a joint Soviet-Mongolian archaeological expedition in the MPR from 1963 through 1972; A. P. Okladnikov, a leader in Siberian archaeology for decades, worked in the MPR in 1949, from 1960 through 1964, and from 1966 through 1968; and L. P. Potapov headed the Sayan-Altai Archaeological-Ethnographic Expedition (Gorno-Altai and Tuva), from 1952 through 1966 (Miliband, *Bio-bibliograficheskii*, pp. 117, 396–398, and 452–453).

26. The text of the 1960 constitution appears in Rupen, *Mongols*, 1:413–426.

27. Jagvaral, "From a Nomadic to a Settled Life in Mongolia"; an extended quotation from this work is in Rupen, *Mongols*, 1:352–353. Lenin advised the Kazakhs of the necessity for them to change from a nomadic to a settled existence in 1920 (*Druzhboi velikoi sil'ny*, p. 208). Note also V. V. Graivoronskii, "Sovetskaya i mongol'skaya istoriografiya o problema osedaniya kochevnikov"; idem., "Pre-obrazovanie kochevogo obraza zhizni v MNR"; a reference to a 1971 dissertation by A. I. Pershits in Miliband, *Biobibliograficheskii*, p. 670; and S. L. Vainshtein, *Istoricheskaya etnografiya Tuvintsev: problemy kochevogo khozyaistva*. A UNESCO symposium was held in Ulan Bator in May 1973 on the "Role of Nomadic Peoples in the Civilization of Central Asia."

28. E. A. Novgorodova, *Syn Khangaiskikh gor;* and B. Shirendyb, *Izbrannye proizvodeniya.*

29. See note 13, Chapter 4.

30. Salisbury (in *War Between Russia and China*, p. 125): "In 1962 the Chinese almost certainly attempted a coup against the Russia-oriented Mongolia government. The effort was thwarted and a vigorous purge of the Mongol Communist Party ensued." See also Tsedenbal, "Toward Socialism, Bypassing Capitalism."

31. Tsedenbal, "Toward Socialism," p. 27. Tsedenbal's report to the Eleventh MPRP Congress in June 1966, included a similar reference: "Through no fault of

ours, rail transit for the past five years has been but one-eighth of what it was formerly, causing serious financial and operational difficulties in our railroad transport" (Tsedenbal *Izbrannye stat'i i rechi, 1962–1973,* pp. 172–173).

32. Rupen, *Mongols,* 1:279, 331, and 338 n. 5; *History of the MPR,* pp. 630 and 835 n. 14.

7. China—Threat and Confrontation: 1963–1973

1. The figures indicated do not include Chinese laborers temporarily in Mongolia or the Soviet military. The trend favoring Russia and working against China was, of course, even stronger when the departure of Chinese laborers and entry of Russian soldiers is taken into consideration.

	1963	1969
Russians	8,900	22,100
Chinese	17,000	7,000

2. Harrison Salisbury, *To Moscow—and Beyond,* pp. 229, 239–240. Similar arguments to the effect that time favors China over Russia appear on pp. 286, 291, in idem, *War Between Russia and China,* pp. 147–148, 207; and in Ferdinand Miksche "Sino-Soviet War in 19xx." Sir Fitzroy Maclean noted that "a frightening imbalance is building up between, on the one hand, the vast empty plains and abundant, scarcely tapped, resources of Siberia, Mongolia and Kazakhstan, and, on the other, the busy, teeming millions of Chinese . . ." (*To the Back of Beyond,* p. 140).

In the 1960s, the population of East Siberia and the Soviet Far East increased by about two million, while the Manchurian and Inner Mongolian population appear to have increased by more than twenty million in the same period.

3. Postwar commanders have included P. A. Belik, commander of the Trans-baikal military district after 1966; V. F. Tolubko, who was named commander-in-chief of Soviet Forces in the Far East in August 1969; Losik, who was replaced by Tolubko; and V. A. Petrov, commander of the Far East military district in July 1975. See John Erickson, *The Soviet High Command, Soviet Military Power,* and "The Soviet Military, Soviet Policy, and Soviet Politics." For military literature, see note 4, Chapter 5.

4. See note 3, Chapter 4 and note 3, Chapter 5. Among those who thought (correctly) Mongolia was of considerable strategic importance were Erickson, *Soviet High Command,* pp. 335, 361, 415; O. Edmund Clubb, *China and Russia,* p. 151; and Salisbury, *War Between Russia and China,* pp. 23, 25–26. Geoffrey Jukes disagreed: "The border with Outer Mongolia—which in view of its weakness, its very close ties with the Soviet Union and relatively poor relations with China, forms an addition to the perimeter which Soviet troops must guard, greater than any contribution Mongolian forces can make to its defense" (*The Soviet Union in Asia,* pp. 68–69).

5. For the Damansky Island incident of 1969, see Roger Glenn Brown, "Chinese Politics and American Policy"; Neville Maxwell, "The Chinese Account of the 1969 Fighting at Chenpao"; and "The Sino-Soviet Dispute" (maps on pp. 68–69).

6. See Salisbury, *War Between Russia and China,* p. 27.

7. *Novosti Mongolii,* May 20, 1975.

8. *Ezhegodnik BSE 1968,* p. 328. See also Paul Hyer and William Heaton, "The

Cultural Revolution in Inner Mongolia"; Tsedenbal, "Toward Socialism, Bypassing Capitalism," p. 26. The MPR also officially protested a Chinese-inspired train delay in February 1969.

9. June T. Dreyer, *China's Forty Millions*, p. 232.

10. Ibid., p. 232; "The Cultural Revolution resulted in minorities losing power and cohesiveness as minority groups." See Rupen, "Peking and the National Minorities," pp. 248-249. The subsequent relaxation in the suppression of minorities in China was reported by Fox Butterfield, "China Calls Meeting With All Minorities—The First Since 1964," *New York Times*, February 25, 1978; and "China Is Seen Easing Attitude on Religion," *New York Times*, March 10, 1978. See also the significant article by Neville Maxwell, "Monks, Who Dominated Tibetan Society, Vanishing Under Communist Rule," *New York Times*, August 19, 1976.

11. See note 14, Chapter 6; Alexander Piatigorsky, "The Departure of Dandaron"; *Index*, no. 1 (1973), p. 9, no. 1 (1975), pp. 92-93, no. 2 (1976), p. 63; Bid'ya D. Dandaron, idem, *Opisanie tibetskikh rukopisei i ksilografov;* and idem, "Aga Monastery." Dandaron is mentioned in D. D. Luvsanov and R. E. Pubaev, "Vostokovedenye issledovaniya v Buryatii," p. 239 n. 9 and n. 10.

12. For a discussion of present-day Buddhism in Buryat Mongolia, see Kevin Klose, "Soviet Buddhist Lamas Dwindle to a Cautious Few," *Washington Post*, March 21, 1978; and David K. Shipler, "In Remote Siberia, a Buddhist Center," *New York Times*, March 20, 1978. For information on Buddhism in Mongolia now, see John Hangin, and Krueger, "The Second International Congress of Mongolists," p. 9, and Owen Lattimore, "Religion and Revolution in Mongolia." See also M. I. Gol'man, *Problemy noveishei istorii MNR v burzhuaznoi istoriografii SShA*, pp. 129-137; and Rupen, "The Fiftieth Anniversary of the MPR, 1921-1971," p. 465 n. 18. The persistence of religion in remote areas in 1960 was noted by Silvio Micheli in *Mongolia*, pp. 130, 271.

13. *Narody Azii i Afriki* lists dissertations and degrees, usually twice a year.

14. Expedition publications were announced as *Trudy sovmestnoi sovetsko-mongol'skii paleontologicheskoi ekspeditsii*. The expedition's first leader was A. G. Vologdin, who died in 1971. See A. K. Rozhdestvenskii, *Na poiske dinozavrov v Gobi*, and G. G. Martinson, *Zagadki pustyni Gobi*. See also A. A. Efremov, M. I. Novozhilov, and A. K. Rozhdestvenskii, "Sbornik rabot po paleontologii MNR."

15. I. N. Kiselev, "Sovetsko-mongol'skoe nauchnoe sotrudnichestvo (na primere AN SSSR i AN MNR)."

16. D. Zagasbaldan, *Problemy sotsialisticheskoi industrializatsii MNR*, p. 110.

17. Lt. G. C. Binsteed, "Mongolia."

18. *History of the MPR*, p. 605.

19. See note 27, Chapter 6.

20. At Shamar Station in the major wheat-growing region, rainfall was 189 mm. in 1958 and 384 mm. in 1959 (*Narodnoe khozyaistvo MNR za 40 let*, p. 20).

21. Daniel Rosenberg, "*Negdel* Development," pp. 64 and 74 n. 2. Silvio Micheli, writing about his trip in 1960, quoted arats: "They say—Ulan Bator no good! Ulan Bator—too much Russian!" (*Mongolia*, page 229).

22. Coal production increased from 740,000 tons in 1961 to 1.9 million tons in 1970.

23. Silvio Micheli visited Dzun Bayan in 1960, and reported that "the refinery was

a genuinely modern and imposing installation" (*Mongolia,* pp. 61–76). The Soviet expert in charge of exploration, V. G. Smirnov, worked in Rumania during the period 1946–1952, in the MPR 1954–1957, and at Tyumen 1957–1970; he then became head of the West Siberian Geology-Petroleum Institute.

Year	Soviet Petroleum to MPR (in thousand tons)	MPR Petroleum Production (in thousand tons)
1959	92.2	-
1960	-	28.6
1963	177.5	-
1964	199.7	-
1965	-	14.2
1966	200.5	12.1
1967	227	9.8
1968	238.9	7.8
1969	265.4	4.5
1970	-	0
1973	323.0	-
1974	347.0	-

24. Rupen, "Fiftieth Anniversary," p. 467 n. 22.

25. See Rupen, *Mongols,* 1:322–323, for information on the December 1963 purge of Tsende.

26. A list of people in the 1963 Central Committee and government appears in Rupen, *Mongols,* 1:393–412.

27. Tsedenbal, Maidar, Dugersuren, and Molomjamts.

28. See Rupen, "Tsedenbal."

29. Note the comments about Sambu by Owen Lattimore in *Nomads and Commissars,* pp. 45–47, and the references in Charles R. Bawden, *Modern History of Mongolia,* especially pp. 308–310. See also "Zh. Sambu (1895–May 21, 1972)," *Bol'shaya sovetskaya entsiklopediya,* vol. 22 (1975), pp. 531–532.

30. Asonov and Petrov, *Ekonomicheskoe sotrudnichestvo Sovetskogo Soyuza s MNR,* p. 152.

31. S. A. Kozin served as Russian adviser to the Mongolian ministry of finance from 1913 through 1916. See Chapter 2.

32. Rosenberg, "*Negdel* Development," p. 66. See George Ginsburgs, "Local Government in the Mongolian People's Republic, 1940–1960," and note 17, Chapter 6. A 1971 *kandidat* dissertation was D. Purev, *Deyatel'nost' MNRP po povyshenie rol' mestnykh khuralov v stroitel'stve osnov sotsializma v MNR (1940–1960 gg.).*

8. Developing Erdenet: 1974–1978

1. *Novosti Mongolii,* Nov. 27, 1974, carried the texts of the speeches by Tsedenbal and Brezhnev. Speeches, photographs, and related material can also be found in *Pod znamanem bratskoi druzhby.* Brezhnev had been in Ulan Bator once before, January 12–17, 1966.

2. *Novosti Mongolii,* Jan. 17, 1975. For a discussion of China's claims to Mongolia, see June T. Dreyer, *China's Forty Millions,* p. 310 n. 119, and *History of the*

MPR, p. 802 n. 85. See the map reproduced in Harrison Salisbury, *War Between Russia and China*, pp. 131–135; Dennis Doolin, *Territorial Claims in the Sino-Soviet Conflict*, pp. 16–18; and Tsedenbal, "Toward Socialism, Bypassing Capitalism," p. 25.

3. *Novosti Mongolii*, Jan. 17, 1975.

4. See a discussion of the exchange between the Jebtsun Damba Khutukhtu and Yuan Shih-k'ai, in Rupen, *Mongols*, 1:61–64.

5. *Novosti Mongolii*, January 14, 1975.

6. *Novosti Mongolii*, Nov. 27, 1974.

7. Tsedenbal, "Toward Socialism," pp. 25, 27.

8. Gerard M. Friters, *Outer Mongolia and Its International Position*, p. 199.

9. The Joffe-Sun Yat-sen declaration of January 1923 and communiqué of January 26 read: "He [Sun] did not find the rapid evacuation of Russian troops from Outer Mongolia an urgent necessity, affecting the real interests of China. . . ." See Friters, *Outer Mongolia*, p. 194; and M. S. Kapitsa, *Sovetsko-Kitaiskie otnosheniya* (Moscow, 1958), p. 94.

10. An early twentieth-century source that compares Khalkhas with Inner Mongols is V. I. Novitskii, *Puteshestvie po Mongolii v predelakh Tushetu-khanovskago i Tsetsen-khanovskago aimakov Khalkha, Shilin-gol'skago Chigulgana i zemel' Chakharov Vnutrennei Mongolii, sovremennoe v 1906 g.*

11. Ross Munro, *New York Times*, Aug. 31, Sept. 1, and Sept. 2, 1975; and Harrison Salisbury, *New York Times*, Oct. 17, 1977.

12. See Rupen, *Mongols*, 1:290; and Owen Lattimore, *Inner Asian Frontiers of China*, p. xxiv.

13. Sir Fitzroy Maclean, *To the Back of Beyond*, p. 78.

14. See A. Kh. Toichiev (Tashkent), "Reshenie natsional'nogo voprosa v MNR (na primere Bayan-Ul'giiskogo aimaka)," *Narody Azii i Afriki*, no. 3 (1973), pp. 120–123. In January 1978 the MPR established consular representation in Tashkent: Consul-General Tseveniin Tseren-Ochir; Consul Sosorbaramyn Bud; and Vice-Consul Damayn Natsag.

15. Ninety-five percent of the territory of Bayan-Ulegei Aimak lies sixteen-hundred meters or more above sea level. For a map and photographs of the USSR's Altai Kray, and of Biisk, see Robert Jordan, "Siberia's Empire Road, the River Ob," *National Geographic* (Feb. 1976), pp. 151, 153, 159. An interesting article from Biisk appeared in *Krasnaya Zvezda*, Aug. 8, 1975; see also Friters, *Outer Mongolia*, p. 141, and other sources he listed there in note 306. A photograph of a section of Chuisk Road appeared in *Sovetskii Soyuz: Zapadnaya Sibir'* (Moscow, 1971), pp. 368–369. The distance from Biisk to the border of the MPR is 617 km. Silvio Micheli described the pass from the MPR into Kazakhstan in *Mongolia*, pp. 270, 289–290.

16. Sir Fitzroy Maclean, *To Caucasus*, pp. 196–197.

17. The actual Mongolian New Man was well described by Silvio Micheli, who met him in 1960 (in *Mongolia*, p. 121):

His character hardened before my eyes, and his simplicity and spontaneity flew out the window. He had obviously been trained in the Party school like the others, and the Party was his sole guiding light. . . . Like many good civil servants with directives and catchwords in their blood, he always assumed a grave and logical manner when talking about official matters, of whatever kind they might be, and became uninhibited and witty when talking about anything else. But this occasional friendly individualism was no more than a narrow clearing in the teeming bureaucratic jungle of his being.

18. B. Tudev submitted a doctoral dissertation entitled *Rabochii klass v bor'be za zavershenii stroitel'stva sotsializma v MNR* in 1975 at the Institute of Oriental Studies in Moscow.

19. Aleksander Solzhenitsyn, "The Smatterers," pp. 229–278. Bawden said many important things about integrity and truth; especially on pp. 23, 87, 246–249, 377, 410–419 in *The Modern History of Mongolia*. There have been signs of at least partial rehabilitation of Jamtsarano: T. Ts. Dudenova, "O fonde Ts. Zhamtsarano"; references in A. V. Burdukov, *V staroi i novoi Mongolii*, pp. 336 and p. 388 n. 4; *History of the MPR*, p. 839 (Baldanjapov); and S. D. Miliband, *Biobibliograficheskii slovar' sovetskikh vostokovedov*, p. 203.

20. *Velikoderzhavnaya politika maoistov v natsional' nykh raionakh KNR* decried the Chinese mistreatment of national minorities in Inner Mongolia (pp. 28–44), Sinkiang (pp. 45–74), and Tibet (pp. 102–125). A similar condemnation appeared in V. A. Bogoslovskii, T. R. Rakhimov, and N. A. Teshilov, "Natsional'nyi vopros." See also S. K. Rozbakiev, "Sud'by uigurskoi literatury v Sin'tszyane."

21. Rinchen referred to the similar destruction during "the events of 1937 and the so-called cultural revolution of Maoists," and noted that "In northern Mongolia [MPR] the native and more than millenial year old tradition of Sanskrit studies was interrupted almost fully in 1937. In South Mongolia [Inner Mongolia] the Maoists put an end to all cultural traditions of learning Sanskrit and Tibetan among the Mongols." (Rinchen, "Sanskrit in Mongolia," pp. 98, 103).

22. *Mongol'skaya narodnaya respublika*, pp. 346–348; B. Gungaadash, *Mongoliya segodnya: priroda, lyudi, khozyaistvo* (Moscow, 1969), p. 96; *Novosti Mongolii*, Aug. 29, 1975.

23. *Mongol'skaya narodnaya respublika*, p. 348; *Novosti Mongolii*, Aug. 27, 1975.

24. It is called the Polytechnical Institute, and it was founded in 1969 with UNESCO assistance. In 1973 an architecture department was established at this institute (*Novosti Mongolii*, July 22, 1975).

25. Information is available for enrollments in the 1960s: Teachers' Institute: 1,300 (1965); Agriculture Institute: 2,000 (1968); finance and economics: 1,200 (1965); medicine: about 1,250 (graduating 250 M.D.s annually); and Higher Party School: 3,000, including 700 in the course for SKhO chairmen and 1,000 in the one for members of the party and state apparatus. *Novosti Mongolii*, Jan. 30, 1976, criticized the Agriculture Institute.

26. In 1965 there were only 171 *kandidat* holders, and but five holders of doctorates.

27. *Novosti Mongolii*, Aug. 22, 1975. See also Urie Bronfenbrenner, *Two Worlds of Childhood: US and USSR* (New York, 1970).

28. Television is now available at Ulan Bator, Darkhan, and the eastern Mongolian city of Choibalsan; Kyakhta, on the Soviet side of the border, broadcasts to the town of Sukhe Bator, five state farms of Selenga Aimak, the new town of Erdenet, and part of Khubsugul Aimak. A statistical handbook listed the total number of Mongolian television sets as just under 15,000 in 1970, and almost 25,000 in 1973. Foreign-trade statistics indicated that the USSR sent over 5,000 sets in 1970; 6,000 in 1973; 3,000 in 1974; 2,000 in 1975; 3,000 in 1976, and 2,000 in 1977.

29. *Novosti Mongolii,* Feb. 6, 1976; Christopher Wren, "Soviet Influence Pervades Ulan Bator," *New York Times,* Dec. 14, 1974.

30. *Novosti Mongolii,* Jan. 9, 1976. Predecessors opened in Prague in 1972, in Budapest in 1974, and in Sofia in 1975.

31. Erdenet is located approximately 400 km. south, and slightly west, of Irkutsk, and 400 km. northwest of Ulan Bator. It lies near the Orkhon River, 64 km. south of the Selenga River. It must be situated at approximately 104°E and 49°N. A rough timetable for its development would be:

1960s—Czech and Mongolian geologists found promising signs.
1970—(October) MPR-USSR joint announcement of serious intent.
1971—(March) detailed Russian geological survey.
    (March 17) First test boring; fourteen holes drilled.
    (June) The Sixteenth MPRP Congress at Ulan Bator announced the favorable results of the geological survey.
1972—(May) Protocol signed in Moscow. High-voltage power lines, railroad, and automobile highway to be supplied by USSR for mines; product of mines to be for export to USSR.
    (June) Announcement of project at the Revsomol Congress in Ulan Bator.
1973—(November) Formal MPR-USSR agreement. The Soviet Union approves the project for the construction of Erdenet; construction begins.
1974—(July 23) Joint meeting in Ulan Bator. Joint Mongolian-Soviet Erdenet Council.
    (August) 750 Revsomols go to construction site.
    (Fall) First pupils attend new Erdenet school.
    (November) Power line from Darkhan is in operation.
1975—(January) Railroad bridge over Orkhon River is completed.
    (June) Population of town of Erdenet reported to have reached 10,000.
    (October 4) Erdenet-Salkhit Railroad opens. Erdenet population reported to be 13,000.
    (December) Erdenet population reaches 15,000.
1977—(February) Water pipeline operational. Mountain top blown off for mining.
    (May) Erdenet population reaches 25,000.
    (June 6) First passenger train to Erdenet.
    (November) Erdenet population reaches 32,000.
1978 or 1979—Operations to begin and first product to be exported to USSR. Population of Erdenet expected to be 60,000.

Alan J. K. Sanders reported on a 1977 visit to Erdenet in "Letter from Erdenet."

About 175 km. north of Erdenet, in the Buryat Republic of the USSR, lies Zakamensk, on the Jida River. It was developed by forced labor in the 1930s—Solzhenitsyn refers to the camp there—as a major source of wolfram (tungsten) and molybdenum. It was connected by a 253-km. highway to the railroad (Jida Station on the line south from Ulan Ude to Naushki to Ulan Bator). The grand plans for massive development and production failed, however, and most of the mines were closed. The population of Zakamen'sk declined from 13,600 in 1959 to 12,000 in 1969.

See G. D. R. Phillips, *Russia, Japan, and Mongolia,* p. 93; idem, *Dawn in Siberia,* p. 159 (with a photograph); Afrikan Bal'burov, *Dvenadtsat' moikh dragotsennostei,* pp. 23–26; *Sovetskii Soyuz—Vostochnaya Sibir'* (Moscow, 1969), pp. 340–341; "Zaka-men'sk," *BSE,* vol. 9 (1972); Violet Conolly, *Beyond the Urals,* especially p. 272; Theodore Shabad, *Basic Industrial Resources of the USSR* (1969), pp. 262–263. See also Yu. D. Kharitonov, "Soderzhaniya vanadiya, molibdena i kobal'ta v pasteniyakh Selenginskogo Aimaka Buryatskoi ASSR," *Mikroelementy v Sibiri* (1974).

32. Salisbury, *To Moscow—and Beyond*, pp. 213–214; idem, *War Between Russia and China*, p. 14.

33. Open coal mines at Sharyn gol and Baganur, and open-pit copper mining at Erdenet, as well as greatly extended farming, suggest the possibility of extensive pollution and erosion, problems previously unknown in Mongolia. A "Section for Protection of the Environment" of the State Committee on Science and Technology has been established, and there is a "Joint Soviet-Mongolian Group to Protect the Natural Resources of the Selenga Basin." The Selenga flows into Lake Baikal, and the purity of that lake could be affected by northern Mongolian mining and industry. See Kevin Klose, "Soviets Gaining on Pollution Problems That Once Threatened Lake Baikal," *Washington Post*, March 5, 1978. The protection of nature and wildlife was discussed in *Novosti Mongolii*, April 15, 1977.

34. The famous 1925 letter from Maxim Gorky to the Mongols advised: "The propagation of the principle of activity," and the letter is often cited in the MPR (Rupen, *Mongols*, 1:351–352).

35. More than twenty-five years ago Herold J. Wiens argued that Mongolia was overgrazed ("Geographic Limitations to Food Production in the MPR"). Some recent dissertations written by Mongols studying in the Soviet Union deal with related matters: B. Jambaljamts, *Klimaticheskoe raionirovanie territorii MNR v svyazi s razmeshcheniem sel'sko-khozyaistva (kandidat* in geography, 1971); A. Damdin, *Nekotorye ekonomicheskie problemy razvitiya obshchestvennogo pitaniya v MNR (kandidat* in economics, 1971); V. Myagmarjav, *Osnovnye problemy ekonomicheskoi otsenko sel'sko-khozyaistvennykh ugodii MNR (kandidat* in economics, 1973); and Sh. Choijilvav, *Zemel'nye fondy MNR i nekotorye voprosy novysheniya ekonomicheskoi effektivnosti ikh ispol'zovaniya (kandidat* in economics, 1974).

36. *Novosti Mongolii*, Dec. 4, 1975.

37. See Rupen, "Tsedenbal."

38. In the USSR, Brezhnev replaced Podgorny as "president" on June 16, 1977, after a month's delay.

39. *Novosti Mongolii*, December 4, 1975.

40. See note 21, Chapter 7.

41. *Novosti Mongolii*, Jan. 21, 1975.

42. This section on the Mongolian elite is based on an analysis of 462 leaders, including all 91 Central Committee members and 61 candidate-members, and all the ministers of the government, whether or not they are Central Committee figures. In addition, the 462 include those whose names have appeared more than once in the Ulan Bator Russian-language newspaper, *Novosti Mongolii*, in the past three years.

43. See note 4, Chapter 5 (where L. Toiv's book is cited). Ravdan published an article: "MNRP—organizator i rukovoditel' narodnykh voisk MNR," *Kommunisticheskie vooruzhenie sil*, no. 5 (1961), pp. 80–83. Shagdarsuren reportedly published his memoirs dealing with Khalkin-gol in 1969, and Lkhagvasuren published his as a study of Mongol-Soviet military collaboration in April 1976.

44. R. Gunsen, *Ugolovno-pravovaya okhrana sotsialisticheskoi sobstvennosti v MNR* (Doctor of Juridical Science, June 1974, Institute of State and Law, Academy of Sciences, USSR); D. Purev, *Deyatel'nost' MNRP po povyshenie rol' mestnykh khuralov v stroitel'stve osnov sotsializma v MNR (1940–1960 gg), (kandidat* in history,

1971, Academy of Social Sciences [AON] of the Central Committee, CPSU, Moscow). See also note 32, Chapter 7.

45. Altunin, the head of Soviet Civil Defense, visited the MPR in 1977.

46. Jalan-Ajav did serve in 1966 as chairman of the Committee for Information and Radio, MPR Council of Ministers.

47. R. Gurbazar was named head of a group to prepare a multivolume Mongolian encyclopedia in December 1976. The project comes under the Institute of Language and Literature of the Mongolian Academy of Sciences.

48. Demichev was appointed Furtseva's successor as USSR minister of culture on November 14, 1974. See the *New York Times* and the *Washington Post*, Nov. 15, 1974.

49. *Far Eastern Economic Review,* Oct. 14, 1977, p. 5.

50. See notes 30 and 31, Chapter 7.

51. Statistics for medical doctors indicate:

Year	Number of M.D.s
1925	2
1930	27
1940	108
1947	134
1952	180
1956	377
1957	547
1958	607
1960	900
1961	870
1967	1820
1973	2700

A publication in 1976 was entitled *Materialy po izucheniyu istochnikov indo-tibetskoi meditsiny.*

52. Russians in the MPR in recent years include: V. N. Kobakhidze, general director of the Erdenet *kombinat;* A. V. Chekashov, chief of administration, "Med'molibden'-stroi"; A. P. Tkachev, chief engineer, Med'molibden'stroi; P. Skupov, chief of Construction Administration, Erdenetenergostroi; P. G. Yushin, deputy secretary, Party Committee of Administration of Med'molibden'stroi; A. A. Vinogradov, head of Soviet Construction Organizations for Darkhan-Erdenet Railroad; V. I. Vasil'ev, head of Soviet Energy Construction Organizations in MPR; I. S. Gur'evich, head of the Irkutsk organization responsible for Darkhan–Sukhe Bator and Darkhan–Ulan Bator high-voltage power line, "Vostsibelektrset'stroi"; S. A. Mel'nikov, head of "Buryatenergo"; N. M. Lunin, general director, Joint Mongolian-Soviet Economic Association and general director, "Mongolsovtsvetmet"; A. Tyuryakov, chairman, Soviet side of Joint Mongolian-Soviet "Mongol'sovtsvetmet": and V. Zaval'skii, chief of Construction Administration, Darkhangor'stroi.

53. Recent dissertations of Mongols studying international relations include: G. Ochirbat (fomer deputy chief editor of *Unen;* chairman of Trade Unions, Central Committee member; member of Presidium of the Great Khural), *Problema sochetaniya internatsional'nogo i natsional'nogo v stroitel'stve sitsializma (na primere*

deyatel'nosti MNRP), Academy of Social Sciences, Central Committee, CPSU, *kandidat* in philosophy, 1972; B. Lkhamsuren (Politburo member purged in 1973), *Printsipy internatsionalizma v deyatel'nosti MNRP*, Institute of Marxism-Leninism, Central Committee, CPSU, *doktor* in history, 1975; B. Ligden, *Mezhdunarodnaya deyatel'nost' MNRP v 1945–1970 gg.*, Academy of Social Sciences, Central Committee, CPSU, *kandidat* in history, 1973; and L. Khashbat (counsellor in MPR embassy in Moscow), *Mezhdunarodno-pravovoe priznanie MNR*, Moscow University, International Relations, *kandidat* in jurisprudence, 1974.

Articles dealing with the MPR's relations with Eastern Europe include: S. K. Roshchin, "MNR–chlen SEV," *Narody Azii i Afriki*, no. 5 (1964), pp. 3–9; M. N. Yumin, "MNR v sisteme mezhdunarodnoi sotsialisticheskoi ekonomicheskoi integratsii"; and idem, "MNR i SEV."

54. See Salisbury, "The Two Mongolias Are Bitter Enemies . . . Borders Are Closed, Hostile," *New York Times*, Oct. 17, 1977. Extreme examples of the polemics in the 1970s include, on the MPR side, T. Nima, "Twenty-Five Years in which Freedom Was Taken Away," where it is alleged that the Chinese practice "appalling discrimination and compulsory assimilation." A Chinese article attacked the alleged Soviet "aim of making the Mongolian people docile slaves" and to "make the Mongolian people serve as cannon-fodder for the Russia of the new tsars" ("New Tsars Step Up Cultural Aggression Against Mongolia," *Peking Review*, no. 10 [March 5, 1976], pp. 17–18).

55. George A. Cheney, "The Pre-Revolutionary Culture of Outer Mongolia," p. 7, citing E. M. Murzaev, *MNR*, p. 13.

56. Phillips, *Russia, Japan and Mongolia*, p. 93. See note 31, Chapter 8.

Bibliography

The most important works of the last fifteen years include Charles Bawden's *Modern History of Mongolia* (1968), which is the very model of a survey—marked by felicity of expression, judicious assessment, and extensive use of Mongolian-language sources. William A. Brown and Urgunge Onon have translated the official *History of the Mongolian People's Republic* (1969), which provides the authorized interpretation of events: a tendentious, propagandistic, and deeply flawed version. The first chapter (pp. 5–44) surveys literature on Mongolia from that same skewed perspective; an extensive bibliography (pp. 713–740) includes many approved Mongolian-language, as well as Russian and other, sources. The translators supplement that bibliography with one of their own (pp. 839–852). The most valuable contribution, however, is in the extensive footnotes provided by the translators (pp. 741–838), wherein Mongolian-language sources and many others provide biographical and other information available nowhere else. A meticulous index provides ready access to this treasure lode.

A. V. Burdukov's memoirs and letters (1969) add significant new information, mostly concerning pre-Communist western Mongolia, but the useful material provided by Burdukov is greatly enhanced by the 317 footnotes (pp. 370–414) compiled by Elena Darevskaya of Irkutsk. She has plumbed East Siberian archives and presented a wealth of unique material. No index eases access to the book, however.

George Cheney's monograph on prerevolutionary culture (1968) provides a convenient summary of much of the standard literature on the subject, but accepts, for example, Maisky's 1918 census figures uncritically. The work is less successful than Bawden's in integrating its varied content, and it presents mainly description, while omitting the critical interpretation which Cheney indicates formed part of his original doctoral dissertation. The availability now in English of Pozdneev's *Mongolia and the Mongols* (1971), including Fred Adelman's useful introduction, provides easier access to a wealth of detail about the traditional society.

George Murphy's *Soviet Mongolia* (1966) is uneven, flawed, and incomplete, but withal it bears the unmistakable imprint of original thought. It is one of the most intellectually stimulating works on Mongolia ever published. S. K. Roshchin, a Russian economist, published an excellent work on Mongolian agriculture in 1971. This is an unusually thoughtful and subtle product of Soviet scholarship.

Collections bringing together several articles by various authors are numerous in the Soviet literature, but the best in many years appeared in 1971. Like many others, it is entitled simply *Mongol'skaya narodnaya respublika*. It includes more careful and thoughtful analysis, and more new information, than almost any Russian book published in the past fifteen years.

Harrison Salisbury's *War Between Russia and China,* published in 1969, has undoubtedly been the most popular, widely read, opinion-forming, and influential work dealing extensively with Mongolia in the last decade and a half. It dramatizes, indeed it overdramatizes, the Sino-Soviet conflict, the role of the MPR, and the racial-prejudice overtones. The book's influence has been pervasive, and to some extent pernicious because of its flamboyance and its extreme presentation of the "Yellow Peril" and the "atavistic" Russian fear of Chinese, Chinggis Khan, and Mongols. According to Salisbury, all Asians are the same to the Russians.

G. K. Plotnikov's 1971 study of the Mongolian army is useful, and of even greater value are N. S. Sorkin's 1970 memoirs of his tour of duty as a military instructor in Ulan Bator in the 1920s. For relevant military strategy, the brilliant forty-page summary by O. Edmund Clubb in Garthoff's 1966 book, *Sino-Soviet Military Relations*, is unique. The USSR's journal of military history, *Voenno-istoricheskii zhurnal*, provides important analysis and information on military-strategic matters.

For general information, the indispensable sources are *Novosti Mongolii*, the Russian-language newspaper published twice weekly in Ulan Bator, and *Narody Azii i Afriki*, the most important Soviet journal dealing with Asian studies. *Novosti Mongolii* not only provides current material, but in marking anniversaries and holidays is often also a significant source for historical data. It is of course an official Communist newspaper, and as such a major vehicle of propaganda. It must be employed carefully, cautiously, and critically.

Miliband (1975) supplies biographical and bibliographical information about most of the Soviet Far Eastern specialists, and may be consulted for further information and references.

Among works dealing with the areas adjoining the Mongolian People's Republic, James Sheridan's brilliant biography of Feng Yu-hsiang (1966), Gavan McCormack's less inspired but nonetheless useful biography of Chang Tso-lin (1977), and Valliant's thirty-page analysis (1972) of the role of Japan in the period 1912–1919, provide much of the information necessary to put Mongolia in the context of the significant events in North China and Japanese activity on the mainland. Japanese works on Mongolia are cited in *Moko kenkyu Bunken Mokuroku: 1900–1972* (Bibliography of Mongolia for 1900–1972).

Doak Barnett's hundred-page record of his travels through Inner Mongolia and Sinkiang in 1948 in *China on the Eve of Communist Takeover* (1963) is packed with uniquely valuable first-hand detail about the realities and dreams of Mongols, Uighurs, and Kazakhs in China. June Dreyer (1976) in effect updates Barnett's material with her study of the Chinese People's Republic's national minorities. Holmes Welch (1972) provides detail and highly intelligent analysis about Buddhism in Mao's China. Edmund Clubb's *China and Russia* (1971) is excellent for the overall context of Sino-Soviet relations, but unique and unrivalled for the material on Sinkiang, which is based on his personal experience. It is convenient that George Moseley undertook a detailed examination of the Ili Kazakh district in Sinkiang (1966), for this is the area that has interacted most closely with the western part of the MPR.

In a whole series of works, Alastair Lamb provides a perspective on the Sino-Indian border that updates the sorts of overall Central Asian comparisons suggested long ago (1940) by Owen Lattimore in his classic *Inner Asian Frontiers of China*. J. R. V. Prescott (1975) fills a great gap by presenting his analysis of Asian border treaties.

Material to compare a minority area that is an integral part of the USSR with the MPR as an independent nation outside the Soviet Union is conveniently available in Rakowska-Harmstone's study of the Tajik Republic (1970). Violet Conolly provides the basis for relating the MPR to East Siberia in *Beyond the Urals* (1967).

One work more than fifteen years old is cited here because it has apparently not been used before: Amur-Sanan, *Mudreshkin syn* (1929). It provides unique information about the relationship between the Kalmyks and Rinchino and the Mongolian Revolution, as well as comparative material on Kalmyk developments. A survey of the mass of the material dating back more than fifteen years once again points up the debt scholars in this field owe to Gerard Friters for his pioneering *Outer Mongolia and Its International Position* (1949).

BOOKS AND ARTICLES

Abasheev, D. A. "Vospominaniya o pervoi mongol'skoi sovetskoi shkole v Urge." In *Trudy buryatskogo kompleksnogo nauchno-issledovatel'nogo instituta.* Vol. 8, pp. 147–150. Ulan Ude, 1962.

Acheson, Dean. *Present at the Creation: My Years in the State Department.* New York, 1969.

Alekseev, V. M. *Kitaiskaya ieroglificheskaya pis'mennost' i ee latinizatsii.* Leningrad, 1932.

"V. M. Alekseev (1881–1951)." In S. D. Miliband, *Biobibliograficheskii slovar' sovetskikh vostokovedov,* p. 192. Moscow, 1975.

Amur-Sanan

———. "The Importance of Buddhist Mongolia to the World Revolution." In *Soviet Russia and the East, 1920–1927,* edited by Xenia J. Eudin and Robert C. North, p. 199. Stanford, Ca., 1957.

*———. *Mudreshkin syn.* Moscow-Leningrad, 1929.

Asonov, B. A. and Petrov, B. M. *Ekonomicheskoe sotrudnichestvo Sovetskogo Soyuza s MNR.* Moscow, 1971.

Atlas Irkutskoi oblasti. Irkutsk, 1962.

Atlas Zabaikal'ya Buryatskaya ASSR i Chitinskaya oblast. Institut geografiya Sibiri i Dal'nego Vostoka. Moscow-Irkutsk, 1967.

"Aviaeskadril'ya 'Mongol'skii arat'srazhaetsya." In *Kniga bratstva,* pp. 346–351. Moscow, 1971.

Baator, Sosorbaramyn, *Problemy razvitiya promyshlennosti po pererabotke selikhozsyrya v MNR. Kandidat* dissertation, Tashkent Institute of Economics, 1975.

Bal'burov, Afrikan. *Dvenadtsat' moikh dragotsennostei.* Moscow, 1975.

Baldaev, R. L. *Sozdanie i razvitie sistemy narodnogo obrazovaniya v MNR (1921–1965 gg.). Kandidat* dissertation, Leningrad University, 1967.

Balkhanov, G. I. "Rol' kommunisticheskoi propagandy v politicheskom vospitanii trudyashchikhsya (Opyt konkretno-sotsiologicheskogo issledovaniya na primere Buryatskoi ASSR)," *Trudy buryatskogo instituta,* no. 20 (1973), pp. 61–69.

Ballis, William B. "The Political Evolution of a Soviet Satellite: the Mongolian People's Republic." *Western Political Quarterly* 9, no. 2 (June 1956): 293–328.

———. "Soviet Russia's Asiatic Frontier Technique: Tannu Tuva." *Pacific Affairs* 14 (March 1941): 91–96.

Baltykov, S-G. "V ryadakh mongol'skoi narodnoi armii. Vospominaniya." In *Kniga bratstva,* pp. 107–110. Moscow, 1971.

---

*Works identified with an asterisk are those cited in the above essay

Bannikov, A. G. "Pervye gody Mongol'skogo universiteta." In *Narody brat'ya,* pp. 101–104. Moscow, 1965.

*Barnett, A. Doak. *China on the Eve of Communist Takeover.* 1963.

Batorov, B. N. "K istorii i bor'by buryatskoi partiinoi organizatsii za preodolenie lamaizma v gody sotsialisticheskogo stroitel'stva." In *Velikii oktyabr' i Vostochnaya Sibir' (materialy yubileinoi nauchno-teoreticheskoi konferentsii v Irkutske 15–17 yunya 1967 g.).* Irkutsk, 1968, pp. 331–344.

Bavrin, E. P. *Mongol'skaya Narodnaya Respublika: Spravochnik.* 1976.

Bawden, Charles R. "An Event in the Life of the Eighth Jebtsun Damba Khutukhtu." *Collecteana Mongolica. Festschrift für Prof. Dr. Rintchen,* pp. 9–19. Wieshaden, 1966.

*——. *The Modern History of Mongolia.* New York, 1968.

——. "Notes on the Worship of Local Deities in Mongolia." In *Mongolian Studies,* edited by Louis Ligeti, pp. 57–66. Amsterdam, 1970.

Belgaev, G. Ts. "K perevodu buryato-mongol'skoi pis'mennosti v russkii alfavit'." *Zapiski buryato-mongol'skogo instituta,* no. 1, 1939, pp. 3–6.

Belikov, P., and Knyazeva, V. *Rerikh.* Moscow, 1972.

Belikov, T. I. *Kalmyki v bor'be za nezavisimost' nashei rodiny (XVII–nachalo XIX vv.).* Elista, 1965.

——. *Uchastie kalmykov v krestyanskoi voine pod rukovodstvom E. I. Pugacheva (1773–1775).* Elista, 1971.

——. *Uchastie kalmykov v voinakh Rossii v XVII, XVIII i pervoi chetvertii XIX vekov.* Elista, 1960.

Bell, Sir Charles. *Portrait of the Dalai Lama.* London, 1946.

——. *Tibet Past and Present.* London, 1924.

Berlin, L. E. "Khambo-Agvan Dorzhiev (k bor'be Tibeta za nezavisimost')." *Novyi Vostok,* no. 3 (1923), pp. 139–156.

——. "U istokov Sovetsko-mongol'skoi druzhby." *Narody Azii i Afriki,* no. 2 (1968), pp. 131–136.

Bertram, James. *Unconquered.* New York, 1939.

Binsteed, Lt. G. C. "Mongolia." *China Yearbook 1914,* pp. 609–643.

Bira, Sh. *Mongolian Historical Literature of the XVII–XIX Centuries Written in Tibetan.* Translated by Stanley Frye and edited by John Krueger. Bloomington, Ind., 1970.

Bisch, Jorgen. *Mongolia: Unknown Land.* New York, 1963.

Bogolepov, M. I., and Sobolev, M. N. *Ocherki russko-mongol'skoi torgovli.* Tomsk, 1911.

Bogoslovskii, V. A., Rakhimov, T. R., and Teshilov, N. A. "Natsional'nyi vopros." In *KNR: politicheskoe i ekonomicheskoe razvitie v 1973 g.* Moscow, 1975, pp. 236–255.

Boloban, A. P. *Mongoliya v ee sovremennom torgovo-ekonomicheskom otnoshenii.* Petrograd, 1914.

Boorman, Howard. "The Borderlands and the Sino-Soviet Alliance." In *Moscow-Peking Axis,* edited by Boorman, pp. 156–173. New York, 1957.

Bor'ba za sovety v Buryat-Mongolii (1918– 1920 gg.). Vospominaniya i materialy. K dvadsatiletiyu razgroma inostrannoi voennoi interventsii i belogvardeishchinu v Buryat-Mongolii. Moscow, 1940.

Borisov, O. *Sovetskii Soyuz i Man'chzhurskaya revolyutsionnaya baza (1945–1949).* Moscow, 1975.

Bradsher, Henry S. "The Sovietization of Mongolia." *Foreign Affairs* 50, no. 3 (April 1972): 545–553.

Brandt, Conrad. *Stalin's Failure in China, 1924–1927.* Cambridge, Mass., 1958.

Brown, Roger Glenn. "Chinese Politics and American Policy: A New Look at the Triangle." *Foreign Policy,* no. 23 (Summer 1976), pp. 3–23.

Bulstrode, Beatrix. *A Tour in Mongolia.* New York, 1920.

*Burdukov, A. V. *V staroi i novoi Mongolii.* Preface by I. Maisky; notes by Elena Darevskaya (pp. 370–414). Moscow, 1969.

Burke, James. "China's Losing Game in Mongolia." *Far Eastern Survey* 17 (July 7, 1948).

Carpenter, Clifton C. "The Inner Asian Frontier—A Cradle of Conflict." *Strategic Review,* Winter 1977, pp. 90–99.

Carr, E. H. *The Bolshevik Revolution, 1917–1923.* 3 vols. London, 1952, 1953, and 1954.

———. *Socialism in One Country, 1924–1926.* Vol. 2. London, 1959.

Chalidze, Valery. *Criminal Russia: Crime in the Soviet Union.* New York, 1977.

Chen, Jack. *The Sinkiang Story.* New York, 1977.

*Cheney, George A. "The Pre-Revolutionary Culture of Outer Mongolia." *Mongolia Society Occasional Papers,* no. 5. Bloomington, Ind., 1968.

Chenkirov, I. V. "Vospominaniya o mongolii." *Trudy buryatskogo instituta,* no. 23 (1974), pp. 224–227.

China Islamic Association. *Chinese Muslims in Progress.* Peking, 1957.

Chinese Buddhist Association. *Buddhists in New China.* Peking, 1956.

Choibalsan. *Novosti Mongolii,* Feb. 8 and 11, 1975.

"Choibalsan." In *Spravochnik propagandista mezhdunarodnika,* pp. 253–254. Moscow, 1974.

Christopher, James W., *Conflict in the Far East: American Diplomacy in China from 1928–1933.* Leiden, 1950.

Clark, Milton J. "How the Kazakhs Fled to Freedom." *National Geographic,* 106, no. 5 (Nov. 1954): 621–644.

*Clubb, O. Edmund. "Armed Conflict in the Chinese Borderlands, 1917–1950." In *Sino-Soviet Military Relations,* edited by R. L. Garthoff, pp. 9–43. New York, 1966.

———. *China and Russia: The 'Great Game'.* New York, 1971.

———. "Manchuria in the Balance, 1945–1946." *Pacific Historical Review* 26 (Nov. 1957): 377–390.

*Conolly, Violet. *Beyond the Urals: Economic Developments in Soviet Asia.* New York, 1967.

———. *Soviet Economic Policy in the East.* London, 1933.

Conquest, Robert. *The Great Terror: Stalin's Purge of the Thirties.* London, 1968.

Consten, Hermann. *Die Weideplätze der Mongolen.* 2 vols. Berlin, 1919 and 1920.

Coox, Alvin D. "*L'Affaire* Lyushkov: Anatomy of a Defector." *Soviet Studies,* January 1968, pp. 405–420.

Cressey, George. "The Ordos Desert of Inner Mongolia." *Denison University Bulletin,* no. 28 (Oct. 1933), pp. 194–196.

Damba Dorji [Ulan Otorchi]. "Ozero Tolbo." *Khozyaistvo Mongolii,* nos. 1–6 (1928). Excerpted in *Kniga bratstva,* pp. 83–89. Moscow-Ulan Bator, 1971.

Damdinsuren, Ts. *Biobibliograficheskaya ukazatel'.* Compiled by A. M. Kaigorodov (announced 1977).

Dandaron, Bid'ya D. "Aga Monastery." *Encyclopedia of Buddhism.* Vol. I, pp. 249–250. Ceylon, 1961.

——. *Index,* no. 1, p. 9 (1973); no. 1, pp. 92–93 (1975); no. 2, p. 63 (1975).

——. *Opisanie tibetskikh rukopisei i ksilografov.* Vol. 1. 1960.

Darbeeva, A. A. "Mongol'skie yazyki." *Sovetskoe yazykoznanie za 50 let.* Moscow, 1967, pp. 276–286.

Darevskaya, E. M. "Obuchenie mongol'skoi molodezhi v Vostochnoi Sibiri (Iz istorii sovetsko-mongol'skikh kul'turnikh svyazei)." *Trudy Irkutskogo gosudarstvennogo universiteta.* Vol. 31, pp. 150–173. Irkutsk.

Dashjamts, D. *Rasprostranenie i utverzhdenie idei marksizma-leninizma v Mongolii,* 1978.

Demidov, V. A. "Istoriografiya bor'by za vlast' sovetov v Gornom Altae." *Istoricheskaya nauka v Sibiri za 50 let.* Novosibirsk, 1972, pp. 187–196.

——. "Sovety v bor'be s natsionalisticheskoi kontrrevolyutsiei v Gornom Altae." *Voprosy istorii Sovetskoi Sibiri,* Istoricheskaya seriya, no. 1, 1967, pp. 25–53.

Doolin, Dennis J. *Territorial Claims in the Sino-Soviet Conflict.* Stanford, Ca. 1965.

Dragunov, A. A., and Dragunova, E. N. "K latinizatsii dialektov Tsentral'nogo Kitaya. Dialekty Syantan' i Syansan (Khunan')." *Izvestiya AN SSSR,* VII seriya. Otdelenie obshchestv. nauk, no. 3, 1932, pp. 240–269.

*Dreyer, June T. *China's Forty Millions: Minority Nationalities and National Integration in the People's Republic of China.* Cambridge, Mass., 1976.

Druzhboi velikoi sil'ny: Istoricheskii opyt KPSS po organizatsii bratskoi vzaimopomoshchi i sotrudnichestva narodov Sovetskogo Soyuza v politicheskom, ekonomicheskom i kul'turnom razvitii Kazakhskoi Sovetskoi Sotsialisticheskoi Respubliki. Alma Ata, 1972.

Dubinin, A. B. *Problemy politiki Kominterna v natsional no-kolonial'nom voprose (na primere Mongolii 1919–1928 gg.).* Kandidat dissertation, Moscow, 1973.

Dubinskii, A. M. *Osvoboditel'naya missiya Sovetskogo Soyuza na Dal'nem Vostoke.* Moscow, 1966.

Dubrovskii, V. A. "Pravovoe polozhenie russkogo naseleniya v TNR." *Uchenye zapiski tuvinskogo instituta,* no. 16, 1973, pp. 276–287.

Dudenova, T. Ts. "O fonde Ts. Zhamtsarano." *Materialy po istorii i filologii Tsentral'noi Azii (psoyashchaetsya pamyati ak.-a V. P. Vasil'eva).* Vol. 4. 1970.

Dylykov, S. D. "Edzhen Khoro." In *Filologiya i istoriya mongol'skikh narodov: pamyati ak.-a B. Ya. Vladimirtsova,* pp. 228–274. Moscow, 1958.

"Sandzhe Dantsikovich Dylykov (b. 1912)." In S. D. Miliband, *Biobibliograficheskii slovar' sovetskikh vostokovedov,* p. 192. Moscow, 1975.

Dylykov S. D., and Gol'man, M. I. "Pamyati A. T. Yakimova (1895–1976)." *Narody Azii i Afriki,* no. 3 (1977), pp. 247–248.

Efremov, A. A., Novozhilov, M. I., and Rozhdestvenskii, A. K. "Sbornik rabot po paleontologii MNR." *Trudy mongol'skoi komissii,* no. 59, 1954.

Egunov, N. P. *M. I. Amagaev.* (Especially "Deyatel'nost M. I. Amagaeva v narodnoi Mongolii," pp. 71–94.) Ulan Ude, 1974.

El'm, L. *Nash sosed—Mongoliya.* Moscow-Leningrad, 1928. [Notebook for the Red Army Man].

Enders, Gordon and Anthony, Edward. *Nowhere Else in the World.* New York, 1935.

Erickson, John, *The Soviet High Command.* New York, 1962.

——. *Soviet Military Power.* London, 1971.

——. "The Soviet Military, Soviet Policy, and Soviet Politics." *Strategic Review,* Fall 1973, pp. 23–36.

Eudin, Xenia J., and North, Robert C., eds. *Soviet Russia and the East, 1920–1927: A Documentary Survey.* Stanford, Ca., 1957.

Eudin, Xenia J., and Slusser, Robert M., eds. *Soviet Foreign Policy, 1928–1934. Documents and Materials.* 2 vols. Stanford, Ca., 1966.

Fainsod, Merle. *How Russia Is Ruled.* Cambridge, Mass., 1953.

Fell, E. Nelson. *Russian and Nomad: Tales of the Kirghiz Steppes.* New York, 1916.

*Friters, Gerard M. *Outer Mongolia and Its International Position.* Baltimore, 1949.

Frynta, Emanuel. *Hasek the Creator of Schweik.* Prague, 1965.

"Bobodzhan Gafurovich Gafurov (1908–1977)," *Novaya i noveishaya istoriya,* no. 6 (1977), pp. 213–214.

"B. G. Gafurov," *Voprosy istorii,* no. 9 (1977), pp. 219–220.

"B. G. Gafurov (b. 1908)." In S. D. Miliband, *Biobibliograficheskii slovar' sovetskikh vostokovedov,* pp. 133–134. Moscow, 1975.

Gardener, William. "China and Russia: The Beginnings of Contact." *History Today* 27, no. 1 (Jan. 1977): 22–30.

——. "Peking to Moscow: The Trans-Siberian Caravan Route." *History Today* 27, no. 4 (April 1977): 211–218.

Garthoff, R. L., ed. *Sino-Soviet Military Relations.* New York, 1966.

Ginsburgs, George. "Local Government in the Mongolian People's Republic, 1940–1960." *Journal of Asian Studies* 20, no. 4 (Aug. 1961): 498–508.

Gobi-Altaiskoe zemletryasnenie. Moscow, 1963.

Gol'man, M. I. "Mezhdunarodnyi kongress mongolovedov [Sept. 2–7, 1970]." *Narody Azii i Afriki,* no. 2 (1971), pp. 229–232.

——. *Problemy noveishei istorii MNR v burzhuaznoi istoriografii SShA.* Moscow, 1970.

——. "III mezhdunarodnyi kongress mongolovedov [Aug. 30–Sept. 3, 1976]." *Narody Azii i Afriki,* no. 4 (1977), pp. 164–173.

"Mark Isaakovich Gol'man (b. 1927)." In S. D. Miliband, *Biobibliograficheskii slovar', sovetskikh vostokovedov,* pp. 145–146. Moscow, 1975.

Gonchigsumla, S. *Mongol'skie narodnye pesni.* Moscow, 1961.

Gonchigsuren, Badarchiin. *Povyshenie roli pervichnykh partiinykh organizatsii MNRP v sozdanii material noteknicheskoi bazy sotsializma (s uchetom opyta KPSS), Kandidat* dissertation, AON TsK KPSS, 1978.

Gongor, D. " 'Khalkh tobchoon'. Mongoliya v periode perekhoda ot rodovogo stroya k feodalizmu (XI–XIII vv.). Doktor* dissertation, Institute of Oriental Studies, Moscow, 1974.

Gorodova, G. S. "Sovetskaya memuarnaya literatura o Mongolii." *Narody Azii i Afriki,* no. 3 (1971), pp. 165–169.

Graivoronskii, V. V. "Preobrazovanie kochevogo obraza zhizni v MNR." *Narody Azii i Afriki,* no. 4 (1972), pp. 21–31.

——. "Sovetskaya i mongol'skaya istoriografiya o problema osedaniya kochevnikov." In *Sbornik, Sovremennaya istoriografiya stran zarubezhnogo Vostoka,* pp. 125–146. Moscow, 1969.

Graves, General William S. *America's Siberian Adventure, 1918–1920.* New York, 1931.

Grumm-Grzhimailo, G. E. *Zapadnaya Mongoliya i Uryankhaiskiy Krai.* Vol. 3, pts. 1 and 2. Leningrad, 1926 and 1930.

Gubel'man, M. I. *Sergei Lazo.* Moscow, 1947.

Gumil'ev, L. N. *Staroburyatskaya zhivopis'.* Moscow, 1975.

Gunsen, R. *Ugolovno-pravovaya okhrana sotsialisticheskoi sobstvennosti v MNR.* *Doktor* dissertation, Moscow, 1974.

Hammond, Thomas T. "The Communist Takeover of Outer Mongolia: Model for Eastern Europe?" In *The Anatomy of Communist Takeovers,* edited by Thomas T. Hammond, pp. 107–144. New Haven, 1975.

Hangin, John. "In Commemoration of the 70th Anniversary of Academician Professor Doctor Yungsiebu Rinchen." *Mongolian Studies* 2 (1975): 7–24 (bibliography).

Hangin, John, and Krueger, John. "The Second International Congress of Mongolists (September 2–11, 1970)." *Mongolia Society Bulletin* 9, no. 2 (Fall 1970): 1–14.

Harrison, Marguerite. *Red Bear or Yellow Dragon.* London, 1924.

Heaton, William. "Chinese Communist Administration and Local Nationalism in Inner Mongolia." *Mongolia Society Bulletin* 10, no. 1 (Spring 1971): 11–47.

——. "Local Nationalism and the Cultural Revolution." *Mongolia Society Bulletin.* 10, no. 2 (Fall 1971): 2–34.

Henze, Paul. "Alphabet Changes in Soviet Central Asia and Communist China." *Royal Central Asian Journal,* April 1957, pp. 124–136.

——. "Politics and Alphabets in Central Asia." *Royal Central Asian Journal,* June 1956, pp. 29–51.

Hindus, Maurice. *Russia and Japan.* New York, 1942.

History of the Mongolian People's Republic. Translated and annotated by William A. Brown and Urgunge Onon. Notes, pp. 741–838. Cambridge, Mass., 1976.

Humphrey, C. *Magical Drawings in the Religion of the Buryat.* Cambridge, 1977.

Hyer, Paul, and Heaton, William. "The Cultural Revolution in Inner Mongolia." *China Quarterly,* no. 36 (Oct.–Dec. 1968): 114–128.

IBZI—Internationale Beziehungen im Zeitalter des Imperialismus. Vol. 1 (i). Berlin.

I. K. Ilishkin. "O nekotorykh voprosakh, svyazannykh s zakonomernostyami rasvitiya kalmytskogo literaturnogo yazyka v sovetskuyu epokhu." In *Razvitie literatur'nykh yazykov narodov Sibiri v sovetskuyu epokhu* (Materialy koordinatsionoi konferentsii, Ulan Ude 22–24 avgusta 1963 g.). Ulan Ude, 1965, pp. 167–172.

Istoricheskii opyt bratskogo sodruzhestva KPSS i MNRP v bor'be za sotsializm. Moscow, 1971.

Jagvaral, N. "From a Nomadic to a Settled Life in Mongolia." *World Marxist Review* 4, no. 8 (Aug. 1961): 50–54.

Jakupov, T. D. *Ekonomika i organizatsiya sel'skogo khozyaistva Mongolii.* Alma Ata, 1972.

Jones, F. C. *Manchuria Since 1931.* New York, 1949.

Journal of the Urusvati Himalayan Research Institute of Roerich Museum 1, no. 1 (Kulu, India, July 1931).

Jukes, Geoffrey. *The Soviet Union in Asia.* Sydney, 1973.

Kartunova, A. I. V. K. *Blyukher v Kitae 1924–1927 gg.* Moscow, 1970.

Kazakevich, V. A. *Poezdka v Dariganggu.* Leningrad, 1930.

"Vladimir Aleksandrovich Kazakevich (1896–1937)." In S. D. Miliband, *Bio-bibliograficheskii slovar' sovetskikh vostokovedov,* pp. 234–235. Moscow, 1975.

Khaptaev, P. T. "Podgotovka molodykh kvalitsirovannykh kadrov rabochikh promyshlennosti v natsional'nykh respublik i oblast'yakh Sibiri (1940–1959 gg.). *Trudy buryatskogo instituta,* no. 20 (1973), pp. 94–105.

———. "Ts. Ts. Ranzhurov." In *Bor'ba za sovety v Buryat-Mongolii,* pp. 233–236. Moscow, 1940.

Kheifets, A. N. *Sovetskaya diplomatiya i narody Vostoka, 1921–1927,* pp. 19–54. Moscow, 1968.

Khomutnikov, V. A. *Novosti Mongolii,* June 21, 1974.

———. *Voennye kalmytskie chasti v boyakh za Sovety, 1919–1922 g.* Elista, 1964.

Kiselev, I. N. "Sovetsko-mongol'skoe nauchnoe sotrudnichestvo (na primere AN SSSR i AN MNR)." In *50 let narodnoi revolyutsii v Mongolii,* pp. 163–179. Moscow, 1971.

Kiselev, S. V. *Drevnemongol'skie goroda.* Moscow, 1965.

Kniga bratstva: Literaturno-khudozhestvennyi i istoriko-publitsisticheskii sbornik. Moscow-Ulan Bator, 1971.

Knight, E. F. *Where Three Empires Meet: A Narrative of Recent Travel in Kashmir, Western Tibet, Gilgit, and the Adjoining Countries.* London, 1897.

Kolarz, Walter. *Communism and Colonialism.* London, 1964.

———. *The Peoples of the Soviet Far East.* London, 1954.

———. *Russia and Her Colonies.* London, 1952.

Kolesnikov, M. S. "Shchastlivyi Oazis." *Dal'nyi Vostok,* no. 1, 1952, pp. 3–93.

Kolokolov, V. S. *Proekt kitaiskogo alfavita na latinskom osnove.* Moscow, 1929.

Kormazov, V. A. "Kochevaya Barga." *Vestnik Man'chzhurii,* no. 8 (1928), pp. 50–58, and no. 9, pp. 35–41.

Korostovets, I. Ya. Dispatch no. 104 (Nov. 16, 1910). In *Graf Benckendorffs diplomatischer Schriftwechsel.* Vol. 1 (1907–1910), pp. 378–383. Berlin, 1928.

———. *Von Cinggis Khan zur Sowjetrepublik: Eine kurze Geschichte der Mongolen unter besondere Berücksichtigung der neüesten Zeit.* Berlin and Leipzig, 1926.

"N. N. Korotkov (b. 1908)." In S. D. Miliband, *Biobibliograficheskii slovar' sovetskikh vostokovedov,* pp. 274–275. Moscow, 1975.

Kotvich, V. L. *Kratkii obzor istorii i sovremennogo politicheskogo polozheniya Mongolii.* St. Petersburg, 1914.

Koz'min, N. N. *K voprosu o turetsko-mongol'skom feodalizme.* Irkutsk, 1934.

Kuchigasheva, N. A., and Chunzhekova, E. N. "Razvitie altaiskogo yazyka v sovetskuyu epokhu." *Razvitie literatur'nykh yazykov narodov Sibiri v sovetskuyu epokhu.* Ulan Ude, 1965, pp. 75–80.

V. A. Kuchumov. "K desyatiletiyu mongol'skoi revolyutsii." *Kommunisticheskii internatsional',* no. 18, June 30, 1931, pp. 14–19.

——. "MNR na novom etape." *Revolyutsionnyi Vostok,* no. 11–12, 1931, pp. 27–41.

Kuznetsov, N. N. *Podvigi geroev Khalkin-gola.* Ulan Ude, 1969.

"Nikolai Vasil'evich Kyuner (1877–1955)." In S. D. Miliband, *Biobibliograficheskii slovar' sovetskikh vostokovedov,* pp. 298–299. Moscow, 1975.

*Lamb, Alastair. *Asian Frontiers: Studies in a Continuing Problem.* New York 1968.

——. *The China-India Border: The Origins of the Disputed Boundaries.* London, 1964.

——. *The McMahon Line: A Study in the Relations Between India, China, and Tibet, 1904 to 1914.* 2 vols. London, 1966.

——. *The Sino-Indian Border in Ladakh.* Canberra, 1973.

Lattimore, Owen. "Inner Asia: Sino-Soviet Bridge." *Nation,* Dec. 6, 1952.

*——. *Inner Asian Frontiers of China.* American Geographic Society Research Series, no. 21. New York, 1951.

——. "Mongolia's Relations with Russia and China." *Manchester Guardian Weekly,* Dec. 4, 1952.

——. *The Mongols of Manchuria.* 2nd. ed. New York, 1934.

——. *Nationalism and Revolution in Mongolia.* New York, 1955.

——. *Nomads and Commissars: Mongolia Revisited.* New York, 1962.

——. "Religion and Revolution in Mongolia: A Review Article." *Modern Asian Studies* 1, no. 1 (1967): 81–94.

——. "Satellite Politics: The Mongolian Prototype." *Western Political Quarterly* 9 (1956): 36–43.

——. "A Treasury of Inner Asian History and Culture." *Pacific Affairs,* v. 50 no. 3 (Fall 1977), pp. 426–444.

Le Coq, Albert von. *Buried Treasures of Chinese Turkestan.* 1928.

Lensen, George. "Yalta and the Far East." In *The Meaning of Yalta: Big Three Diplomacy and the New Balance of Power,* edited by John Snell, pp. 127–166. Baton Rouge, 1956.

Leong, Sow-theng. *Sino-Soviet Diplomatic Relations, 1917–1926.* Honolulu, 1976.

Lias, Godfrey. *Kazakh Exodus.* London, 1956.

Lichtman, M. M. "Nicholas Roerich and Science." *Art and Archaeology* 29, no. 5 (May 1930): 209–214.

Luria, A. R. *Cognitive Development: Its Cultural and Social Foundations.* Translated from the 1974 Russian original. Cambridge, Mass., 1976.

Luvsanov, D. D., and Pubaev, R. E. "Vostokovednye issledovaniya v Buryatii." *Narody Azii i Afriki,* no. 5 (1970): 237–241.

Mackintosh, J. M. "The Soviet Generals' View of China in the 1960's." In *Sino-Soviet Military Relations,* edited by R. L. Garthoff, pp. 183–192. New York, 1966.

Maclean, Sir Fitzroy. *To the Back of Beyond: An Illustrated Companion to Central Asia and Mongolia.* Boston, 1975.

——. *To Caucasus: The End of All the Earth.* Boston, 1976.

Maclean, Veronica. "A Woman in Outer Mongolia." *Geographical Magazine,* Feb. 1965, pp. 740–753.

*McCormack, Gavan. *Chang Tso-lin in Northeast China, 1911– 1928: China, Japan, and the Manchurian Idea.* Stanford, Ca., 1977.

Mänchen-Helfen, Otto. *Reise ins asiatische Tuwa.* Berlin, 1931.

Ma Ho-tien. *Chinese Agent in Mongolia.* Baltimore, Md., 1949.

Maisky, I. M. *Sovremennaya Mongoliya.* Irkutsk, 1921. (Reprinted in abridged form as *Mongoliya nakanune revolyutsii;* Moscow, 1959).

Maksanov, S. A. "Ideino-politicheskaya podgotovka komunistov i komsomol'tsev v Buryat-mongol'skoi oblastnoi partiinoi organizatsii v period stroitel'stva sotsializma (1923–1937 gg.)." *Trudy buryatskogo instituta,* no. 20 (1973), pp. 49–60.

Malakshanov, K. L. *Deyatel'nost' KPSS i MNRP po ukrepleniyu druzhby i sotrudnichestva sovetskogo i mongol'skogo naroda v period zaversheniya stroitel'stva sotsializma v MNR.* Kandidat dissertation, Irkutsk, 1967.

———. "Rol' sovetskoi buryatii v dele ukrepleniya bratskogo soyuza SSSR s MNR (1920–1930 gg.)." *Trudy buryatskogo instituta,* no. 23 (1974), pp. 63–69.

Malozemoff, Andrew. *Russian Far Eastern Policy, 1881–1904, With Special Emphasis on the Causes of the Russo-Japanese War.* Berkeley, 1958.

Mamet, L. P., *Oirotiya. Ocherk natsional'no-osvoboditel'nogo dvizhenii i grazhdanskoi voiny v Gornom Altae.* Moscow, 1930.

Mamuu, A. *MRSM i ego deyatel'nost' v gody obshchedemokraticheskogo etapa revolyutsii (1921–1940).* Kandidat dissertation, Moscow, 1960.

Mamuu, A., and Ustinov, V. M. "V institute istorii partii pri TsK MNRP." *Voprosy istorii KPSS,* no. 5 (1969), pp. 152–154.

Mangadaev, M. N. "Russkyi yazyk v shkolakh Buryatskoi ASSR." *Razvitie literatur'nykh yazykov narodov Sibiri v sovetskuyu epokhu.* Ulan Ude, 1965, pp. 149–156.

Mao I-heng. *O-meng Hui-i-lu* [Reminiscences of Russia and Mongolia]. Hong Kong, 1954.

Markelov, V. N. *Ugolovnoe pravo MNR.* Moscow, 1960.

Martin, Christopher. *The Russo-Japanese War.* 1967.

Martinson, G. G. *Zagadki pustyni Gobi.* Leningrad, 1974.

Mashlai, T. *Razvitie obshcheobrazovitel'noi shkoly Mongolii (1911–1940 gg.).* Kandidat dissertation, Moscow, 1965.

Materialy po izucheniyu istochnikov indo-tibetskoi meditsiny. Moscow, 1976.

Matveeva, G. S. "V. I. Lenin i mongol'skie revolyutsionary." *Narody Azii i Afriki,* no. 2 (1970), pp. 146–151.

Maxwell, Neville. "The Chinese Account of the 1969 Fighting at Chenpao." *China Quarterly,* Oct.–Dec. 1973, pp. 730–739.

Mehra, P. L. "Tibet and Russian Intrigue." *Royal Central Asian Journal,* no. 45 (Jan., 1958): 28–40.

Mel'nikov, S. A. "Sotrudnichestvo energetikov Buryatii i Mongolii." *Trudy buryatskogo instituta,* no. 23 (1974), pp. 228–229.

Mergen, Gombojab. *Slovar' orfografii toli* (latinizirovannyi). n.d.

Merse (Kuo Tao-Fu). *Meng-ku wen-t'i chiang-yen lu* [Discussion of the Mongolian Question]. Mukden, 1929.

Meshcheryakov, M. V. *Ocherk ekonomicheskogo sotrudnichestva sovetskogo soyuza i MNR.* Moscow, 1959.

Mezhdunarodnye otnosheniya. Politika. Diplomatiya XVI– XX veka. Sbornik statei k 80-letiyu ak.-a I. M. Maiskogo. Moscow, 1964.

Micheli, Silvio. *Mongolia: In Search of Marco Polo and Other Adventures.* Translated by Bruce Penman from 1964 Italian original. New York, 1967.

Miksche, Ferdinand. "Sino-Soviet War in 19xx?" In *Sino-Soviet Military Relations,* edited by R. L. Garthoff. New York, 1966.

*Miliband, S. D. *Biobibliograficheskii slovar' sovetskikh vostokovedov.* Moscow, 1975.

Misshima, Yasuo, and Goto, Tomio. *A Japanese View of Outer Mongolia.* 1942.

Moko kenkyu Bunko Mokuroku. 1900–1950. Mongoru kenkyu Bunken Mokuroku. 1900–1972. [Bibliography of Mongolia, 1900–1972]. Kyoto and Tokyo, 1973. (See a review of the book in *Mongolian Studies* 1 (1974): 98–102.

Molokov, I. "Voennaya i ekonomicheskaya pomoshch' RSFSR DVR-e (1920–1922 gg.)." *Voenno-istoricheskii zhurnal,* no. 10, October 1972, pp. 75–79.

Mongol'skaya narodnaya respublika. Moscow, 1971.

Mongush, D. A. "Razvitie tuvinskogo yazyka v sovetskuyu epokhu." *Razvitie literatur'nykh yazykov narodov Sibiri v sovetskuyu epokhu.* Ulan Ude, 1965, pp. 53–60.

Montagu, Ivor. *Land of Blue Sky: A Portrait of Modern Mongolia.* London, 1956.

Morley, James W. *The Japanese Thrust into Siberia, 1918.* New York, 1957.

Moseley, George. *The Party and the National Question in China.* Cambridge, Mass., 1966.

*———. *A Sino-Soviet Cultural Frontier: The Ili Kazakh Autonomous Chou.* Cambridge, Mass. 1966.

Moses, Larry. "Inner Asia in International Relations: The Role of Mongolia in Russian-Chinese Relations." *Mongolia Society Newsletter* 11, no. 2 (Fall 1972): 55–75.

———. "Nomadism and Revolution." *Mongolia Society Bulletin* 10, no. 2 (Fall 1971): 35–41.

———. "Soviet-Japanese Confrontation in Outer Mongolia: The Battle of Nomonkhan-Khalkin-gol." *Journal of Asian History* 1, pt. 1 (1967): 64–85.

Moskovskaya torgavaya ekspeditsiya v Mongoliyu (MTE). Moscow, 1912.

*Murphy, George G. S. *Soviet Mongolia: A Study of the Oldest Political Satellite.* Berkeley, 1966.

Murzaev, E. M. *MNR: fiziko-geograficheskoe opisanie.* 2nd ed. Moscow, 1952.

———. *Nepotorennymi putyami: Zametki geografa,* pp. 267–384. Moscow, 1954.

"Eduard Makarovich Murzaev (b. 1908)," In S. D. Miliband, *Biobibliograficheskii slovar' sovetskikh vostokovedov,* pp. 371–372. Moscow, 1975.

Namsrai, Tsogtyn. *Sotsialisticheskaya nadstroika v strankakh, minovavshikh kapitalizm (na opyte MNR).* Moscow, 1976.

Narodnoe khozyaistvo MNR za 40 let. Ulan Bator, 1961.

Narody brat'ya. Moscow, 1965.

Natsagdorj, D. *Biobibliograficheskii ukazatel'.* Moscow, 1975.

Natsokdorj, Sh. "The Economic Basis of Feudalism in Mongolia." *Modern Asian Studies* 1, no. 3 (1967): 265–281.

"Neiman, K. A." *Novosti Mongolii,* August 20, 1974.

Nekapitalisticheskii put' razvitiya i opyt MNR. Moscow, 1971.

Nekrich, Alexander M. "The Arrest and Trial of I. M. Maisky." *Survey* 22, no. 3/4 (Summer/Autumn 1976): 313–320.

——. "What Happened in the Kalmyk ASSR." In *The Punished Peoples: The Deportation and Fate of Soviet Minorities at the End of the Second World War*. New York, 1978, pp. 66–85.

Nima, T. "Twenty-Five Years in Which Freedom Was Taken Away." In *Meng-ku Hsiao-hsi-pao*. Ulan Bator, 1972.

Norton, Henry K. *The Far Eastern Republic of Siberia*. London, 1923.

Novgorodova, E. A. *Syn Khangaiskikh gor (Ocherk o zhizni i deyatel'nosti akademika B. Shirendyba)*. Moscow, 1976.

"Eleonora Afanas'evna Novgorodova (b. 1933)." In S. D. Miliband, *Biobibliograficheskii slovar' sovetskikh vostokovedov*, p. 391. Moscow, 1975.

Novitskii, V. I. *Puteshestvie po Mongolii v predelakh Tushetu-khanovskago i Tsetsen-khanovskago aimakov Khalkha, Shilin-gol'skago Chigulgana i zemel' Chakharov Vnutrennei Mongolii, sovremennoe v 1906 g*. St. Petersburg, 1911.

Nurmekund, P. P. "O reforme kitaiskoi pis'mennosti." *Keel ja kiriandus* [Language and Literature], no. 4–5, 1958, pp. 313–316. (In the Estonian language.)

Ocherk istorii MNRP. Moscow, 1971.

Ocherki istorii Kalmytskoi ASSR: Epokha sotsializma. Moscow, 1970.

Ocherki istorii kul'tury MNR. Buryatskii institut obshchestvennykh nauk [BION], buryatskii filial, Sibirskoe otdelenie, Akademiya nauk SSSR. Ulan Ude, 1971.

Olgin, V. "Expansionism in Peking's Border Policy." Far Eastern Affairs, no. 3 (1975), pp. 36–46.

Onon, Urgunge, ed. and trans. *Mongolian Heroes of the Twentieth Century*. New York, 1976. (Among the leaders discussed are Togtokho [translation of Navannamjil's account]; Maksorjav [translation of Choibalsan's account]; Sukhe Bator; Ayush; and Damdinsuren.)

Orlov, A., and Plotnikov, G. K. "Slavnyi syn mongol'skogo naroda (k 80-letiyu so dnya rozhdeniya marshala MNR Kh. Choibalsana)." *Voenno-istoricheskii zhurnal*, no. 2 (1975), pp. 120–123.

"Osnovnye napravleniya vostokovednykh issledovanii v Institute obshchestvennykh nauk buryatskogo filiala SO AN SSSR." *Narody Azii i Afriki*, no. 4 (1976), pp. 213–214.

Parkin, P. *Voenno-istoricheskii zhurnal*, no. 3 (March 1974), pp. 123–126 (about Sergei Lazo).

Pasqualini (Bao Ruo-Wang) and Chelminski. *Prisoner of Mao*. Penguin, 1976.

Pershin, D. P. *Baron Ungern, Urga and Altan-Bulak. An Eyewitness Account of the Troubled Times in Outer (Khalkha) Mongolia During the First Third of the Twentieth Century*. Manuscript at Hoover Institution; written in 1933.

"A. I. Pershits." In S. D. Miliband, *Biobibliograficheskii slovar' sovetskikh vostokovedov*, p. 670. Moscow, 1975.

Petrov, Yu. P. *Stroitel'stvo partiino-politicheskogo apparata Sovetskoi Armii v gody inostrannoi voennoi interventsii i grazhdanskoi voiny*. Moscow, 1952.

Petryaev, E. D. *Kraevedy i literatory zabaikal'ya. Materialy dlya biobibliograficheskie slovar'ya*. Irkutsk-Chita, 1965.

Phillips, G. D. R. *Dawn in Siberia: The Mongols of Lake Baikal*. London, 1942.

——. *Russia, Japan, and Mongolia*. London, 1942.

Piatigorsky, Alexander. "The Departure of Dandaron." In *Kontinent 2*, pp. 169–179. New York, 1977.

Pierce, Richard A. *Russian Central Asia, 1867–1912: A Study in Colonial Rule.* Berkeley, 1960.

*Plotnikov, G. K. *Mongol'skaya narodnaya armiya.* Moscow, 1971.

Pod znamenem bratskoi druzhby: Vizit sovetskoi partiino-pravitel'stvennoi delegatsii vo glave s General'nym sekretarem TsK KPSS L. I. Brezhnevym v MNR, 25–27 noyabrya 1974 g. Moscow, 1974.

Polivanov, E. D. "Osnovnye formy graficheskoi revolyutsii v turetskikh pis'mennostyakh SSSR." *Novyi Vostok,* no. 23–24, 1928, pp. 314–330.

——. *Problema latinskogo shrifta v turetskikh pis'mennostyakh.* Moscow, 1923.

"E. D. Polivanov (1891–1938)." In S. D. Miliband, *Biobibliograficheskii slovar' sovetskikh vostokovedov,* pp. 443–444. Moscow, 1975.

Polyakova, E. I. *Nikolai Rerikh.* Moscow, 1973.

Pomus, M. "Sergei Shirokikh-Polyanskii." In *Bor'ba za Sovety v Buryat-Mongolii,* pp. 237–242. Moscow, 1940.

Pond, Alonzo W. *Andrews: Gobi Explorer.* New York, 1972.

Popov, V. L. *Uryankhai'skii pogranichnyi vopros. Doklad.* Irkutsk, 1910.

Potabenko, S. I. "Konferentsiya, posvyashchannaya stoletiyu so dnya rozhdeniya N. K. Rerikha." *Narody Azii i Afriki,* no. 3 (1975), pp. 239–241.

Potapov, L. P. *Ocherki narodnogo byta tuvintsev.* Moscow, 1969.

"Leonid Pavlovich Potapov (b. 1905)." In S. D. Miliband, *Biobibliograficheskii slovar' sovetskikh vostokovedov,* pp. 452–453. Moscow, 1975.

Powell, J. B. "The Soviet Atrocities in Barga" and "The Sino-Russian-Mongolian Struggle in Barga," *The China Weekly Review* 1, no. 9 (Nov. 2, 1929): 337–340; no. 13 (Nov. 30, 1929): 486–488. (Based on Kormazov.)

*Pozdneyev, A. M. *Mongolia and the Mongols.* Edited by John Krueger and Fred Adelman. Bloomington, Ind., 1971.

*Prescott, J. R. V. *Map of Mainland Asia by Treaty.* Melbourne, 1975.

Price, Ernest B. *The Russian-Japanese Treaties of 1907–1916 Concerning Manchuria and Mongolia.* Baltimore, 1933.

Price, Julius. *From the Arctic Ocean to the Yellow Sea.* London, 1893.

Pubaev, R. E. "Nekotorye dannye o razvitii ekonomiki i kul'tury Selenginskogo aimaka MNR (Po materialam istoriko-etnograficheskoi ekskursii BKNII SO AN SSSR v okt.-noyabre 1963 g.)." In *Materialy po istorii i filologii Tsentral'noi Azii.* Vol. 2, pp. 14–23. Ulan Ude, 1965.

*Rakowska-Harmstone, Teresa. *Russia and Nationalism in Central Asia: The Case of Tadzhikistan.* Baltimore, Md., 1970.

Red Sun Rising. "Rules of Play" for SPI War Game (Russo-Japanese War), pp. 24–25.

Rinchen, Y. "Books and Traditions (From the History of Mongolian Culture)." *Mongolia Society Occasional Papers* no. 8, pp. 63–76. Bloomington, Ind., 1972.

——. "Sanskrit in Mongolia." In *Commemoration Volume on the 71st Birthday of Acharya Raghuvira,* vol. 3 in *Studies in Indo-Asian Art and Culture.* New Delhi, 1974.

——. *Zum Kult Tschinggis-Khans bei den Mongolen,* pp. 9–22. Budapest, 1959.

(Attacks on Rinchen include articles in *Unen,* Ulan Bator, August 19, 1959; *Sovremennaya Mongoliya,* no. 10 (23), October 1959, pp. 26–27; *Problemy*

Vostokovedeniya, no. 2, 1960; and *Novosti Mongolii,* March 26, 1976.)

Roerich, George (Yu. N. Rerikh) "Indology in Russia." *Journal of the Greater Indian Society* 12, no. 2 (1945): 69–98.

———. "Mongolo-Tibetskie otnoshenii v XIII i XIV vv." *Sbornik. Filologiya i istoriya mongol'skikh narodov.* Moscow, 1958.

———. "Mongolo-Tibetskie otnoshenii v XVI i nachalao XVII vv." *Mongol'skii sbornik.* Moscow, 1959.

———. *Tibetskii yazyk.* Moscow, 1961.

———. *Trails to Inmost Asia: Five Years of Exploration with the Roerich Central Asian Expedition.* New Haven, 1931.

"Yu. N. Rerikh." *Narody Azii i Afriki,* no. 4, 1962, pp. 247–252.

"Yu N. Rerikh (1902–1960)." *Bol'shaya sovetskaya entsiklopediya,* vol. 22, 1975, p. 43.

"Yurii Nikolaevich Rerikh (1902–1960)." In S. D. Miliband, *Biobibliograficheskii slovar' sovetskikh vostokovedov,* pp. 471–472. Moscow, 1975.

Roerich, Nicholas. (N. K. Rerikh) *Altai-Himalaya: A Travel Diary.* New York, 1929.

———. *Shambhala: The Resplendent.* New York, 1930.

"N. K. Rerikh (1874–1947)." *Bol'shaya sovetskaya entsiklopediya,* vol. 22, 1975, pp. 42–43.

Roerich, Svyatoslav. "S. N. Rerikh (1904–   )." *Bol'shaya sovetskaya entsiklopediya,* vol. 22, 1975, p. 43.

Roerich Museum: A Decade of Activity, 1921–1931. New York, 1931.

Rokossovsky, K. K. "My vsegda vmeste." In *Narody brat'ya,* pp. 5–11. Moscow, 1965.

Rosenberg, Daniel. "*Negdel* Development: A Socio-Cultural Perspective." *Mongolian Studies* (1974): 62–75.

*Roshchin, S. K. Sel'skoe khozyaistvo MNR na sotsialisticheskom puti. Moscow, 1971.

Rossabi, Morris. *China and Inner Asia from 1368 to the Present Day.* New York, 1975.

Rozbakiev, S. K. "Sud'by uigurskoi literatury v Sin'tszyane." *Narody Azii i Afriki,* no. 5 (1973), pp. 153–157.

Rozhdestvenskii, A. K. *Na poiske dinozavrov v Gobi.* Moscow, 1965.

Rupen, Robert A. "The Absorption of Tuva." In *The Anatomy of Communist Takeovers,* edited by Thomas T. Hammond, pp. 145–162. New Haven, 1975.

———. "The Buryat Intelligentsia." *Far Eastern Quarterly* 15, no. 3 (May 1956): 383–398.

———. "The City of Urga in the Manchu Period." In *Ural-altaische Bibliothek,* vol. 5, pp. 157–169. Wiesbaden, 1957.

———. "The Fiftieth Anniversary of the MPR, 1921–1971." *Asian Survey* 13, no. 5 (May 1973): 458–469.

———. "Inside Outer Mongolia." *Foreign Affairs* 37, no. 2 (January 1959): 328–333.

———. "Mongolia and the Sino-Soviet Dispute." *China Quarterly,* November–December 1963, pp. 75–85.

———. *The Mongolian People's Republic.* Stanford, Ca., 1966.

———. *Mongols of the Twentieth Century.* 2 vols. Bloomington, Ind., 1964.

———. "The MPR and Sino-Soviet Competition. "In *Communist Strategies in Asia,* edited by Doak Barnett, pp. 262–292. New York, 1963.

——. "Peking and the National Minorities." In *Communist China 1949–1969: A Twenty-Year Appraisal,* edited by Frank Trager and Henderson, pp. 243–258. New York, 1970.

——. "A Soviet Historical Novel about Mongolia [Kolesnikov]." *Far Eastern Quarterly* 14, no. 4 (August 1955): 553–557.

——. "Tsedenbal." In *Leaders of the Communist World,* edited by Rodger Swearingen, pp. 414–423. New York, 1971.

——. "Tuva." *Asian Survey* 5, no. 12 (December 1965): 609–615.

Salisbury, Harrison. *Black Night, White Snow: Russia's Revolutions 1905–1917.* New York, 1978.

——. *To Moscow—and Beyond.* New York, 1960.

*——. *War Between Russia and China.* 1969.

Salomon, Hilel. "The Anfu Clique and China's Abrogation of Outer Mongolian Autonomy." *Mongolia Society Bulletin* 10, no. 1 (Spring 1971): 67–86.

"Zh. Sambu (1895–May 21, 1972)." *Bol'shaya sovetskaya entsiklopediya,* vol. 22, 1975, pp. 531–532.

Samdandeleg, Ts. *Istoriya mongol'skoi narodnoi armii, 1921–1924 gg.* Dissertation, Moscow, 1960.

Sanders, Alan J. K. "Mongolia 1976: Drawing Together Frankly with the Soviet Union." *Asian Survey* 17, no. 1 (Jan. 1977): 27–33.

——. "Mongolia 1977: Directive No. 14." *Asian Survey* 18, no. 1 (Jan. 1978): 29–35.

——. "Letter from Erdenet." *Far Eastern Economic Review,* Oct. 28, 1977, p. 58.

Sangidanzan, Dashdondovyn, *Osnovnye funktsii narodnogo gosudarstva na demokraticheskom etape revolyutsii v MNR (1921–1940 gg.). Kandidat* dissertation. Institute for State and Law. Moscow, 1976.

Sanjeev, Garma. "Weltanschauung und Schamanismus der Alaren-Burjaten." *Anthropos* 22 (1927): 576–613 and 933–955; 23 (1928): 538–560 and 967–986.

Sanzhiev, B. S. *Yaroslav Gashek v Vostochnoi Sibiri.* Irkutsk, 1961.

Sapozhnikov, V. V. *Po russkomu i mongol'skomu Altayu.* Moscow, 1949.

Savin, A. "Podgotovka Yaponii k voine protiv SSSR v 1941 g.." *Voenno-istoricheskii zhurnal,* no. 6 (June 1971), pp. 38–47.

Schurmann, Franz, and Schell, Orville. *The China Reader 3: Communist China: Revolutionary Reconstruction and International Confrontation: 1949 to the Present.* New York, 1967.

Schwartz, Henry G. *Chinese Policies Toward Minorities: An Essay and Documents.* Bellingham, Washington, 1971.

Semenev, A., and Dashtseren, B. *Eskadril'ya "Mongol'skii Arat."* Moscow, 1971.

Semennikov, V. P. *Za kulisami tsarizma. Arkhiv tibetskogo vracha Badmaeva.* 1925.

Semenov, G. M. *O sebe: vospominaniya, mysli i vyvody.* Harbin, 1938.

Serdobov, N. A. *Istoriya formirovaniya tuvinskoi natsii.* Kyzyl, 1971.

Serdyuchenko, G. P. "Iz istorii sozdaniya alfavitov na osnove russkoi grafiki." *Kratkie soobshchenie IVAN,* no. 12, 1955, pp. 62–76.

——. *Kitaiskaya pis'mennost' i ee reforma.* Moscow, 1959.

——. "O novom mongol'skom pis'me." Manuscript, Peking, May 7–11, 1956. (In this author's possession.)

———. *Russkaya transkriptsiya dlya yazykov zarubezhnego Vostoka.* Moscow, 1963.

———. "Spisok osnovnykh nauchnykh rabot doktora fileologicheskikh nauk G. P. Serdyuchenko." *Narody Azii i Afriki,* no. 2 (1964), pp. 228–231.

"Georgii Petrovich Serdyuchenko (1904–1965)." In S. D. Miliband, *Bio-bibliograficheskii slovar' sovetskikh vostokovedov,* pp. 507–508. Moscow, 1975.

Shagdarov, L. D. "Razvitie buryatskogo literaturnogo yazyka v sovetskuyu epokhu." *Razvitie literatur'nykh yazykov narodov Sibiri v sovetskuyu epokhu.* Ulan Ude, 1965, pp. 36–47.

"Shamany i shamanstvo." In *Ateisticheskie Chtenie,* vol. 3, pp. 32–43.

Shastitko, I. M. "Novye materialy o vzglyadakh V. I. Lenina u natsional'no-kolonial'nomu voprosu." *Narody Azii i Afriki,* no. 5 (1971), pp. 140–146.

Shcherbakov, Yu. *Pisatel', Agitator, Boets* [Hashek]. Moscow, 1966.

"Fedor Ippolitovich Shcherbatskoi (1866–1942)." In S. D. Miliband, *Bio-bibliograficheskii slovar' sovetskikh vostokovedov,* pp. 612–622. Moscow, 1975.

Sheng, Yueh. *Sun Yat-sen University in Moscow and the Chinese Revolution: A Personal Account.* Lawrence, Kansas, 1971.

Shereshevskii, B. M. "Iz istorii bor'ba za ukreplenie partiinogo rukovodstva DVR (yanvar'–fevral' 1921 g.). *Voprosy istorii Sovetskoi Sibiri.* Istoricheskaya seriya, no. 5. Novosibirsk, 1972, pp. 17–35.

———. "Iz istorii ekonomicheskogo stroitel'stva v DVR." *Voprosy istorii Sovetskoi Sibiri,* Istoricheskaya seriya, no. 1. Novosibirsk, 1967, pp. 54–72.

*Sheridan, James E. *Chinese Warlord: The Career of Feng Yu-hsiang.* Stanford, Ca., 1966.

Shirendyb, B. *Izbrannye proizvodeniya.* Moscow, 1973.

Shishkin, S. *Khalkin-gol.* Moscow, 1954.

Shoizhelov [Natsov]. "Sotsial'no-ekonomicheskie korni pravyi opasnosti v MNRP." *Kommunisticheskii internatsional',* no. 31 (209), (Aug. 9, 1929), pp. 38–47.

Shprintsin, A. G. "Iz istorii novogo kitaiskogo alfavita (1928–1931 gg.)." *Narody Azii i Afriki,* no. 6, 1961, pp. 126–135.

———. "Kitaiskii novyi alfavit' (latinizatsiya), dialekty i obshcheliteraturnyi yazyk." In *Strany i narody Vostoka,* vol. 15, pp. 309–321. Moscow, 1973.

———. "O literature na kitaiskom yazyke, izdannoi v Sovetskom Soyuze (20-30-e gody)." *Izucheniya kitaiskoi literatury v SSSR. Sbornik statei k 60-yu N. T. Fedorenko.* Moscow, 1973, pp. 242–266.

"A. G. Shprintsin (1907–   )." In S. D. Miliband, *Biobibliograficheskii slovar' sovetskikh vostokovedov,* p. 618. Moscow, 1975.

Shulunov, N. D. "Obrazovanie buryatskoi ASSR." *Trudy buryatskogo instituta,* no. 20 (1973), pp. 5–15.

———. *Stanovlenie sovetskoi natsional'noi gosudarstvennosti v Buryatii (1919–1923 gody).* Ulan Ude, 1972.

"The Sino-Soviet Dispute." *Strategic Survey 1969,* pp. 66–72. London, 1969.

Slusser, Robert M., and Triska, Jan F. *A Calendar of Soviet Treaties, 1917–1957.* Stanford, Ca., 1959.

Sobolev, A.I., and Iskrov, M.V. (USSR); Minis, A. and Damdinsuren, S. (MPR), eds., *Rol. mezhdunarodnogo kommunisticheskogo dvizheniya v stanovlenii i razvitii MNRP,* announced 1978.

"Soderzhanie zhurnala 'Khozyaistvo Mongolii' (Ulan Bator, 1926–1931 gg.)" *Bibliografiya Vostoka*, no. 1. Leningrad, 1932.

Solzhenitsyn, Aleksander. *Gulag Archipelago Two.* New York, 1975.

———. "Nations in Exile." In *Gulag Archipelago Three,* pp. 385–405. New York, 1978.

———. "The Smatterers." In *From under the Rubble,* pp. 229–278. Boston, 1974.

*Sorkin, N. S. *V nachale puti (zapiski instruktora mongol'skoi armii).* Moscow, 1970.

Sosorbaram, P. *Bukhgalterskii uchet v MNR.* Moscow, 1975.

Stephan, John J. "The Tanaka Memorial (1927): Authentic or Spurious?" *Modern Asian Studies,* no. 4 (1973), pp. 733–745.

Strong, Anna Louise. *China's Millions.* Book 2: *Across China's Northwest and Gobi Desert to Moscow with Borodin and Marshal Feng,* pp. 225–413. New York, 1928.

Sushanlo, M. *Dungane—istorika-demograficheskii ocherk.* Frunze, 1971.

Suyin, Han. *Lhasa, The Open City: A Journey to Tibet.* New York, 1977.

Tang, Peter S. H. *Russian and Soviet Policy in Manchuria and Outer Mongolia, 1911–1931.* Duke University Press, 1959.

Tastanov, Kh. "Kul'tura mongol'skikh kazakhov" [in Kazakh language]. *Zhuldyz,* no. 11 (1963), pp. 135–140.

Tillet, Lowell. "The National Minorities Factor in the Sino-Soviet Dispute." *Orbis* 21, no. 2 (Summer 1977): 241–260.

Timofeeva, N. N. "KUTV (1921–1925)." *Narody Azii i Afriki,* no. 2 (1976), pp. 47–57.

Todaeva, B. Kh. *Mongol'skie yazyki i dialekty Kitaya.* Moscow, 1960.

Tsedenbal, Yumjagün. *Izbrannye stat'i i rechi. 1941–1958.* Moscow, 1962. *1959–1961.* Moscow, 1962. *1962–1973.* Moscow, 1974.

———. "Toward Socialism, Bypassing Capitalism." *Far Eastern Affairs,* no. 1 (1975), pp. 8–29.

Tsendee, Damdiny, *Ispol'zovanie opyta raboty sovetskikh profsoyuzov MNR po kommunisticheskomu vospitaniyu Trudyashchikhsya.* Kandidat dissertation, Higher Trade-Unions School. Moscow, 1976.

Tsibikov, B. D. *Razgrom ungernovshchiny.* Ulan Ude, 1947.

Tsydypov, Ts. Ts. "Buryatskii yazyk v shkole." *Razvitie literatur'nykh yazykov narodov Sibiri v sovetskuyu epokhu.* Ulan Ude, 1965, pp. 167–172.

"Mikhail Izraelevich Tubyanskii (1893–1943)." In S. D. Miliband, *Biobibliograficheskii slovar' sovetskikh vostokovedov,* p. 557. Moscow, 1975.

Tuchman, Barbara W. *Stilwell and the American Experience in China, 1911–1945.* New York, 1971.

Tudev, B. *Rabochii klass v bor'be za zavershenii stroitel'stva sotsializma v MNR. Doktor* dissertation, Institute of Oriental Studies. Moscow, 1975.

Ubryatova, E. I. *Nekotorye voprosy grafiki i orfografii pis'mennosti yazykov narodov SSSR, pol'zuyushchikhsya alfavitami na russkom osnove.* Moscow, 1959.

Uchebnik mongol'skogo yazyka (latinizirovannyi), 2 vols. Moscow, 1933.

Udval, S. "Stroitel'stvo sotsializma i formirovanie novogo cheloveka v MNR." *Kommunist,* no. 7 (1967), pp. 86–90.

Ugolovnyi protsess MNR. Moscow, 1974.

Ulymzhiev, D. B. "MNRP—ispytannyi avangard mongol'skogo naroda." *Trudy buryatskogo instituta,* no. 23 (1974), pp. 31–50.

"Urginskaya obshchestvennaya trudovaya shkola 1-i i 2-i stepeni (1920/21 uchebn.

god)." *Izvestiya Gosudarstvennogo instituta narodnogo obrazovaniya v g. Chite.* Book 1 (1923), pp. 292–295.

Vainshtein, S. I. *Istoricheskaya etnografiya Tuvintsev: problemy kochevogo khozyaistva.* Moscow, 1972.

*Valliant, Robert B. "Japanese Involvement in Mongol Independence Movements, 1912–1919." *Mongolia Society Newsletter* 11, no. 2 (Fall 1972): 1–32.

Vandanov, B. M., and Mende. *Revsomol Mongolii.* Moscow, 1931.

Velikoderzhavnaya politika Maoistov v natsional'nykh raionakh KNR. Moscow, 1975.

Vilenskii, V. "Mongoliya protiv iga imperialistov." *Izvestiya,* Nov. 2, 1923.

——. "Sovetskaya Rossiya i Mongoliya." *Izvestiya* Nov. 2, 1920.

Vitebsky, Piers. "Some Medieval Views of Mongolian Shamanism." *Journal of the Anglo-Mongolian Society* 1, no. 1 (May 1974): 24–42.

Vneshnyaya politika KNR: o sushchnosti vneshnepoliticheskogo kursa sovremennogo kitaiskogo rukovodstva. Moscow, 1971.

Von Kyachta bis Darchan. East Berlin, 1971.

Warner, Denis, and Warner, Peggy. *The Tide at Sunrise: A History of the Russo-Japanese War, 1904–1905.* New York, 1974.

Weale, Putnam [Bertram Lennox Simpson]. *Chang Tso-lin's Struggle against the Communist Menace.* Shanghai, 1927.

Weigh, Ken S. *Russo-Chinese Diplomacy, 1689–1924.* Bangor, Maine, 1958.

Weiske, Fritz. "Die wirtschaftlichen Verhältnisse in der Äusseren Mongolei." *Osteuropa,* no. 4, 1928, pp. 149–165.

*Welch. Holmes. *Buddhism Under Mao,* Cambridge, Mass., 1972.

Whiting, Allen S. *Sinkiang: Pawn or Pivot?* East Lansing, Michigan, 1958.

——. *Soviet Policies in China, 1917–1924.* New York, 1954.

Wiens, Herold J. "Geographical Limitations to Food Production in the MPR." *Annals of the Association of American Geographers* 41, no. 4 (Dec. 1951): 349–369.

——. "The Historical and Geographical Role of Urumchi, Capital of Chinese Central Asia." *Annals of the Association of American Geographers* 52 (1963): 441–464.

Wolff, Serge. "Mongolian Educational Venture in Western Europe (1926–1929)." *Mongolia Society Bulletin* 9, no. 2 (Fall 1970): 40–100.

Wren, Christopher. "Kazakhstan Beckons Refugees from China." *New York Times,* April 24, 1976.

Yakimov, A. T. "Bratstvo po oruzhiyu (Vospominaniya politrabotnika)." In *Kniga bratstva,* pp. 58–62. Moscow, 1971.

——. "MNRP—organizator i vdokhnovitel' pobed mongol'skogo naroda." *MNR: Sbornik statei* (Feb. 1964), pp. 68–70.

——. *Voenno-istoricheskii zhurnal.* no. 2 (Feb. 1964), pp. 68–70 (about Sergei Lazo).

"Aristarkh Tikhonovich Yakimov (b. 1895)." In S. D. Miliband, *Biobibliograficheskii slovar' sovetskikh vostokovedov,* pp. 634–635. Moscow, 1975.

(See also article in *Narody Azii i Afriki,* no. 5, 1965, p. 226.)

Yanguzov, Z. Sh. *OKDVA na strazhe mira i bezopasnosti SSSR (1929–1938 gg.).* Khabarovsk, 1970.

Yumin, M. N. "Khozyaistvennye reformy v MNR." *Narody Azii i Afriki,* no. 2 (1976), pp. 156–163.

——. "MNR i SEV," *Narody Azii i Afriki* no. 3 (1977), pp. 17–28.

———. "MNR v sisteme mezhdunarodnoi sotsialisticheskoi ekonomicheskoi integratsii." *Narody Azii i Afriki,* no. 1 (1973), pp. 3–11.

Zagasbaldan, D. *Problemy sotsialisticheskoi industrializatsii MNR.* Moscow, 1973.

Zagd, Bochoogiih, *Tvorcheskoe voploschenie leninskikh printsipov sotsialisticheskoi demokratii v usloviyakh MNR. Kandidat* dissertation, MGU, 1978.

Zhalsobon, V. D. "Kitaiskaya kolonizatsiya vnutrennei Mongoliya v 20–30-kh godakh XX veka." *Trudy buryatskogo instituta,* no. 23 (1974), pp. 129–143.

Zhalsonova, R. Zh., and Shagdyrov, B. B. "Mongolrabfak." *Trudy buryatskogo instituta,* no. 23 (1974), pp. 89–98.

"Tsyben Zhamtsavanovich Zhamtsarano (1880–1937)." In S. D. Miliband, *Biobibliograficheskii slovar' sovetskikh vostokovedov,* p. 203. Moscow, 1975.

Zlatkin, I. Ya. "Ak. B. Ya. Vladimirtsov—istorik-vostoved." *Narody Azii i Afriki,* no. 6 (1975), pp. 201–217.

———. *MNR—strana novoi demokratii. Ocherk istorii.* Moscow, 1950.

———. *Ocherki novoi i noveishei istorii Mongolii.* Moscow, 1957.

"Il'ya Yakovlevich Zlatkin (b. 1898)." In S. D. Miliband, *Biobibliograficheskii slovar' sovetskikh vostokovedov,* pp. 216–217. Moscow, 1975.

Zubkov, N.P. *Rukovodshchaya rol' MNRP o sushchestvlenii nekapitalisticheskogo puti razvitiya Mongolii.* Dissertation, Moscow State University, Moscow, 1974.

PERIODICALS AND SERIALS

The Canada-Mongolia Review. Canada-Mongolia Society, Saskatchewan, Saskatoon, Canada.

Ezhegodniki BSE.

Far Eastern Economic Review (Hong Kong).

Mongolia Society, Bloomington, Indiana—various publications: *Bulletin, Studies, Newsletter,* for example.

*Narody Azii i Afriki.

New York Times.

*Novosti Mongolii (Ulan Bator).

Peking Review.

Trudy buryatskogo instituta obshchestvennykh nauk [BION] buryatskogo filiala sibirskogo otdeleniya AN SSSR (Ulan Ude).

U. S. Department of State. *Foreign Relations of the United States.*

*Voenno-istoricheskii zhurnal.

Index